Managing Information in Complex Organizations

Semiotics and Signals, Complexity and Chaos

Kevin C. Desouza and Tobin Hensgen

M.E.Sharpe
Armonk, New York
London, England

Library of Congress Cataloging-in-Publication Data

Desouza, Kevin C., 1979–
Managing information in complex organizations : semiotics and signals,
complexity and chaos / by Kevin C. Desouza and Tobin Hensgen.
  p. cm.
Includes bibliographical references and index.
ISBN 0-7656-1360-3 (hardcover : alk. paper)
 1. Communication in organizations. 2. Complex organizations. 3. Information theory.
4. Information resources management. I. Hensgen,Tobin. II. Title.

HD30.3.D47 2004
302.3′5—dc22   2004014841

Printed in the United States of America

The paper used in this publication meets the minimum requirements of
American National Standard for Information Sciences
Permanence of Paper for Printed Library Materials,
ANSI Z 39.48-1984.

BM (c)   10   9   8   7   6   5   4   3   2   1

Advance Praise for *Managing Information in Complex Organizations*

"If information is to be treated as 'real,' then *Managing Information in Complex Organizations* is a solid guide to that aspect of reality. The essence of information's managerial challenge is the recognition of what has and has not been communicated. Desouza and Hensgen put that challenge in context so that the practicing manager can develop the necessary tools for its mastery. . . . Information is a vital element in decision-making and without its mastery the practicing manager's abilities are greatly reduced. This text aims to correct that deficiency. Its success in doing so depends on the willingness of the reader to admit that merely broadcasting data is not the same as communicating. Too many managers hold tight to that false belief. Desouza and Hensgen describe the risks in doing so and alternatively the potential rewards from embracing context in communication."

—Dr. Michael Lissack, Institute for the
Study of Coherence and Emergence

"This innovative book will be essential reading for academics and researchers in information and knowledge management studies. No significant work can be done in these areas without reference to Desouza's and Hensgen's book. Because of its readable style and wellspring of examples, both graduate and undergraduate students will find the book useful. A groundbreaking book as such is essential to any person who is serious about conceptualizing the notion of semiotics, complexity, and chaos surrounding the information in organizations."

—Sajjad M. Jasimuddin, School of Management
University of Southampton, United Kingdom

"This book explores the concept of information in the most realistic setting — 'a complex world.' The authors do an excellent job bringing together diverse literature in a cohesive and symbiotic manner; they have managed the complex academic literatures to generate information and knowledge that is of interest to both academicians and practitioners. This book is a must read for practitioners and students in the disciplines of information management, strategic management of technology, and information integrity, assurance, and audit."

—Madhavan Nayar, President, Unitech Systems, Inc.,
and Cofounder, Information Integrity Coalition

"Hindsight has been said to be 20/20—especially when applied to recent disasters where warning information was present before the actual event. This book posits a new model that enables practitioners to avoid traps in processing information and to illuminate this warning information for decision makers. The authors use the model to show how critical information was mishandled in several recent crises. Other case studies describe how optimal information processing using this model may have actually evaded the crisis. One enlightening recommendation is the concept of virtual crisis centers for monitoring key elements of the organization itself. These remote internal centers sense forthcoming organizational crises in order to mitigate or even avoid the events. This scholarly book provides practical guidelines for the information manager dealing with situations where the mishandling of even small bits of information can be large consequences."

—Dr. Robert J. Harden, United States Army
Research Laboratory, Department of Army

Contents

Figures

Preface

In October 2002, while a PhD candidate at the University of Illinois at Chicago, a colleague and mentor, Dr. George Kraft, suggested we meet for lunch at a local Mexican restaurant. Having lunch with George is always a pleasant event; we have the opportunity to exchange ideas on what is current, he generally selects the fare, and he always picks up the tab. On this particular occasion, George wanted me to meet one of his former MBA students, Tobin Hensgen, a doctoral student from Loyola University who had had some questions regarding the work on an information theory piece by Claude Shannon of Massachusetts Institute of Technology (MIT). In 1948, Shannon had written a pivotal piece related to the technical side of communications, in which he demonstrated how an effect common to thermodynamics could be applied to information.[1] The effect described was entropy, which, as a concept, is a measure of disorder and uncertainty within a system.

Tobin was working on an information piece related to communication failures involving the September 11 attack on the World Trade Center and felt that the effects of entropy had played an important part in why vital information that could have better prepared the United States was either delayed or lost completely. Because my interests involved signal, or message, transfers in information systems, it became immediately and refreshingly apparent that we spoke a variation of the same language. Some of my recent work dealt with a semiotics approach to information flow that charted the transfer of data-to-information and information-to-actionable knowledge. When I presented the five steps of this process to Tobin, he thought for a moment and then began sketching something on a napkin. Once finished, he passed a rendering to me that depicted a perfect overlay of the semiotic model against a time line that reflected the effects of entropy and information during the events leading to September 11. George suggested that combining these ideas might make an interesting paper. The product stemming from this first meeting made our first article in *Emergence* and a subsequent smaller piece in *IT Professional*.[2]

But a central question kept resurfacing during our mutual research, which centered on the use of information by organizations: *Why do organizations continue to fail to process available information optimally in order to evade conditions related to impending crises*? In an effort to address some of these concerns, we collaborated on a dozen or so papers over the following months. I admit some surprise in the fact that each of these papers drew immediate editorial interest from a wide range of periodicals and journals. Citations from some of these works had been referenced by other sources within months of publication. It was clear we were on to something that had peaked the interest of many people involved in the fields of information systems, emergence, cybernetics, knowledge management, and crisis management. As we continued our work, it became apparent that much of our research would be tied in with emerging ideas in communications that were being developed by others. While academic journal articles are nice per se, they present certain understandable constraints. Size and space limitations are major concerns with publications, as such pieces must be limited in length. Additionally, the time required for peer review makes it nearly impossible to disseminate current information. It is unfortunate that most academic journals today take around six months on average to review an article, then an additional six to nine months to publish it. During this time, much of what the article has to say or report starts to become obsolete. This is especially true when the information presented involves dynamic fields like information systems and management. Additionally, many of the ideas we address involve a multidisciplinary overview that simply cannot be thoroughly discussed in the context of an article. They may, however, be presented with some confidence in a book.

While much of what we present has appeared in scientific and business journals to which we have contributed, our goal will be to *integrate* a variety of themes and blend them with the existing literatures on systems, organizations, philosophy, and information processing. This approach is based on two existing conditions: first, we want to call attention to the inadequacies plaguing current methods of information management in many organizations today. Additionally, we wish to shed some light on how organizations might better manage and leverage available information and transform such information into knowledge that is useful, valuable, and actionable. Our intention is to provide and connect associated references in this text in pursuit of new theories on information. Many of the founding principles to which we pay homage as well as some methodologies that this text addresses have been in existence for years, in some cases centuries, but the ways they are connected are distinct and related to new models developed by the authors.

Who Should Read This Book?

We expect the people who would benefit from this book to fall into two general categories. The first category includes scholars and managers who are engaged in information processing as a matter of their daily routine. Scholars include both current professors and graduate students involved in the area of information systems, semiotics, complexity theory, knowledge management, and computer sciences. We believe the greatest interest will be from practitioners and executives interested in information systems, knowledge management, and strategic planning, especially for those concerned with traditional contingency planning. An important secondary audience for our book will include members of law enforcement, national infrastructure protection, and defense organizations, all of whom seek better ways to gather, manage, and share information. Regardless of whether one is researching how organizations manage information or actively engage in the management of information, we feel that this text will provide new avenues of perception and encourage further research on information management. For researchers, we expect the text will provide a good reason as to why one must look at *allied*, seemingly unrelated disciplines, for answers to questions on issues involving information. We have adopted frameworks and arguments presented from nearly a dozen different scientific disciplines and have integrated them into a single text. This exercise has furthered our understanding of information and organizations.

Since this discourse on information processing is based on new applications as applied to a variety of organizational concerns and involving case studies, we anticipate great interest. Beyond theory, our work provides actual "how-to" approaches related to case studies in the areas of cyberterrorism, intelligence failures, and crises associated with medical errors. We encourage readers to question some of the fundamental assumptions of how information needs to be managed in their own organizations, and we hope to provide some of the tools to better manage information in order to develop sustainable and agile organizations.

As we will argue throughout the text, information shapes an organization. Information can shape an organization to be agile and adaptable to the environment, and the same information if not properly processed can lead to the demise of an organization. This book is not an "easy" read and may require time for reflection, even rereading, in order to fully grasp the concepts behind the topics discussed. We know of no other text that attempts to join the variety of topics related to information presented between these covers. We encourage readers to make use of the references provided to expand their grasp of the principles involved. And we hope this introduction to the fields that have a direct bearing on information will encourage further research into the implications and effects on organizations. But, before we begin, we would like to acknowledge those who helped chart the course for this journey by reminding us that while we might not be able control the wind, we certainly could adjust our vessel's sails to steer a better course.

Acknowledgments

Writing a book is very much like running a marathon. Our race began in October 2002 over lunch. George Kraft, who served as a professor, mentor, and colleague to the two of us while we were students at the Illinois Institute of Technology, invited us to this esteemed luncheon at a local tavern. We thank him for recognizing the fact that an exciting synergy could be generated by the synthesis of our individual research interest.

Our marathon has been composed of multiple stages. Each stage was defined by the shaping of one or more research ideas and insights that eventually entered this text. At each stage we have had the pleasure of collaborating with a number of distinguished scholars. We have coauthored several papers with George Kraft, Roberto Evaristo, and Yukika Awazu, and we have certainly gained from their experiences. Yukika Awazu deserves special thanks for research assistance in the preparation of the text. We wish to thank Eliezer Geisler for extending a warm invitation for us to present some of our findings at the Stuart Graduate School Research Colloquia and during meetings with the Information Integrity Coalition. Editor Eric Valentine saw value in our work early on and helped us bring it to fruition. On numerous occasions he has challenged us to make our ideas more easily digestible; we thank him for his generosity of time and energy.

We have been fortunate to have optimal sources of energy, support, and motivation for running this marathon. We would like to acknowledge some of those who contributed to the strength we needed to complete the run.

Kevin Desouza—My colleagues at the Department of Information and Decision Sciences, University of Illinois at Chicago, of whom there are too many to mention individually, but I would like to single out and thank— Mary Beth Watson-Manheim, Arkalgud Ramaprasad, Yair Babad, and Robert Liden, who have been a valuable resource of ideas, critiques, and suggestions. Research and consulting collaborators—Thomas Davenport,

Robert J. Thomas, Mark Power, Carlo Bonifazi, Shigetaka Yamakawa, and Margaret Kraft, who have all helped some part of my research agenda and improved my understanding of information and organizations. A special thanks to Thomas Davenport, who invited me to spend the summer of 2002 as a visiting research fellow at Accenture's Institute of Strategic Change. During the course of writing this text, I have had the support of some great friends who patiently put up with some rather tedious discussions on the topics of the book—Artur Arciuch, Hector Vielma, Philip Waitzman, and Anuradha Jayaraman. Last, but definitely not least, I would like to thank my family for being patient and supportive as I dedicated time and effort to this project. I dedicate this book to my sister, Karishma Desouza, who one day promises to write her own book.

Tobin Hensgen—Among the things on which Einstein has commented, two things immediately come to mind. First, *"The significant problems we face cannot be solved at the same level of thinking we were at when we created them,"* which was one of the main reasons for attempting this book, and second, *"A hundred times every day I remind myself that my inner and outer life are based on the labors of others,"* which summarizes the source of the drive that helped complete this book. From the Illinois Institute of Technology, Loyola University of Chicago, and Xavier University, my thanks and appreciation to Scott Peters and Mike Marcus, dedicated instructors and mentors who introduced me to a broad range of organizational theorists and practitioners; Chris Barlow, who truly understands, studies, teaches, and practices creativity in management; Michelle Engstrom, whose contributions, critiques, and insights on information flow and technical applications as well as on matters involving practicality have been singularly invaluable over the past year; Arup Varma for his quiet but fiercely focused support from across several continents; Barney Berlin for his patience, guidance, and quiet management associated with a variety of difficult tasks; and Kate Watland for her assistance, advice, and encouragement in support of my dissertation. On a personal note, I would like to pass on a note of remembrance for my brother, Mike, who was always smarter than me.

We thank all of you for your generosity and support, and know that we can count on you as we continue running this marathon; it is to you that this work is dedicated.

Managing Information in Complex Organizations

1

Introduction

The dynamics related to today's informational environments are far more complicated than those of fifty years ago. To a large extent, technology that provides "real time" or instant access to information greatly contributes to this complexity. More important, human reaction and the ability to process new information compound these conditions of complexity. Paradoxically, the causes for dilemmas in how information is handled also provide the solutions to resolve problem issues. First, however, we must understand the relation of information and data to information systems. This text provides a step approach intended to attain such an understanding. Each chapter will attack a discrete aspect of information handling, and the lessons learned will serve as a foundation for subsequent chapters.

Information failures bind commonalities in the events surrounding both World Trade Center attacks (1993, 2001), the fiascos involving Enron, Tyco, and Arthur Andersen, the crises and disasters of the *Challenger*, Chernobyl, Union Carbide (Bhopal), the Moscow Opera hostage situation, Waco, the Concorde, *Exxon Valdez*, and any number of other events that have commonly been lumped together under the category of disaster resulting from crisis. In each instance, information existed that might have assisted in lessening and possibly evading the impending crisis. In contrast, and possibly more important, examples exist that underscore success when information is handled properly. This book is about information and organizations. Specifically, the notion of how information affects and defines an organization is explored. One recent event involves the 2003 incursion of Coalition forces into Iraq. The military campaign provided evidence that information properly handled can produce successful results.

During the incursion of Coalition forces into Iraq in 2003, for example, we witnessed how information served to positively influence an organization and its mission. Before the conflict was begun, Allied information resources so outweighed that of the Iraqis that the outcome of the engagement was an almost certain foregone conclusion. A little later in the book we refer to *temporal* information processes upon which an organization may depend because these represent an archive of best practices and experiences "known" to the organization when faced with new challenges; these represent *organizational memory*. As a result of effectively drawing from the wealth of information contained within the organizations' temporal archives, casualties and damage were kept to a minimum while nearly all goals and objectives were efficiently achieved.

However, once the major military phase of the campaign had concluded, so too did the type and source of information that might prove of value to an "occupying" army. Attention shifted from archives that provided uncertain or dated information with reference to the new tasks; the focus was now on *spatial* information, represented by the reception of new information from a variety of sources, many of which are *uncertain*. By November, intelligence resources and processes showed signs of rapid constriction, which resulted in poor information gathering, questionable processing, and a less confident information distribution mechanism. This in turn led to more casualties and more material damage to the Coalition's resources than had been experienced *during the phase of major combat*. During the initial phases of the campaign in Iraq, intelligence was focused on a single objective. Once that objective was accomplished, not only were there more objectives, some of which had been expected, but there was also a need for many more sources of information, which may not have been anticipated. This condition, despite other resources, produces an untenable position for an offensive military machine that is suddenly required to assume the role of peacekeeper in an unpredictable environment.

These two extremes underscore a critical point this book will make, that is, information and organizations are inextricably related. The survival and growth of organizations is tied directly to information processing capacities and capabilities. But before we begin examining nuances that bind information and organizations, we must first address the concept of contemporary information use.

The term "information" is often overused and consequently becomes diluted. Phrases such as "information economy," "information systems," "information society," and "information management" are used in a myriad of applications.[1] As a concept, "information" tends to serve as rhetoric rather than as an analytical or insightful *function*.[2] For practitioners and scholars the term becomes the proverbial conundrum inside a puzzle surrounded by a riddle, and *meaning* itself becomes entirely lost in the realm of etymology, that is, the history of words. This condition distorts both the representation and the reality of meaning to the extent that relations between a word and its meaning frequently become disparate. This forces limits in language and has a corresponding impact that limits thought.[3] In a world where almost everything is immediately regarded as information, the *word* itself loses value. Without value, the motivation for purposeful research is severely restricted. In a sense, this notion revisits Hardin's "Tragedy of the Commons" in which public pastures were opened to all and the motive for conservation was lost. The remaining motive of self-interest resulted in overgrazing to such an extent that the saturated resource is lost to everyone.[4]

One point we wish to address in this context is the issue of "neutrality" as it exists between information and knowledge. Because data and information must be synthesized in the effort to achieve knowledge, both data and information must be regarded as neutral and unbiased. Knowledge on the other hand is rarely neutral. Without this distinction, information alone may become the basis for acting reactively and prematurely. The news media, for example, often presents information-as-knowledge, and organizations continually struggle with myth-information generated from *rumor-central*, that "invisible" group within organizations often found around company watercoolers that perpetuates gossip. While the politically correct phrase "We support the troops but not the war" was bantered along the Beltway, much of the popular press depicted the U.S. involvement in Iraq as a precursor to another Vietnam. While not particularly creative, this type of editorialized "information" violates the rule of neutrality in information and is akin to propaganda.

Similarly, during 2003 the media broadcast the notion that a condition known as severe acute respiratory syndrome (SARS), which originated in China, home of the Hong Kong flu, represented a global threat rivaled only by the "black death" plague of the Middle Ages. Despite the fact that there was no statistical information to bolster this "information," the city of Toronto was figuratively "quarantined," and students were being held out of school because their teachers had recently returned from the People's Republic. If one were to use the same faulty logic that applied to the popular "troops-to-war" comparison about Iraq, one might, based on the SARS misinformation, state that they "support the disease but not the virus."

Organizations are complex generators and dissipaters of information. This is central to issues involving the attainment of organizational goals and survival. The generation of information involves creating information and knowledge for an organization, and dissipation is the process of modifying the organization through use of information.[5] Effective and efficient generation and dissipation of information is a proven key determinant for competitive advantages. Organizations will generate and collect information about their constituent parts and process it in a number of ways. Behavior within an organization will be modified by the effects of information. But if information is mishandled by the organization, its potential value will be lost.

Information systems scholars have emphasized a need to make the role of information more *visible* in order to enable information sharing so that information can be leveraged, created, or expanded. This requires the construction of novel frameworks and systems if we are to understand the information processing function and understand the role played by information overload.

The main focus of this book is to present a diligent investigation into the role and concept of information and to map a more effective model for the use of information. This map will include management techniques involving the notions and practices associated with such topics as emergence, values-based leadership, and complexity. These concepts are being addressed individually in the literature, but this is the first attempt to bring them together in a purposeful, *cybernetic* approach. Cybernetics is derived from the Greek word *kybernetes*, which means "steersman" or "the art of steering" and refers to the idea of how things are interrelated. It is founded on the works of Wiener, von Bertalanffy, and Ashby, who, in the 1940s–1950s, developed theories to investigate communication systems that involved the transfer of information between systems and the environment, within systems, and the role of control or internal or external feedback in modifying its function.[6] The topic represents an excellent start for many of the ideas put forth in this text and underpins our central assertion that information in various stages, that is, generation, movement, and dissipation, govern organizational actions and in turn performance.

This book will explore the intricacies of information processing rather than the more common "black box" approach. The text will serve to expand the boundaries of information sciences and be useful to practitioners and advanced students in a variety of related courses and fields. Entropy, the state of *disorder*, or uncertainty, within a system *that ultimately maximizes* and *from which there is no return*, while founded in physics as the second law of thermodynamics, is equally applicable to other disciplines when the principle is applied to information. This is a strong concept for an IT professional, but it carries the same impact for second-year biology students, philosophers, military personnel, or public sector practitioners. Traditional approaches to information are bound by inflexible theories. Our approach requires the user to develop new theories as the facts change.

Navigating This Book

The first section of this text establishes the preliminaries. Chapter 2 introduces some of the key terms we use through out the text—semantics, cybernetics, entropy, and signals. In chapter 3 we will discuss information forms and dependencies. Specifically, we begin to explore the many forms information can take and how dependencies in the organization are affected because of information forms. It is here that we introduce the three dimensions of information processing—evolutionary, spatial, and temporal.

The second section of the text explores these three dimensions of information processing further in terms related to organizational memory, how unreliable information may be detected, and steps required to move organizational information to organizational knowledge. Chapter 4 grounds the concept of "information" using the sciences of semiotics (signs) and the concept of *emergence*. Charles Sanders Peirce (1839–1914), the scientist and logician, established semiotics to represent information flow from data capture through to some actionable event, for example, decision-making. The use of the semiotic discourse is relevant here, as information is nothing more than a collection of signs which, if interpreted correctly, produce value for the organization. Specifically, we explain information flow using a semiotic model. Information is no more than a collection of signals organized in a logical fashion. Building on our semiotic model in chapter 5, we cover concepts of coupling and cohesion in the organization's "information space." Here we conduct a discussion of problems on organization faces when trying to comprehend, generate, and act on signals. We look at the role various organizational devices and agents play in the generation and dissipation of signals. The work here draws from the theories in electrical, communication, and systems engineering. It is our contention that over the past two decades society has made great advances related to signal processing and communication systems in the field of engineering science and as a result, at least on the technical side, we have been able to do more with less. Broadband, wireless, and remote computing advances have all furthered the science of signal transfer and recognition. But as *organizations* have attempted to embrace these technologies, they seemed to become worse at implementing them. This failure is related to techniques that are shortsighted. In chapter 6 we discuss alternatives to correct this problem that include challenges to organizational learning and the effects of *emergent information*, a topic of recent interest among information theorists, on organizational hierarchies.

The third section, covered in chapters 7 and 8, presents some of the traditional problems associated with crisis planning and how they tie in with misconceptions involving information processing. Given that all crises are predicated on warning signals, it is surprising how much of the literature deals exclusively on crisis containment and recovery *after the fact* rather than on the development of programs dedicated to crisis evasion. We contend that the information processing frameworks put forth in the first half of the book will help move thinking from crisis containment to the practice of crisis evasion. We look at how organizations can hurdle many of the traditional information processing barriers associated with the human side of information technology—cognitive dissonance, errors, illusion information processing, and information bottlenecks.

In the final section of the book we present steps that organizations can take to optimize their information processing activities. In chapter 9 we outline steps on organization needs to take in order to establish an adequate information architecture. In the concluding chapter we conduct a discussion on advances in science related to computing and on how organizations can benefit from our recommendations as they continue to process information.

The appendix provides case studies as illustrations of how optimal information processing could prevent disastrous conditions or evade the effects of crises. Additionally, we investigate crisis implications associated with the cyberworld, a largely neglected topic. This discussion examines the meaning of cyberterrorism, the forms it may take and how it can occur, and safeguards, using a semiotic model, that should be considered. A similar discussion is conducted to elaborate on the issues related to medical errors and how they might be obviated. Medical errors, for example, result in malpractice litigation and patient deaths, and are a common source for negative press in the health care industry. We show how the various types of medical errors can be mapped on a semiotic framework.

This provides the introduction on our initial thoughts to information and suggests a "road map" for this text. In the next chapter we will explore the foundations of several notions presented throughout the text—semantics, cybernetics, entropy, and signals.

2

Organizations of Information
Semantics, Cybernetics, Entropy, and Signals

For our purposes, information is regarded as a vibrant entity composed of data sets related to a particular topic. Any of Roget's *Thesauruses* provides an entire page of synonyms under the word *information* and related uses of the word; each of them in some context is correct. The nuances related to the word *information* in definitions are those of semantics, that is, the contextual use of the word related to the topic or setting in which it is used.

This notion sets the basis for the discussion in this chapter. Initially we will discuss some of the issues related to semantics that deal with literal meanings corrupted during incidents of translation. While this point underscores what can happen when semantics is complicated across language barriers, it is intended to remind the reader that similar issues exist under any conditions during which the information recipient is obliged to interpret the intention of information received. In this sense then, the "vibrancy" of information takes on another dimension in that it appears capable of "adaptability," a feature generally reserved for living creatures. To address this new feature, we review the field of cybernetics, which seeks to compare the similarities between living beings and machines.

Finally, this chapter reexamines notions related to concepts found in other disciplines that relate to information. Specifically, we will refer to the concept of *entropy*, or "disorder," that can occur when information is mismanaged or poorly developed. Additionally, we will present some initial ideas regarding *emergence* and "discovery" related to information systems. The uses of these terms will be explored in more depth in later chapters, but it is important for the reader to have some familiarity with them early on. The references cited will provide those interested with a deeper understanding of the subjects used that are related to our discussion of information.

The notion that information provides value to organizations crystallized in the late 1950s when a Vienna-born professor, Peter Drucker, advanced the notion that the future's real accomplishments would result from the efficient use of a class of people he referred to as *knowledge workers*. Peter Drucker described this class of workers as those who respond to the demands placed on them through the use of information rather than arbitrary schedules attached to them by bosses; information and knowledge is either relevant to task fulfillment or it is not. Drucker argued that, in the new economy, knowledge is not just another resource like other factors of production—land, labor, and capital—but it is *the* resource. He currently contends that the use of knowledge and information has become the resource that makes today's society unique.[1]

A half century later, organizations are still unclear of how knowledge and information management can be used effectively. The two most prominent and determinant concerns affecting performance in today's society relate to the function of organizations and information. As environmental complexity increases, an advancing trend is taking place that folds models of organizations and information in such a manner so that the success of one becomes inextricably bound to the other. At the same time, each serves as a relational barometer on the success of the other. Effective and efficient use of information bolsters an organization and promotes longevity while the organization that turns a blind eye to the importance of information use flirts with atrophy. Organizations are ultimately judged by performance, not intentions, and if intentions stifle the flow of information, problems and the potential for crisis ensue.

Polaroid discounted the impact of the digital revolution because it regarded information transmitted in bytes as a separate medium.[2] As a result, they were not prepared for the economic impact digital cameras had on the "instant picture" market they had dominated for so long. In 1967, Swiss technicians at the research institute in Neuchâtel developed an electronic quartz movement that was suitable to power a wristwatch, but Swiss watch manufacturers rejected the concept. As a result, during the annual Swiss watch conference they had regarded the device as a toy while a group of convention visitors from Japan's Seiko Epson Corporation was receiving a different message based on the same information.[3] In each of these examples, how information was handled shaped the respective future for each of the organizations. In each instance, information was available and dispatched, but the manner in which the information was used or synthesized became the seminal consideration as to whether there was something to be gained for the organization. How information is interpreted represents a new type of currency in the marketplace. The value of this currency is reflected by how it is spent on the decisions, right or wrong, that affect behavior within the organi-

Figure 2.1   **Information Lost In Communications**

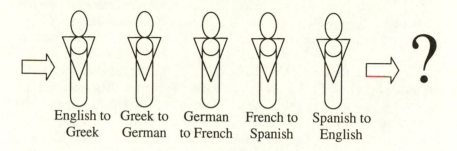

English to	Greek to	German	French to	Spanish to
Greek	German	to French	Spanish	English

zation. Ultimately, information is always measured in terms of decisions.[4] A salient function of information is to reduce uncertainty associated with the execution phase of the decision-making process.

Information is that which bridges the gap between intention and interpretation (Figure 2.1). While this notion seems simple at first blush, the process required to achieve the desired result is at once both subtle and complex. On a popular TV variety show from the 1950s, the *Gary Moore Show*, the host would invite bilingual audience members onstage to convey a joke. The joke would be told in English to someone who would translate it to another language, Greek for example, to the next person. That person would translate from Greek to German, and then from German to French, and so on down the line. The last person would translate the same joke back into English. The results of this exercise were always incomprehensible, but the illustration serves a point.

Semantics

The literal definition of semantics is "meaning." In our example the participants understood the concept of the exercise and, significantly, everyone worked in an effort to make the exercise succeed. Yet somehow the results were disastrous. This same principle is constantly and consistently set in motion in organizations and relates not to the intention of information, but to its interpretation. The exercise was destined to fail because it is obvious that the idiomatic and semantic differences that exist in five different languages would distort the original intention of the message. Word-meaning in various contexts belongs to the study of semantics, as "neutral" words gather their meaning based on the speaker's inflection or emphasis. Words need to be in "context" when spoken to have meaning. Analyzing words without the appropriate context renders them ineffective, sometimes useless, and in many cases can result in negative interpretations.

Similarly, confusion in information is compounded when culture preferences enter the mix. Years ago, in an effort to promote democracy among a largely illiterate Navajo group, Indian Services employees came up with the idea to use colored ballots to represent different candidates.[5] But the Navajo attribute an intense value system to colors, and results of the election were in this instance determined by cultural values ascribed to colors and not the qualifications of the candidates.[6] To the dismay of Indian Services, their well-intentioned plan misfired as they were unable to present their intentions in terms of semantics. Semantics then, a topic of variation and interpretation, impacts more than just language; it affects behavior. An integral part of semantics involves the actors (mechanical or human) that synthesize data that is intended to evolve into information; the results of the synthesis must be neutral and unbiased. Humans have a capacity for complexity with regard to semantics because they ascribe a wide range of possible affective, emotional attachments to meanings.

Affective stipulations involve emotions, feelings, and attitudes. Consider two people receiving the same information from their boss. One person loves his/her boss and hangs onto every word that is communicated while the other hates the boss and, while fixated on hatred, misses most of what is being conveyed. The mechanical world functions differently because a computer, a light switch, or some other device generally complies with the information it receives for a neutral, predesigned purpose without regard to emotions. Unless intentionally instructed to do otherwise, a mechanical device will accept or pass information as a function of purpose, nothing less, nothing more. Semantics represents a view of things from within a system's framework that comprises of the actors, the message, the medium, and the environment. The interaction among these variables results in semantic interpretation.

As with the translation example presented earlier, distinctions and breakdowns occur as signals and messages are transferred through organizations. While semantics may define word meanings in a particular context, semantics also dictates the type of *exclusivity* that "rules out" some interpretations. In the Navajo example, a cultural bias involving colors precluded the purpose of the ballots, and the bridge between intention and interpretation was never crossed. In our TV translation example, the breakdown between intention and interpretation may be traced to human interaction, which was based on incomplete information. Had the breakdown been related to some devices used to count ballots or on a glitch in a software program used to tabulate results, the breakdown would have been considered *mechanical* in nature. In the 2000 U.S. presidential election, we saw elements of both conditions that produced a serious state of confusion. Sometimes similar breakdowns are related to mechanical limitations and sometimes the problems are human in nature and, as such, information specialists often consider conditions believed to be common to both. One condition common to most systems involves the idea of hierarchy.

Hierarchy determines purpose in a number of ways; through the biological code of a DNA strand or by the instructions to an automated application. Coding translates information from one representation to another. Within chromosomes that reside within living cells, DNA uses a messenger RNA—a single-strand molecule acting as an intermediary between DNA and the protein-synthesizing machinery that dictates what cell function is in operation. Automated applications are programs engineered in sequential algorithms intended to produce specific results. Both examples require a hierarchy of sequences (codes) that determine all subsequent actions. Similarly, in organizations, hierarchy, usually vertical, determines mission statements from on high. In the objective sense, hierarchies define the way things ought to be, while in reality the world is full of subjective semantics capable of modifying organizational intentions. And while the principles of hierarchy can be stated verbally, they are evaluated in terms of abstractions associated with "meaning" that function according to the order or level of the abstraction. For example, candidates at various stages of an organizational training program are presented with data related to an organization's perceived best practices intended to demonstrate the correct way in which to conduct business, only to be later told by field practitioners, "This is how we do it here. . . ."

This relates to the concerns of "coupling" and "cohesiveness," which are determined by the *relation* of agents within a system, a notion that will be discussed at greater length later in the text. For now it is sufficient to understand "coupling" in terms of how closely the relation between agents working on the same task is tied and which of the agents has overall control of the task. "Cohesiveness" relates to the type of functions conducted by agents in a group that is dedicated to ensuring a common goal or outcome. In the mechanical world, systems too tightly coupled may be highly *efficient* at what they accomplish but completely *ineffective* in the cooperative processes that lead to meaningful, cohesive results. In each of the instances cited above, semantics within the system serves to define terms in a particular context and acts as an inhibitor to an organization's intentions. An organization would not be involved in training it did not expect to be used, and a system designer would not intentionally develop a bottleneck. Unfortunately, this is exactly what happens more often than one might expect, and the consequences are always bad.

Semantics then is also a process that requires the integration and summarization of previous experiences, considerations bounded by the actor's capacity for abstraction, and a system structure. Semantics affects interpretation and meaning. Once meaning is determined, the basis for whether information will lead to knowledge is established. We will explore this evolutionary process in chapter 4 in greater detail, but for now the reader should understand that what has been interpreted through the use of semantics is often the focus of review after things go wrong.

What If: Information Gathering and Sharing in Law Enforcement

While semantics and meaning are important conditions affecting information value, it is action, not words, that determines truth and the value of information. Often the results of action are determined by how tightly coupled the players within an organization are bound. Tight coupling occurs when individual organizational units are restricted because of a centralized authority governing all aspects of an operation. Organizational problems often stem not from an ability to *obtain* data, but from the inability to *share* information or from methods used to dissipate information related to data.

For the purpose of illustration, consider the following:[7] Assume, for the moment, you are a member of a state or local law enforcement agency assigned to the task of intelligence gathering on matters related to a new phenomenon likely to affect our state of domestic tranquility: terrorism directed at U.S. targets. The year is 1992, and the Allies under Generals Norman Schwarzkopf and Colin Powell have recently completed a successful campaign against the Stalinist regime of Iraq. Kuwait has been liberated, and while the infrastructure of Iraq has been reduced to the extent that they no longer pose a military threat in the region, their political structure remains virtually intact.

Just as the introduction of the new narcotic crack cocaine during the late 1980s changed forever the way the police would be involved in the drug war, you suspect that counterterrorism activities are likely to have a great impact on the future of law enforcement, so you do your homework. That homework includes checking with a newly formed European counterterrorism information exchange, the Trevi Group, which informs you that radical religious fundamentalists from the Middle East, sponsored by "invisible" countries, appear to pose the greatest threat to their respective country's security. You convince your boss of the need to work with federal authorities because of terrorism-related information available through their networks. On the executive side you establish contacts with the FBI and INS, while on the judicial side you make contacts with the Justice Department. Additionally, you begin to establish an informants' network.

From the resources now available, you begin structuring a database related to terrorism. The U.S. embassy in Amman, Jordan, provides you a list of recent applicants who, while living in various Middle Eastern countries, were born in the United States and have applied for and been granted American passports. While cross-checking data, you find certain anomalies involving Middle Easterners who have entered the United States with Iraqi passports but no U.S. visas, and who have been allowed to remain in the states pending administrative hearings. Because individuals with such a status are required to provide a contact address, you find that a number of these people reside at the same addresses. Some have declared addresses, which indicates that they reside at three principal addresses, two of which are in town while another is in a town just over the state border.

Of the two in-town addresses, one is a vacant lot and the other is the address of a local college that knows nothing of the subjects you are tracking. The third address is an apartment complex, and the building management provides you a list of tenants. None of your subjects' names appear on any of the leases, but several apartments in one complex are leased to people who have distinctive Middle Eastern names. Name checks on these individuals are inconclusive, but the local phone company provides you with the records of phones listed to some of the subjects at that address. Among the phones listed, one has been disconnected, according to the phone company, because of unpaid bills amounting to thousands of dollars stemming from dozens of calls over the past weeks to Iraq. Based on this information, you are successful in securing a warrant, which is based on the fact that some of the foreign occupants who might be in the apartment have falsified their entry documents. Upon executing the warrant, you discover the people you are seeking as well as plain-view evidence of a bomb-making factory.

While the *details presented in this scenario are factual*, the sequence related to law enforcement activities, while viable, never occurred. The semantics of this scenario provided meaning for our investigator, but in reality, the context of the culture, like the Navajo colors, greatly diminished his effectiveness to act. Under conditions that existed then, some of which still exist, optimal information processing could not occur. Proper handling of information could have led to preemptive action by those members of law enforcement who are constitutionally charged with providing for the public good. As a result of the events characterized by this scenario, the first World Trade Center (WTC) bombing took place on February 26, 1993. Similar scenarios with similar results would play out in Oklahoma City in 1995, Atlantic City in 1996, and again in New York City, Pennsylvania, and Washington, DC, on September 11, 2001. Each of these incidents supports a common notion that can be traced to the *meaning*, or interpretation, of the information collected. The interpreted value of the available information altered both the priorities and perceptions involved in these situations long before the meaning of the information had been determined.

The consequence of semantics leads to organizational issues of *complexity*, *adaptation*, and *semiotics*, which involves the meaning of signs. The intention of an organization to focus on the possible effects of semantics (meaning) relates directly to a probability that the greatest amount of information will be transmitted. Whether this can or will be accomplished is determined by cybernetics.

Cybernetics

Cybernetics is derived from the Greek *(kybernetes)* and refers to the person who steers the boat. Literally it means "steermanship," which connotes control of the direction in which one is headed. In the English vernacular, cybernetics relates to the theory of messages.[8] The condition of control is critical to the idea of cybernetics, although the command side of the control issue is often more common with machines than humans. Cybernetics is the theory of messages. The theory maintains that it is possible to determine the probability of the maximum information carried by a channel of a communication apparatus.[9] Such apparatuses include the channels of communication between humans whether or not the transmission is mechanically assisted. *First-order cybernetics* sought to contrast living systems with artificial ones and stressed control over the transfer of clear messages between the sender and receiver; the most effective models use cybernetics to *bridge* the gap between what is *intended* and what is *interpreted.* This was accomplished through engineering (controlling) a system design in such a manner that a high degree of certainty in results is nearly always guaranteed. Naturally, because of the variables involved, the degree of control is more effective when instructing machines or computers than when dealing with humans.

By the late 1960s, advances in technology allowed for fairly stable system actions, that is, those that could be coded and programmed into a system were also predictive. An engineer could program robot arms of an assembly line to comply with instructions that provided predictive outcomes. Similarly, procedures could be developed in computer programs to create simulations on a screen before production was begun on a project. In a sense, the first order of cybernetics, while actively seeking to contrast living systems with artificial ones, became subsumed by elements of predicable determinism in which only inevitability existed. Without uncertainty, there was no concern for probabilities. For example, if I already "know" tomorrow's lottery numbers will be 1–2–3–4–5–6, uncertainty regarding the selection of the numbers does not exist, so there is no need for me to consider the probabilities associated with drawing random numbers from a pool; there is no need for new information.

At this stage of development in cybernetics, the system *model* rather than the *engineer* controlling the model becomes the point of focus. Informational input alters the system environment from its current state to a future state, which in turn modifies the organization of the system. The certainty of information is predetermined by programming techniques that leave nothing to chance. Chance, however, plays a large part in human systems and information flow. This compelled cyberneticists to consider "second-level" processes for systems, which, because of a high number of associated variables, required a broader approach. This need evolved as *second-order cybernetics.*

Second-order cybernetics evolved to consider the effect of cybernetics on social systems. Generally speaking, the externalities or unforeseen consequences that affect a system cannot be programmed because they are too random. Contingency planning is founded in a cybernetic (control) approach to predictive probability that often produces little more than a "best guess" manual. In a later chapter we will address issues related to probability and consequence, but for now we address the class distinctions between first- and second-order cybernetics. The first-order approach focuses on the results of a design with no regard for characteristics that have no bearing on the process; the study is passive and purely objective. Second-order cybernetics melds the observer and that which is observed with the understanding that results are dependent on interaction between the two. The first order allows for the efficient production of a handgun without regard to how the weapon might be used. The second order realizes that the use of the weapon will produce certain consequences, some of which the producer may wish to avoid. The purpose of the second-order approach includes the intention to alter the system, or organization, which is being observed. Such changes are accomplished with the use of information.

Cybernetics then involves an attempt to create predictive models based on the use and control of information. Today's technology affords first-order developers tools that have a distinct advantage that was unavailable when British psychiatrist W. Ross Ashby[10] first considered the concept in the middle of the last century. The second order of cybernetics further developed notions that considered similarities between living and mechanical systems that emphasized *interdependency in autonomy*, information effects on organizations, the environment in which they function, and the importance of cognition, or learning, to the organization. Each of these factors relates to information and how it is used to change organizations. And the misuse of information is most apparent during conditions of crisis, especially those leading to disaster.

Disasters such as the *Challenger*, Chernobyl, Union Carbide (Bhopal), and the Moscow Opera hostage situation, Waco, the Concorde, and *Exxon Valdez* can be attributed to poor management of information. In each of the instances cited above, information related to warnings was present well before the eventual catastrophe.[11] However, because there was either (1) no organizational response plan or, (2) an inappropriate understanding of some existing plan, the probability that a crisis would occur was enhanced. We maintain that the appropriate use and management of the available information would have, in most cases, served to *evade* the crisis conditions that precipitated. At various stages that led to each crisis, available information was "missing." Missing is not the same as lost; missing implies some chance for recovery. In some cases recovery means the simple act of locating, while in others the conditions involved with the location can impede or defeat recovery. For organizations, available information that "goes missing" supports uncertainty in the system. Uncertainty resides in the realm of entropy.

Entropy

Rudolf Clausius (1822–1888) reduced the science of thermodynamics to two laws. The first states that matter can neither be created nor destroyed, and the second states that while the *quantity* of energy may not be changed, its *quality* may be reduced.[12] Clausius proposed that energy is constant, but entropy tends to maximize. His second law defines the term entropy as a *measure of disorder in a system.* Near the turn of the century, Ludwig Boltzmann (1844–1906) statistically asserted that entropy increases almost always, rather than always, and, importantly, established the probability that the effects of entropy are *irreversible* once equilibrium, or maximum entropy, is achieved.[13] By example, if an ice cube is deposited into a glass of water, two states within the glass are observable; the form of the ice cube and that of the surrounding liquid. As the cube melts, however, the certainty associated with the ice cube is less orderly. Eventually the cube dissolves into the water and is unobservable; maxim entropy has been achieved and is, without the introduction of another energy source, irreversible. By irreversible we mean that the two observed components, the water and the ice, will never revert to their original states. The resultant water-ice combination does not allow the observer to clearly identify with any certainty what was ice and what was water prior to their combination.

The ideas of disorder and irreversibility associated with entropy have profound implications for information. This concept applies to information and data that recombine across a communication channel. So the greater the increase in entropy (toward maximization), the less observable certainty exists in an information system; less certainty means less information. Assume that three sources within an organization have data, collected separately, that, when combined, produces information of importance to the organization. Two weeks before a planned conference, one of the sources is burdened with an unrelated task, which draws it away from its initial work before the data can be used. The second source becomes the victim of company "rightsizing" and is let go. At this stage, the information opportunity to generate something that might have resulted from combining the data from the three sources has suffered the effects of maximum entropy. The next opportunity these sources *may* have to be joined again is at the conference, at which time the informational impact that may have been obtained by combining the data is past. Interestingly, in 1894, Boltzmann remarked that he felt entropy was directly related to "missing information." In the Victorian age of deterministic ideals, this was an idea far ahead of its time, which would not be given any serious attention for another sixty years.[14]

By the halfway point of the twentieth century, the United States enjoyed unprecedented prosperity largely because its economy was bolstered during the effort to rebuild the world after a major global conflict. American scientists had helped decide the war and had ushered in the atomic age. While New Age authors like Aldous Huxley and Peter Drucker wrote of the need and future importance of "knowledge workers" in preparation of the impending "information age," few took note; after all, America was the epicenter for all things good and new. Things changed though, on October 4, 1957.

The Soviet Union orbited a small transmitting satellite into space, which they dubbed *Sputnik (Traveler)*. Almost overnight the impression of superiority in the American way of life was noticeably shaken. Terms like "brain drain" and descriptions of our educational system as a "vast wasteland" began to creep into the vocabulary of both scientists and reactionists. The system that had buoyed the American experience since after World War II was demonstrating instability, uncertainty, and disorder; it was displaying the affects of entropy. The notion of "missing information" contributing to this state of affairs clearly indicated that bias was in part responsible for the prevailing condition. The lexicon that had existed before *Sputnik* did not consider or allow for the probability that technology under Communist influence might surpass the science guided in a democracy. But such limits demonstrated that our information was inadequate, and in an effort to counter the impact that had been experienced, all principal disciplines were reevaluated and new approaches to information were sought. In 1958 the government established the Advanced Research Projects Agency (ARPA) to assist in fulfilling these needs, and the race toward information and information systems had begun.

The specifics on how information flow should be handled were still unclear. Then in 1959, Claude Shannon and Warren Weaver of MIT, among others, revisited work related to the field of thermodynamics while seeking possible answers. Specifically, Shannon's work was related to signals and how they were influenced as they coursed through communication channels. As had been noted in physical systems, there was evidence that signal transfers were subject to disturbances that affected the information to be conveyed through a channel.[15] Depending on the variables at work during the transmission of a signal, information in a message was subject to conditions of uncertainty. Shannon considered the measure of uncertainty in a message in terms of entropy. For him, information involved revelation in that to be useful, information must be "unexpected" in the sense that it was not previously known while at the same time being universal. In the universal sense, a mathematical expression can be recognized as such by mathematicians throughout the world regardless of language differences. The idea that information should be "unexpected" means that it should be unique. Revelation from information leads to the lowering of uncertainty (entropy) in the environment. A message is informative if the chance of its predictability is small. If, by contrast, a message is very predictable, it has a small amount of information—one is not surprised to receive it.[16] If the information receiver is aware the information conveyed, it has little additive purpose and changes nothing. Information is more a matter of process than storage.[17] The process is dynamic, always changing, and though information will be stored for the purpose of reference, new and unique information that is received during the process has a bearing on what has come before. This is the basis for cognitive learning, which will be discussed further in later chapters. New information has the ability to change the perspective of information that has been stored. Without the characteristic of uniqueness in information, the course of action in information gathering in organizations can begin to "loop," that is, recycle that which is already known so the process begins to gravitate to a condition of equilibrium. Once this occurs, the information process can become stalled, which indicates the onset of entropy within the system.

Once entropy in information is maximized, disorder and uncertainty within the system become the order of the day. Recovery from such a condition requires a reorganization that precludes the existence of the previous system. Like a booster rocket that propels a craft toward space, a system suffering from maximum entropy is best ejected or it merely rides along as baggage. It should be noted that in the context of the information, meaning, that is, *semantics*, is irrelevant.[18] What is important is that the transfer of discernable information is accomplished. When Alexander Bell communicated to Watson via a prototype of the first telephone, the content of the message was less important than the fact that a voice message had been conveyed through a mechanical device.

Signals versus Information versus Knowledge

Information can be said to be a logical collection of rudimentary elements assimilated in some logical fashion. But what comprises a rudimentary element? We assert that such elements are *signals*.

The *Merriam-Webster Dictionary* defines a signal as:

- an act, event, or watchword that has been agreed on as the occasion of concerted action: something that incites to action;
- something (as a sound, gesture, or object) that conveys notice or warning;
- the sound or image conveyed by telegraphy, telephony, radio, radar, or television; a detectable physical quantity or impulse (as a voltage, current, or magnetic field strength) by which messages or information can be transmitted.

It follows then that one *makes* information from a logical comprehension of signals. In a 1981 article, Martha Feldman and James March rightfully argue that information in organizations can be examined as signals and symbols. Information represents a commodity that can be interpreted in a variety of ways.[19] Yet both data and information in their purest state are consummately objective.[20] The value of available information should be represented in terms of relatively low, fixed costs. It is only after information has been synthesized that it attains value. Once synthesized, information should provide the basis for the action related to behavior modification; it becomes knowledge. Too often, however, information is treated as knowledge, and actionable events are founded on premature assumptions; this practice exposes any existing conditions to critical faults. The effects of such faults are particularly evident during impending crisis. Today's dynamic environment mandates that information must flow along lines of certainty and through channels that maximize technical assurance. Organizations are consumers and producers of information. Information makes the organization, and organizations are a product of information.

Ultimately the synthesis of information yields knowledge that may be distinguished from data or information in that it serves as the basis for an actionable event. An actionable event is intended to modify some behavior of organization members. Knowledge, as opposed to information, is rarely neutral because the system has synthesized it. The need to manufacture a product (knowledge) from information in a biased manner is important to the success of business missions and organizational agendas. It represents the result of interpretation by the knowledge-user. The generation and dissipation of information in organizations is all geared toward improving the process and outcomes of decision-making.[21] The cost of gathering and processing information must be lower than the value it will derive from optimal decision-making using the information. The epistemological discussion of knowledge may be traced back to the days of Plato and Aristotle. They studied the sources and types of knowledge that humans acquired over time. Attempts to classify knowledge can be looked at considered from two perspectives: explicit and tacit, based on communicability of knowledge[22] and individual and collective knowledge, based on the knowing entity.[23] Explicit knowledge can be expressed in words and numbers and shared in the form of data, scientific formulae, product specifications, manuals, universal principles, etc. This kind of knowledge can be readily transmitted across individuals formally and systematically. Also, it can easily be processed by computer, transmitted electronically, or stored in databases.

Tacit knowledge based largely on experience is highly personal and hard to formalize, making it difficult to translate or share with others. Subjective insights, intuition, or hunches fall into this category. Tacit knowledge involves ideals, values, and emotions. The subjective and intuitive nature of tacit knowledge makes it difficult to process or transmit the acquired knowledge in any systematic or logical manner.[24] For tacit knowledge to be communicated, it must be converted into words, models, or numbers that anyone can understand—a difficult task. For example, master craftsmen develop a wealth of expertise only after years of experience. This knowledge is difficult to articulate and highly subjective. Personal insights, intuitions, hunches, and inspirations derived from experience are all part of tacit knowledge, which also serves to shape the way we perceive the world around us.

Reductionism versus Emergence

As with other facets of the connected universe, the foundations of information theory are grounded in a variety of disciplines. We often find the influence of one discipline's theory is not confined to a particular area of study but rather is capable of positing some residual influence on other fields. In one sense then, we observe the notion of reductionism, which maintains that "we're all connected" in that all objects and events may be reduced down to their ultimate elements or indivisible parts.[25] This idea is fundamental to the practice of "reengineering," during which a product or process is taken apart in an attempt to improve it before it is reassembled. This concept is opposed, however, by a systems theory that maintains that properties defining higher-order systems *should not be reduced* to the properties of the lower-order subsystems or component parts; this is the concept of emergence. In the first instance the thought is to understand the whole; it should be reduced and its parts inspected. In the second, the belief is that any disassembly of the whole defeats the idea of inspecting the workings of the whole. In information, traditional approaches in search of answers have relied on a reductionism approach, but in most instances the results have produced little more than a revisit to the original system under observation.

Reductionist methods require the observer to inspect the past. In organizations, decisions on inventory levels may be based on a regression model of past product performance. Preparation for the next game requires professional athletes and coaches to pore over films involving the upcoming opponent. Insurance actuaries review past experience to help to determine premium rates. Each instance provides a sound basis for the beginning of information analysis, but none relates to current environmental dynamics. To capture current data and information, organizations must employ an emergent approach.

The emergent view of a system is all-encompassing. It takes into account the multilevel hierarchy that exists in systems and organizations and views subsets of the structure in terms of independent building blocks or components that contribute to the organization as a whole. The subsets may reasonably be expected to demonstrate similar, though not necessarily identical, characteristics as the whole. This concept is based in part on the work of Benoit Mandelbrot, who defined *fractals* as objects that display characteristics of self-similarities at various levels within a hierarchy of a system.[26] These ideas contribute to the notion of complexity, or interrelated layering, in an organization. While variety can be represented in the hierarchy, it is commonly held that subsets, which conform to principles defining the welfare of the whole, are most likely to survive. Rogue subsets generally destabilize and dissolve and may develop as fodder for some future part of the hierarchy. This principle commonly occurs in nature and is part of the evolutionary cycle, which is generally distributive, that is, there is little room for distinction between the system environment and the system itself. A common example of this relation occurred about 65 million years ago when nearly 70 percent of earth's species were extinguished as the result of cataclysmic changes in the environment, and yet, life continued.

Information may be thought of as the nutrients that feed or energize a complex system, and any contribution at any level of the system has the potential to benefit the entire organization. As in biology, nutrients fuel system growth and encourage the chances for adaptation that may be required. With dynamic emergent-oriented designs, spontaneous adaptability is possible. This form of change (reorganization) is predicated on the fact that the organization receiving information will use it. Information deprivation has the opposite effect, and the results are not confined to the issue of data or information availability, but rather are related to how the system handles and manages the information that is available. As we will see in later chapters, information obtained and not used is worthless, regardless of its otherwise perceived intrinsic value.

In summary, reductionist doctrines are passive and rely on determined information while emergent concepts are "working" and actively seek information. Future information systems will be focused on emergence as a tool for the analysis of real-time (occurring) developments related to organizational well-being. The reductionist uses information to reach defined and predictable objectives as part of solution or goal. Emergence seeks information that otherwise cannot be predicted at any level of search, and so fulfills Shannon's expectations of information. The discovery of information of use to the organization contributes to solutions and is a property of an emergent process.

In this chapter we have established some of the groundwork that will be revisited and built upon in subsequent chapters. We also understand that for many, some of what has been addressed is difficult because it may be new and can appear quite abstract. But it is important that the reader become familiar with the terminology and concepts presented, as their use becomes clearer as we share illustrative examples for each of the points raised throughout the book; your indulgence will be rewarded. In the next chapter we will address some of the barriers and forms associated with information transfer. Within organizations, how information is handled is generally addressed in some broad sense of policy or form, but often without regard as to how methods and actors within the organization are capable of distorting the intention of the information being provided.

3

Information Forms and Dependence

As we have seen in chapter 2, information can be affected, if not distorted, for a variety of reasons that may include conditions of poor signal transfer, conditions in which the information is incomplete, or conditions in which the recipient, whether intentional or not, alters information so that its intention is lost. We must also consider issues related to *when* information becomes valuable, *where* it is received and stored, and *whether* if stored the information is subject to review. The problems related to the information that impact organizations may certainly occur if the information received is incomplete or inaccurate, but they may also result if an organization's knowledge base, its archive of stored information, is deficient because of the methods used by the company to create or review knowledge. A form of information that is useful to an organization will evolve in stages; first it is received and assessed, then it may be stored if it is considered valuable. Thereafter, information both received and stored should be routinely compared against each other for new dimensional values. Dimensions are represented by a scale, or range, and these comparisons are intended to uncover similarities between new and existing information. Issues related to *spatial* (newly arrived) and *temporal* (storage) processing of information are addressed in this chapter. Additionally, we consider an *evolutional* hybrid to processing information intended to address delays that otherwise exist in the normal processing of information. Finally, the philosophy of perception that affects information is addressed to remind us that subjective interpretation will affect information.

If one were to regard information flow in the same way that some billing arrangements seem to be handled, interesting similarities are evident. It has been suggested that if a *bill payment,* say for a credit card, and a *bill for payment* from the credit card company are mailed between the same respective parties at the same time, the former will take twice as long to be received as the latter. Literally, while this may not be entirely accurate, the process and forms involved with payment are considerably less complex than the dependent procedures, for example, billing cycles, required to credit an account. In other words, the payee gets a bill, writes a check, and mails it. The company that receives the check must be concerned with applicable interest, financial credit restrictions, mailings, posting, and any number of matters related to accurate credit transactions.

Let us assume that information travels in the same way, so that only half of what is transmitted is received before the receiver, dependent on the information, begins acting. Assume further that neither side has any regard for the disparity in the content lag. In short order the dependent group will reach a state of confusion based on the fact that, as "late" information arrives, plans that have been started will require alterations. If this kind of process continues, it is likely that the receiving group will eventually be unable to manage any changes that the information might require.

Our investigation into organizations of information begins by looking into the forms and dependencies that affect the efficient transfer of information. This is important to understand because some of the dependencies in information relationships can lead to a distortion of information. Similarly, the manner in which information is displayed, that is, its form, will affect its impact on the organization. While most forms are efficient and productive, many are misleading; consider an IRS tax form or some software manuals for example. People who write such things usually have a pretty good understanding of their content, but they often expect the consumer to have a similar level of understanding. With information, things get more complicated because the forms in which information is received are always varied, sometimes unreliable, and always subject to interpretation. In the final analysis, information should always lead to actionable knowledge, and the action is always exhibited by behavior.

The results and effects of how information is absorbed, synthesized, and used will always be evident in behavior in individuals and organizations. In the event that information is received and not used, behavior will not change. A principal function of information is to accede to actionable knowledge, that is, behavioral changes are observable in the actions of those who receive and use information: the purpose of actionable knowledge is to modify the behavior of individuals, groups, organizations, or machines.

While information can be intentionally channeled, as through the specific instructions of a concerned parent to a child in need of direction or in a code sequence through a directed pipeline to a computer, there is also a question as to whether expected behavior changes can be anticipated or predicted. In mature organizations, systems, or people, it has been argued that conventional activities can be reduced to *routines* of operation that are preformed over and over again.[1] The results in such routines are then predictable. If this were the case universally, there would be no need for information, as real information should be regarded as unique such that it generally predicates change. New information can threaten routines and raises the possibility of unanticipated behaviors in both organizations and individuals. Unexpected behavior is usually associated with the *reaction* to new information when *adaptation* is required. In later chapters we discuss crisis situations in which the effects of *reaction* contribute to the problem under review while *adaptation* might have provided more constructive solutions to the problem. Successful adaptation to information makes the adaptor better fit to compete within the environment, and successful adaptation is exhibited through behavioral change. In the nineteenth century the British naturalist Charles Darwin explained the process of adaptation in biology in terms of the *interaction* between a species and its environment. While we address certain parallels that exist between this theory and information in the next chapter, our initial approach to information in organizations deals with how information that is received by the organization is ultimately handled. Information considered useful is processed and regarded in three ways: evolved, spatial, or temporal. To help illustrate this idea, we will use a familiar analogy.

Although you may not drive a car of this particular design, the instrumentation should be familiar (Figure 3.1). The large dial to the left is a tachometer, the one to the right a speedometer. Other dials might indicate oil pressure and electrical discharge fuel reserves, engine temperature, or an odometer to measure miles traveled. If the driver is the chief decision-maker and the car is the organization, these dials would provide both temporal and spatial representations of important information. Spatial information processes represent the most current, often changing, information available and is that which the decision-maker monitors closely while the engine is running. Temporal is "stored" information, for example, the mileage on the odometer, and would be monitored less frequently and is available whether the engine is running or not. Such information may provide the decision-maker a guide as to when certain maintenance should be performed on the vehicle. Due diligence requires that when the odometer advances about 4,800 kilometers or so, it is time to change the oil, but the decision-maker has some degree of flexibility with this time frame. If, however, while cruising at 120 kilometers per hour the tachometer points wildly to the right and the oil pressure gauge reads zero, the decision-maker should know there is a problem that, if left unattended, will lead to engine failure. Spatial information, like the pointer on

Figure 3.1 **Dashboard of a Classic Car**

Source: Courtesy of Art Today.

the tachometer, must be attended to in real time. Failure to do so will result in immediate disruptions to the organization.

Now assume that the instruments are individuals providing feedback to the organization. Each dial represents a different department, and some departments require closer monitoring than others. When acting in concert, the instrumentation will indicate that the organizational engine is running smoothly and the decision-maker can enjoy the ride. But if the instruments provide feedback that requires action and such information is ignored, the decision-maker can expect problems. By example, the driver who flirts with risk by driving as the dial on the fuel gauge bounces atop "E" should not be surprised if the vehicle comes to a halt. This analogy illustrates the importance of balance in the processes, spatial and temporal, used to frame feedback in the form of information for the decision-maker.

Communications theorist Harold Innes saw information in terms of immutability and mobility and advanced the idea that information may be *spatially or temporally* bound.[2] The immutable, or temporal, aspect of this idea refers to an organization's ability to archive information for future reference. Archived information is sometimes referred to as an organization's "memory." Spatial, or mobile, information refers to data that has the ability to push the message it attempts to communicate to increasingly broader audiences. This

Figure 3.2 **Aspects of Information Processes**

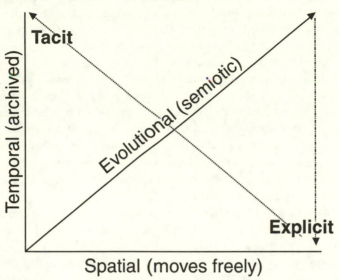

type of information is received by a variety of sources, some of which will prove unreliable.

We introduce a third facet to this information processing scheme that combines elements from both the temporal and spatial realms. This other processing scheme contributes a semiotic (literally "the study of signs") aspect to provide a more contextual complement on both the mobility and immutability in information (Figure 3.2). By contextual we mean new information is qualified immediately as to whether it is relevant to the receiver. The relation of the information to the receiver determines whether behavioral adaptation should be anticipated as an option. The notion of semiotics recognizes that meaning is often tied to the context of the environment, that is, information, regardless of its source, may have important meaning in one environment but none in another.

Certainly people are familiar with street signs as instruments that convey meaning related to a particular environment, for example, an intersection or railway crossing. The red octagon-shaped sign that "means" stop at an intersection carries a different (or no) meaning when it is mounted on some fraternity house wall. Some ascribe meaning to astrological signs as an indicator of their own or others' mannerisms or to future events as prescribed by the stars. A picture can convey meaning beyond aesthetics and will be judged according to the viewer's environment. A picture of the Kaiser during World War I meant entirely different things depending on one's view of global conditions at the time. Language, either verbal or of the type associated with gestures or posturing, involves semiotics in that the interpretation of the "signal" being communicated is related to the circumstances of the environment. In each of these situations the conditions under which some forms of information were conveyed determined how that information would likely be interpreted and if it was of value. Semiotics involves information in relation to the environment in which it is presented and expects changes in behavior to occur based on the analysis of the "signs" presented by the information. Information that is irrelevant to one environment may be disregarded in one set of circumstances and passed on to another environment that finds it useful. This allows information to continue to move freely under most circumstances while at the same time capturing the most task-related data for synthesis under specific circumstances.

While each of the processes mentioned will be covered in more depth in the next three chapters, for now we will address how information barriers in organizations can influence or impede desired behavior. Specifically, we will focus on common practices found in organizations that impede the use of information—myth-information, hoarded information, and distorted information. Later we will review behavioral reactions to information that can affect its usefulness because of interpretation that is affected by cognitive dissonance, perception, and the inability to properly use feedback (see chapter 8).

The Three Dimensions of Information Processing

Of the three informational dimensions (spatial, temporal, and evolutionary) we have presented, organizations are mostly involved with spatial information processes. The spatial realm feeds the modern information engine in organizations with a constant flow of new information from a variety of sources, and the information engine is designed around electronic technology. It should be remembered that there was a time in the not-too-distant past when, in order to obtain information, one was required to seek the information, perhaps by visiting a library. In today's environment, information comes to the seeker via interconnected Web delivery systems.

Collection of information is easy; making sense of it presents the challenge. Spatial information involves the distribution of data along those paths that are the fastest and furthest-reaching. While spatial information appears to react quickly in a dynamic environment, that is, as the environment changes, so too the information that is released changes, and some concern must be given regarding the reliability of such information. Once, information sources were thoroughly checked before information was released, but today there seems to be more information available than time, and "questionable" data is always in the information pipeline. Competitive organization demands place the greatest emphasis on the newest information and data, which in turn places conditions on the use of all the information in the pipeline, for example, what is useful and what is not? Spatial processes seek to impact and alter the environment with the most recent available information long before it is archived. This practice makes sense in a supply chain environment, that is, Dell Computers, where Just-In-Time inventory practices are employed. The same practice can have an awkward effect if employed in a task in which cumulative research or testing for validity is required and such tasks are associated with new information. This process is complex and requires timely analysis and detailed comparisons between new information and the existing repertoire of information present in the organization. For example, during the late 1950s, thalidomide, a "new drug," was prescribed as a sedative for pregnant women, but unforeseen side effects produced children who were unintentionally maimed because the drug was marketed before all the information was available.[3]

Because spatial information represents the "newest" data, it can have a tendency to "shake things up" as users are anxious to be first to glean anything that might be useful for the organization. During the Iraqi Freedom campaign, there were at least two instances where "new" information triggered missile attacks on "targets of opportunity" thought to be sanctuaries of Iraqi "command and control" personnel. These attacks represented a "flexible response" to the spatial information that "stuck"; this was less credible information, which failed to produce less dramatic results. Typically, in the business world, a legislative or regulatory change affecting an organization provides a good example of spatial information that will impact the business environment. Subsequent organizational changes will be reflected *explicitly* through policy or procedure changes. Explicit expressions of information and subsequent knowledge, as we will see, should be easily transmittable and presented in an easily understandable form. Because of obsession with the "need for speed" by most users, the use of spatially processed information will continue to be the most widely used by organizations.

The temporal aspect of information contrasts to spatial processes because temporal information has been synthesized and accepted as reliable; it becomes a candidate for storage in the organization's memory. Individuals display temporal information processes when demonstrating certain skills or abilities that are based on their own experience and memory. Such information or knowledge often represents the "value" in what an employee brings to an organization. It is interesting to note that some companies are very guarded about allowing the competition to inspect their facilities while others are not. In the latter case, the organization understands that the competition is likely aware of their processes, but the real knowledge, that which the competition would like to "uncover," resides within their employees.

Information that is archived in a temporal repository presents another level of information complexity. Archived information implies that the data collected has meaning. Having achieved the characteristic of meaning, the collection becomes the basis for knowledge creation in organizations. Additional complexity is indicated in how, or if, the archive is used. The tendency to efficiently use information reflects the social value of the information to the organization. Conversely, to take archival information for granted ignores a valuable contention that to know where you are, you must first review where you have been.

The efficient use of information requires the recognition of meaningful trends as the information is synthesized and linked in an effort to establish value-results by establishing a relation between spatial and temporal processes. The foundation of this process requires *semiotics,* the study and correct interpretation of signs related to the information, which will be discussed in greater depth in the next chapter. This connection between information that is bound between spatial and temporal processes allows organizations the ability to establish information "cascades" for the purpose of transforming information to action based on knowledge. Without this step, there is a tendency to give the impression that fundamentally, all information processes should be categorized under conditions of either temporal or spatial. Put another way, organizations have a tendency to pigeonhole information as either spatial *or* temporal and seldom appreciate the fact that information can possess qualities of both.

Because spatial processes emphasize seeking, delivering, and churning new information, the cost in terms of lost information *value* can be high. When the most current information is regarded as the most valuable, prior information drops back in the queue and may be overlooked, even lost. This approach in spatial processing can leave essential information buried as newer information builds, and this delays the opportunity for linking any relation to the equally important temporal processes that have already been stored. It is important to weigh the new information received against the organizational memory to determine if existing archives of information may have to be modified. Organizations that combine spatial and temporal processes develop their own type of *evolution* of information, that is, information capable of adapting to organizational requirements survives and that which does not, will not. The semiotic aspect of the process provides a faster method in terms of recognition of "signs" associated with information that will be useful to the organization. This *evolutionary* processing synthesizes spatial information and quickly forges the link to temporal processes.

Information and Behavior

Individuals and organizations focus on ways to resolve problems by attending to a *problem space* in which all elements related to a given question reside. Problem space is represented by the convergence of the task environment, that is, the conditions representing the task problem, the known or available strategies to address the problem, and a problem-solver or team assigned to resolve the problem. While this space represents the convergence of the principal factors that affect problem or issue resolution, it *is not* the only space affected by information flow. Too often, personnel working on tasks requiring decisions or solutions channel their attention into the problem space without regard to other equally important parts of the information processing system.

In later chapters we will address the specifics of the *task environment* and *available strategies* section of an information processing system, but for now it is important to understand that each of the three parts of the information processing system, that is, task environment, strategies available, and the problem-solver, is in itself a distinct system distinguishable from the entire system (Figure 3.3). As such, there are pressures, real or assumed, that come to bear on each of these separate parts. Our initial concern for organizations and individuals is what can happen to information that is intended for the *problem-solver.*

Organizations are often likened to machines, and machines are expected to break down at some point. With machinery, the response to breakdowns is always reactive, that is, bring in the mechanic or replace the equipment. Often, machinery is scheduled for preventive maintenance (PM) with the expectation that such service will prolong machinery life. Organizations provide some of the same type of "maintenance" through employee training programs, but more often than not they too wait for something to break before the fix is attempted. The distinction here is that the organization-as-machine is not likely to throw out what does not work, but is encouraged to find a better way to make the best use of what is present, even if the part, or unit section, does not function correctly. This may require other units to compensate for the known organizational weaknesses. To accomplish this, the organization as a whole must find and use a better way to (1) gather more valuable information while (2) simultaneously creating the ability to dissipate that information throughout the organization.

There are those who discount the need for processing information beyond the point of receiving and relegating it to some convenient pigeonhole. For them, we point to information failures that result in the breakdowns for most contingency plans and occur in most disaster scenarios. One notable example

Figure 3.3 **Information Processing System**

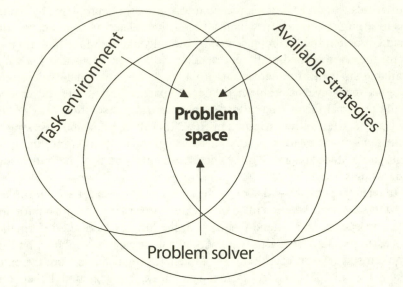

occurred during the events leading to the World Trade Center disaster of September 11.[4] Information in and of itself should be represented only in various stages of a data flow that leads to a contribution in an organization's or individual's knowledge base. Information exists independently from meaning. Meaning is derived from an understanding of the relations between the information pieces. By example, chess masters briefly exposed to an arrangement of playing pieces on a board that simulate an actual endgame could accurately reconstruct the boards after the pieces were removed but were unable to provide similar results when the original pieces were placed at random.[5] The information provided, in either case, was neutral, and meaning came only in the first instance, when the observer was able to cognitively establish a relation to something that was understood. Similarly, there is meaning in the expression $e = mc^2$ but its information is independent and must rely on who receives the information and how the relation between the variables is understood. Once meaning is obtained, the information's importance can be decided. Thereafter, the ultimate value of the information is subject to change for a variety of reasons. Despite the fact that information should be neutral, the social or cultural climate within an organization can work to inflate or deflate the importance of information by ascribing meaning.

In 2003, Operation Iraqi Freedom provided several extreme examples of this notion. On the Coalition side, new information from a variety of sophisticated as well as conventional sources provided real-time spatial data that could be immediately compared to temporal archives in activities intended to resolve such matters as target acquisition or supply logistics. During tactical exchanges, new information could at least combine, if not supplant, existing information and thereby alter its significance by providing new meaning. This approach is supported by Chris Argyris's perspective on double loop learning, which requires the invention of new meanings in order to modify earlier assumptions.[6] The practice proved to be eminently successful. In contrast, Iraqi minister of information Mohammed Saeed al-Sahaf, a.k.a. "Baghdad Bob," regularly appeared on the Al-Jazeera satellite TV network declaring that Coalition forces were doomed and totally incapable of breaching Baghdad's defenses. Many of these reports were given as British and U.S. tanks were rolling, unimpeded, along the streets of Iraq's capital city. While "Bob's" pronouncements were obviously intended as blatant propaganda, his panache was such that he evolved into a quasi-cult hero whose popularity was founded in myth-information.

Myth-Information

Myth-information is always incomplete because its foundations are generally so untenable that they avoid serious scrutiny. Myths generally involve deeply held convictions that are founded more in faith than reality and are common to most cultures and all organizations. The most natural way for myth to enter the information stream is through repetition, since humans have a tendency to be influenced by that which is seen or heard most frequently, regardless of its source. There is the possibility that the use of myth-information can produce unintentional results. Hussein's 1991 "mother of all wars" subsequently served as a parody in the West, although the despot's intention was to impart contempt, vainglory, and portent to his words. It is likely that the same words were more effective during the 1980s when Iraq faced off against Iran. Something that made perfect sense in the lexicon of desert peoples, that is, a reference to chopped-up snakes, the burning of an enemy's vital organs in hell, or terms of evisceration, have a way of losing their effect when crossing cultural and mythical lines. A common ditty heard at computer conventions of the eighties *"DOS isn't done until Lotus won't run"* represented a little lighthearted banter between companies who were establishing their own myth culture. Inventive language is often used in support of myth-information. Euphemisms like "downsizing" or "rightsizing" may help perpetuate the myth that an organization is being managed properly, while expressions such as "collateral damage" may be used to veil the unsavory though inevitable consequences of an armed conflict. Myth-information is often related to organizational social knowledge with an intention to hide particular facts from certain groups.[7] The distinguishing feature that separates myth-information from other errors-in-information is a tightly held social context that binds the progenitors of this type of information to self-interests.

Myth-information can involve data that is intentionally withheld, thereby fostering rumors, another type of myth combining organizational culture and supposition. "Hoarding" information transcends the conventional culture of organizations in that it is usually never condoned but often widely practiced and can occur at any level within the organization.

Information Hoarding

Information that is held is sometimes referred to as "information-in-jail" because of the custodial trait of the information holder. In such instances, information is hoarded so effectively that it would appear as if it does not even exist. On occasion, useful information is held with the intention of orchestrating an advantageous announcement intended, for example, to coincide with the release of earning statements or to introduce an important organizational restructuring. Unfortunately, this is not always the case.

In our present context, held information is not of the type that is intentionally detrimental, that is, we choose not to focus on the closeted skeletons that every company hopes to shelter from the view of the general public. Rather, we are addressing useful information that is held by those who reside behind "high walls" or within the confines of departmental "silos." Because information is often equated with power, held information may be construed as a valuable commodity, most often by the entity that is withholding it. Still, the motivations for holding information are mixed. In most environments such activities are the most damaging form of information delay or denial. The issue of delay recognizes that held information is likely to surface at some time. By example, in January 1986, information regarding NASA's *Challenger* was intentionally withheld despite the fact that, for safety reasons, had the information been divulged, the mission would have been scrapped.[8] Within two minutes of launch the *Challenger* exploded, killing all aboard, and shortly thereafter the whistles started blowing as NASA employees produced documents that indicated that faulty equipment was likely to produce disastrous consequences if the mission were allowed to proceed. When the fingers start pointing, the rate at which the high walls begin to tumble can be quite startling. Going into projects, members are often reminded that there is no "I" in the word *team*. They should also be aware, possibly apprehensive, that in the event a project failure, without "U" there is no *fall guy!* If information hoarding results in problems, one finds the people who are quickest to take the credit for success are often the quickest to look for scapegoats. And any held information by one part of an organization can have a ripple effect that results in multiple errors occurring throughout the organization.

Information Distortion

But assuming everyone is freely willing to share information, another aspect of information impedance relates to distortion. In its purest form, distortion occurs when the channel carrying the information is congested with background noises sufficient to defeat the message. As we have seen earlier, because spatial information processes seek the newest information, conflicts and distortion can occur if new information conflicts with archived information. A change in union rules or ERISA requirements that impacts employees will immediately give rise to a distorted version of which set of guidelines relates to whom and when they apply. Both myth-information and held information produce distortions. Conversations around the proverbial company "watercooler" provide an excellent place for information distortion. Here people gather to share their opinions on any number of matters for which they are generally ill equipped, whether it be the weather, sports, politics, or interoffice intrigue. Here a form of social knowledge, generally devoid of verifiable facts, is openly exchanged, and the seeds of rumors are sown. In an effort to address this type of activity, many companies provide a "rumor central" extension to their intranet sites, where concerns raised at informal gatherings may be addressed.

Organization executives should be conscientious in their choice of words or phrases when addressing groups lest they convey, intentionally or otherwise, reasonably unacceptable policy. In 1997 a Texaco executive made an unadvised reference to "black jellybeans" in a jar, which connoted organizational racism and led to a series of costly investigations into the company's policies of promotions and rewards for minorities.[9] Texaco's policies were found wanting in that a critical distortion existed and had been tolerated until an intentional effort was made to bring the company in line with accepted legal standards.

What the Blind Men Saw?

Beyond the problems that deal with the *physical transfer* of information mentioned in the preceding paragraphs, organizations are impacted by the cognitive restrictions they will face in their personnel. The notion of cognition separates the rational processes involved with the acquisition of information from *affective*, emotional processes including such attitudes or inclinations. Cognitive maturity establishes a *schema*, or mental path, under which individuals function. This mental path is a way of thinking that determines the perspective on how one expects to respond to an issue.

A useful analogy in describing *schema* involves the story of the elephant and the three blind men, each of whom in using his remaining senses, interprets the beast to be three different objects, none of which is an elephant.[10] This exercise demonstrates the effect of cognitive dissonance and is the foundation on which most excuses are grounded.

Cognitive dissonance is a theory proposed by Leon Festinger in 1957 and is based on the notion that people *prefer* their cognitions, or beliefs, to be consistent with their behavior.[11] If the balance required under such conditions is lacking, one experiences dissonance and will strive to resolve the conflict. This is a common dilemma found among problem-solvers and decision-makers who are exposed to new, unsettling information that requires action leading to change. Only two things can resolve inconsistencies related to dissonance: either change one's thinking or one's behavior so that one is in line with the other. Because behavior is more difficult to change than attitude, it is more likely that the problem will be resolved in the way the situation is viewed. Any adjustment in beliefs will do the trick. The smoker who is informed that the EPA has determined that secondhand smoke is harmful may go to great lengths to dispute the reported findings so as to avoid behavior modification such as refraining from smoking in the presence of others because it is the "right" thing to do. Dissonance occurs when people cannot personally justify their actions if requested to act in some manner that is contrary to their beliefs, as when they are exposed to new information. Dissonance can also occur in a group situation if core beliefs are affected by outside conditions. For example, following the events of September 11, Americans' basic beliefs in domestic safety were visibly shaken. But information can also work in a positive fashion to alleviate dissonance. New information can serve to reconcile conflicts associated with dissonance. The use of feedback also provides a remedy for dissonance in that the *mutual* exchange of information is one method for bringing participants closer to being "on the same page."

Information in feedback *always* signals conditions related to change. It must be remembered if the feedback is "stabilizing," that is, the indications do not reflect any need for change, the decision should be to maintain the status quo. By definition, if "new data" that is received actually contains nothing that is not already known, it contains no "useful" information, and again, the status quo will be maintained. Consequently, information involved with feedback is "negative" in the sense that it seeks to "disturb" the status quo and cause a shift in behavior. The use of feedback is critical to the information chain in order to determine that what has been intended has been interpreted correctly. The use of feedback is an essential tool for converting data to useful information so that it may be communicated throughout the system or organization.

Tacit versus Explicit Information

Like knowledge, information contains characteristics that can be described as explicit or tacit. Information that is explicit is easily described and easily passed on to others. Tacit information is subjective and related to the experience of an organization or individual and is therefore more difficult to convey. Some consider a demonstration of tacit information an expression of knowledge. The expression "If it were easy, everyone would be doing it" conveys the sense of tacit knowledge. Because tacit knowledge, based on a unique synthesis of information, is considered as an asset to organizations, it bears a short revisit here.

The information conveyed to Michael Jordan regarding basketball or to Muhammad Ali regarding boxing is about the same information available to all athletes at their respective level of participation, and yet the names of these athletes stand out because of the unique way they managed the information. Certain franchise or branded successes take this idea to the same level in organizations. Their commonality here in the use of information suggests the ability of Jordan or Ali to demonstrate "ownership" of the product represented as knowledge. This "ownership" signifies an important distinction between information and knowledge.[12] Information may be available to all, but only some can use information to develop a knowledge base. For our purposes, the significance of information as the preliminary device leading to knowledge, tacit or explicit, is key. While we have discussed some of the common traps and solutions to the way in which information is handled in the social sense, there is another, more subliminal consideration that needs addressing: the perception of information.

Perception

Plato's *Republic*, Book VII, provides one of the earliest accounts devoted to perception and the related distortion of information as he discusses the Shadows of the Cave.[13] In this work, the philosopher imagines a group of shackled people who are raised in an "underground den" so that they can see only what is in front of them. What rests before them is a high wall that displays the shadows cast by things that move behind them. In time, the group gives meaning to the shadows, which, to them, represent what is real in the world. As adults, the shackles are removed and the people are reintroduced to actual representations of the things that have passed before them as shadows. The immediate reaction, of course, is one of disbelief; the information presented to them does not conform to the world that they had always perceived.

Perception represents an observation or awareness based on the sensitivity and discernment of the viewer. The Platonic perspective on perception dealt with *objects* that resided in the realm of Forms; a realm that held the one-Chair, the one-Cup, the one-Truth, and so forth. Objects known to man were mere representations of those in the Forms' realm and were therefore represented by small-case letters, for example, chair, cup, or truth. Another way of stating this is to say there is no "real" truth among humans, just a representation of Truth. Because this dualism is tied to the *object* that is being perceived and not the viewer, the basic presumption becomes difficult to work with in any but the most general senses. The chair presented to a group is recognized by all not as a chair but rather as an icon qualitatively linked by characteristics associated with a chair.

Concepts related to perception can affect decisions to a greater degree than information or knowledge. A classic example of this effect involves use of the first commercial computer, the UNIVAC, which had been used with some success by the U.S. government in the early 1950s for census analysis. During the 1952 presidential election, CBS television news anchor Walter Cronkite shared the screen with the huge computer as viewers were informed that the machine would be used to tabulate and "predict" the winner of the Eisenhower–Stevenson race. While the machine appeared at rest during the broadcast, leaving viewers to accept the newscaster's contention that even a computer seemed incapable of calling the contest, it was later divulged that UNIVAC had already projected the winner: with only 5 percent of the returns counted, the UNIVAC predicted a landslide victory for Eisenhower.[14] The news media, many of whom were sympathetic to the Stevenson platform, felt the result was too unbelievable and delayed reporting it for fear of embarrassing themselves by informing the public that a machine had, with little effort, accomplished something of which most political forecasters were incapable.[15] In this instance the information provided from synthesized data merely provided a fact, which appeared to be newsworthy but was nevertheless withheld because of perception. If the results of the UNIVAC projection had been reported during the newscast, it likely would have had no effect on the outcome of the 1952 election. An effect that was created, though, was that UNIVAC, and the ability of computers to make an impact on decision-making generally, was greatly enhanced.

This example illustrates conditions under which empirical observation, a

Figure 3.4 **Three Realms of Information Organization**

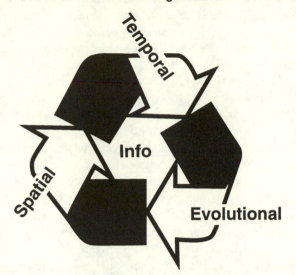

source of information, conflicts with rational or experiential judgment, which is the basis for perception. Empirically, the UNIVAC computer produced results based on what it was given. Rationally, these results were not considered significant by the media. In the first instance, theories of science and applied engineering provided the product, that is, an analysis produced by a computer. In the second instance, social constraints related to rationality and a conscious organizational bias caused the product to be shelved. For information to succeed beyond perception there is a need for some middle ground between empiricism and rationalism. Better still would be a method that effectively combines both notions in a efficient manner. This method exists in phenomenology.

The Austrian philosopher Edmund Husserl (1859–1938) developed phenomenology as a means to resolve the opposition of empiricism and rationalism by considering all disciplines equally and with relation to one another (Figure 3.4). This approach was intended to relate specifically to the human condition of consciousness and perception and in so doing expanded considerably on the works of other German philosophers, for example, Kant. Rather than separating what is observed from that which is thought, Husserl interprets the combined process in terms of wholeness, or *Gestalt,* thereby viewing the input-output system as one, each with its own weight and impact on the resulting perception. In doing so, phenomenology is able to view interdependent functionalities not derivable from either the parts in separation or in summation alone. This "big picture" approach suggests that difficulties associated with behavior during information processing should not be restricted merely to what is observed or by what is reasoned; there will be times when such difficulties might simply be the result of a "bad hair day" on the part of one of the decision-makers. Phenomenology respects the fact that we all see things differently. Our purpose here is to develop a method that allows us all to be focused on the same thing, that is, information, and in doing so, establish a stronger basis for perceptions.

Having briefly addressed the forms and dependencies that affect information, we will now turn our attention to the notion of *semiotics*, the analysis of the signs conveyed through information. Signs and signals appear everywhere as an expression of communication, yet few are consciously aware of how prevalent the impact of signs can be when regarded as phenomena. For example, one body of evidence supports the contention that "body language" can convey a "sign" more indicative of what a person thinks than is conveyed by what they say. Trained observers interpret signs for direction or as barriers to information through an understanding of the common structures associated with the information process. Such structures are common to individuals, organizations, and machines and will be addressed in the next chapter. Following that, chapter 5 will focus more closely on the spatial aspects to information processing in a discussion of channels of information transfer and how the notion of the "message is the medium" is most important. In chapter 6 we will discuss the temporal aspect of information processing. How an organization learns from its past experiences, the role of feedback, and memories will be our principal items of coverage. In the second part of the book we will revisit the issues involved with the processing of information in detail.

In the next chapter we address the seminal section of this text, the semiotic model as a method for channeling information from data to actionable knowledge. Earlier we discussed the notion of cybernetics, which seeks to establish common ties between living and mechanized systems. An essential feature common in these comparisons relates to the ability to adapt in order to survive in any environment. For this reason we review evolutionary theory to discover how principles associated with living beings also apply to information.

4

Evolutionary Dimension of Information Processing

Semiotics

Having reviewed some of the things that hinder the effective use of information in organizations, we turn to methods intended to guide information from its inception, as raw data, to a phase where it is most useful, that is, the pragmatic stage of actionable knowledge. Actionable knowledge represents that point at which information has evolved to what may be considered a reliable, valuable product: knowledge. It is knowledge, not information, that should always be acted upon. To accomplish this transformational task we will introduce a model based on semiotics (signs) to outline the necessary steps of informational transformation.

In the previous chapter we contended that information processing in organizations should be regarded as *spatial, temporal, or evolutionary.* This chapter will focus exclusively on developing the third axis while introducing the reader to the notion of semiotics (signs) used in an approach to develop information. Our choice of the word "evolutionary" is not casual. The roots of the word *evolution* are derived from Latin and literally mean an "unrolling." To evolve implies continuous change from a lower, simpler, or worse to a higher, more complex, or better state.[1]

The notion of Darwin's evolution is well known and has applications in almost all sciences. His theories on evolution address the matter of survival when species compete.[2] Only the most adaptable candidates, through a process of "exaptation," survive in the world today. It is interesting that Darwin cited Robert Malthus, a political economist, who wrote *The Essays on Population.*[3] In this critical essay, Malthus argued that the geometrical power of increase in human numbers, and an arithmetical growth in agricultural production, would regularly combine to produce famine, increased mortality, and longer hours of work. Darwin argued that creatures multiplied in numbers beyond the capacity of their environment to sustain them. The struggle for survival was bound to occur, with only the most adaptive species surviving long enough to reproduce.

If one thinks of the variety of information in organizations as being in competition for attention, certain similarities begin to take shape. Organizations are constantly inundated with competing information signals. Such signals are commonly referred to as data. The organization's task is to produce knowledge from these signals, and that knowledge should be used to modify the behavior of organizational members. To do so, the various data elements (species) have to compete in the organization (environment), and the most adaptable among the data elements have to survive to evolve into knowledge. The evolution of organizational knowledge can be viewed as a process of *reduction*. From many data elements, few information items are generated and even less knowledge. What Malthus anticipated for society, we see in organizations facing exponential increases in data and information while knowledge increases arithmetically. The evolutionary aspect, from data generation through the dissipation of adaptive information in the knowledge systems of organizations, is the focus of this work.

We look to evolution to see how signals develop, or survive, in order to yield knowledge that will be recognized through the action of behavior modification of members within the organization. In evolution, successful species survive their environments through adaptation at least long enough to propagate. Similarly, information survives and progresses through an organization if it is adaptable. Because of the similarities between the theory of evolution and information processes, which include adaptation as a response to the environment, we will review conventional evolutionary theory, and its relation to information.

Theoretical development in any science is often a reflection of the prevailing doctrine from other disciplines. At the turn of the nineteenth century, for example, the prevailing thoughts regarding society and science first indicated an escalating information base founded in principles related to the interaction of systems, behavior, and the environment. At that time, all things, it seemed, could be described in terms and theories that dealt with evolution.

Evolutionary Theories

The two men who contributed most heavily to theories associated with the current views on evolution were Jean Baptiste Lamarck and Charles Darwin. There was a third evolutionary theorist, Charles King, who speculated that changes in species were the direct result of some exposure to some cataclys-mic event.[4] Lamarck proposed his theories during the mid-eighteenth and early nineteenth centuries and is probably most noted for his theory on how *necessity* compelled generations of a certain species to produce the long neck commonly associated with giraffes.[5] According to Lamarck, if an animal were required to exercise and stretch its neck in order to reach its food source, the next generation would reap the benefit of any beneficial physiological change. This benefit would in turn be further enhanced through similar practices of successive generations until what is recognized as a giraffe is produced. Darwin's contention includes the idea that the survivors displayed a definite tendency for adaptation, which assists a species, and that this ten-dency is genetically passed through generations. Species without this ten-dency have a far less chance for survival.[6] Both organisms and information exist in a state of competition with their respective environments. Organisms must adapt to climate changes, food scarcity, and rivalry from other organ-isms. Information must contend with competing information, methods of delivery, and interpretation in order to survive. As with information, this idea places the species in direct competition with its environment. In each case, the idea of "survival of the fittest" does not mean the strongest; it means the most adaptable. If an organization is required to consume and process infor-mation in order to survive, what features must it exapt or develop? As will be seen later in the chapter, we argue that while many of the *features* used in information processing may be in place in an organization, the adaptive skills required to optimize deployment for organizational goal attainment are often missing. To ensure longevity, organizations must understand the function of successful adaptation to informational changes.

At the beginning of the last century, Marconi and Morse contributed to the beginning of the "new" information age. Their work provided the method and means for information delivery that allowed consistent transfer at un-precedented speed. Here also we witness the first example using an elec-tronic medium. The delivery of deciphered code represented information that could be easily passed to others. The ability to deliver and decipher informa-tion was a skill among those who manned the wireless sets. In our examina-tion of information boundaries, we first consider information that may be easily passed on to others because it is explicit, as opposed to information derived from experience, which is unique, personally held, or tacit.

Information that is explicit is easily identified because it is easily passed on to others. Tacit information is more subjective and often related to experi-ence, which makes it unique. Philosopher Michael Polanyi gives an example of someone using a dictionary.[7] A dictionary contains not only word mean-ings but also correct word spellings. The person who knows *what* a dictionary is used for may be at a loss as to *when* to use the book if they do not have the tacit information required to "know" if a word is spelled wrong because of the feeling that the word "just doesn't look right."[8] Applying Lamarck's evolutionary views to information, there would be *no distinction* between what is tacit and what is explicit in either information or knowledge. Information and experience would be inseparable and could be passed easily to successive generations in organizations or people. Oddly, this is exactly how some organizations believe their knowledge base is passed, though in fact this is not the case. It may apply to certain rules, procedures, and policies that are constantly distributed throughout an organization, but it is not so clear that any requisite knowledge or essential information is similarly retained or passed. One distinguishing feature that separates information from knowledge is *ownership*, and it is unclear if organizations per se own all of their knowledge. A large part of it lies with employees.[9] If so, the case for efficient and effective information processing becomes of greater importance for organizations. The ability to capture, synthesize, and disperse valued information, that which is capable of underpinning the knowledge base of the organization, becomes crucial. The process of accomplishing this task involves the study and understanding of semiotics.

Semiotics

Semiotics is concerned with the meanings and interpretations of signs or signals and therefore fits perfectly in the study of information flow. Semiotics involves the theory and the analysis of signs and is regarded as having developed from two originating schools of thought. The first may be traced to Charles Sanders Peirce (1839–1914), mathematician and logician, who referred to semiotics as the "formal doctrine of science." The domain of semiotics can be broken down into three distinct sections: *syntactics*, which deals with relationships or linkages between various components; *semantics*, as discussed in chapter 1, with the additional purpose of establishing relationships through common meaning among components; and *pragmatics*, which deduces meaning or insights from relationships found in the context of semantics and seeks to apply such insight through actions. Signs in and of themselves represent articles or objects and are intended to convey meanings as *interpretants*, that is, distinct representations for the viewer. Because meaning is subjective, representation by signs is rarely absolute. Without this ability, the sign at the gate saying ENTRANCE FORBIDDEN might lead one to then wonder why such a sign is on a gate when, if entrance were absolutely and always forbidden, the sign would be better suited on a brick wall. The "silent alarm" triggered by an intruder would have little value if it were in fact silent. The *interpretant* associated in each of these examples then conveys additional meanings. Peirce developed qualitative relational categories for signs, which he placed in three broad groups as follows: [10]

- Icons: these are *interpretants*, that is, the "sense" made from a sign. Icons hold strong qualitative relations to the object. A picture of someone who is well known represents this qualitative relation, so that a photo of Ronald Reagan in the 1950s would be interpreted as "the actor, Ronald Reagan" while the same man in the 1980s would be interpreted as "the President, Ronald Reagan." Maps are icons of a spatial rendering of some known, recognizable area. In most religions, icons are strongly identified with qualitative characteristics associated with particular beliefs and practices.
- Indexes: establish a qualitative relation through association to an object as in the expression "Where there's smoke [association], there's fire [object]." Indexes usually convey a message specifically related to an object or experience. A small child is reminded to avoid the stove, whether the stove (object) is on or not, because it is "hot" (association).
- Symbols: The most general *interpretant*, that is, the sense made of a sign, in which there is no qualitative association between the object and the sign, although meaning is still conveyed because of a familiar context. Most words function as symbols since they connote meaning but have no direct qualitative connection to the object, for example, the *word* "football" without additional qualifiers does not distinguish between the European and American variety of the game. Without qualifiers, the reaction of two people to the same word may be quite different.

Peirce coined the word *virtual* to represent something that is not actual.[11] In the context of Peirce's semiotics, information represents an object (an idea, thought, or sensation) to be judged or interpreted in the minds of those who will review the information and in turn create new signs related to the *information-object*. The cognitive properties related to this process are based on the successive development and nurturing of sign interpretations.

While signals and signs may be represented in a variety of ways, most of us feel familiar, possibly confident, with the common signs used in language, that is, words. At about the same time Peirce was formulating his theories, a Swiss linguist, Ferdinand de Saussure, was using semiotics to link signs that demonstrated the similarities and differences in language. Based in part on Saussure's work, A.J. Greimas developed a diagram, the *semiotic square*, to represent a syntactical arrangement within the meaning of words. Greimas specifically addresses the essence of transformational meaning in words to

Figure 4.1 **Semiotic Square**

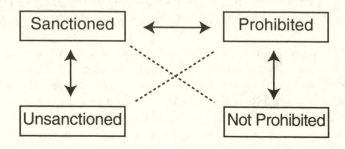

demonstrate variety and richness in language.[12] Relations must exist between the parts of the model in a word's meaning, which is affected during the trajectory of discourse between the parts. Greimas's use of the semiotic square to analyze paired relational concepts results in a wide variety of effective interpretations, which may serve to fill a semantic gap in an otherwise static environment. For example, the meanings of the word *sanctioned* are more deeply understood when scrutinized in opposition to itself as represented above in the *semiotic square* model (Figure 4.1).

The square places terms in opposition, which become mutually defining. This notion states that if one understands word meaning in terms of the *semiotic square*, they will have a far deeper understanding of the contextual meaning of the original word. The space between the squares represents variety in language including variations of the words presented. The use of the semiotic square develops a concept of distinction in word meanings. Greimas seeks meaning deductively through associations between paired concepts represented in an example using a semiotic square. We choose to reason inductively in an effort to represent a totality. This simple model provides a basis for introduction to some of the concepts related to semiotics. This basis is intended to explore the possibility for significant variations that exist in words, messages, signals, and information. Case studies provided later in this text provide examples, which demonstrate that the failure to regard such distinctions can have dire consequences.

The use of semiotics as a tool for meaning subsequently found roots in literature, the arts, philosophy, and psychology. The French critic Barthes found use of semiotics for ascribing a deeper meaning to literature and society, American linguist Noam Chomsky used it to attribute relationships between language and psychology, and Nobel laureate Umberto Eco found semiotics useful in decoding communication within society. A central feature of semiotics is the ability, through analysis and reconstruction of signs, to generate innovation in the field related to the original object and the interpretation of that object. As stated by Eco, "Semiotics is concerned with everything that can be taken as a sign."[13] New interests in semiotics have emerged in the latter part of the last century and are based on concepts related to information transfer in both mechanical systems, for example, in computers, and in human interaction, including brain functions employed during communications. Our approach in the use of semiotics is pragmatic and embraces features common to both man and machine. We present a model concerned with the causal relations that are predicated on signs during the transfer of information.

An Informational Semiotic Framework

Our work in developing a functional model to aid the synthesis of information in a knowledge creation process flow is experience-based. The authors have worked with the law enforcement intelligence community to augment the capabilities of information gathering and sharing as well as with private sector intelligence groups concerned with competitive intelligence and corporate espionage activities. In working with these organizations, we have discovered common points of interest, which indicate the need for such a model. Later in this chapter we will present a quintessential case study while using the model process as a means that might have evaded elements of disaster associated with the case. It is not our intention to weigh in on the politics or policies of the organizations represented in the case scenario, since interest in such facets have been covered in other works.[14] Rather, we present the case as a rationale for the need to address some of the issues presented in another manner. Our suggestion includes use of a model that employs a five-step "semiotic ladder" (Figure 4.2).

Previous works on semiotics that have been applied to information systems and management arenas are scant and have focused heavily on devising or enhancing existing system design methodologies.[15] Ramaprasad and Ambrose deviated from this approach and devised a four-stage (morphological, syntactical, semantic, pragmatic) one-dimensional model to explain knowledge management in organizations.[16] The model we present may be viewed as an extension of this framework for two reasons. First, we have added another layer—*empirics*—to explain the observations of data classes that will be deemed useful to the organization. Second, we divide task efficiency and effectiveness at specific levels, as it is expected that efficient data collection will lead to more effective use of information at the higher levels. It is also important that we consider this model to be quasi-transitory by

Figure 4.2 **Semiotic Ladder**

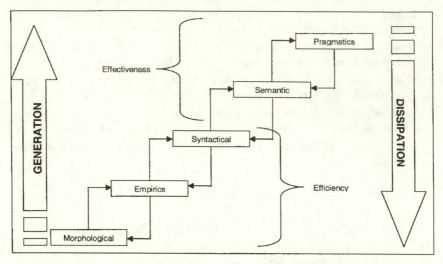

design, that is data and subsequent information that is synthesized on the *generation* side of this process is ultimately intended to develop some actionable knowledge base by the time it attains the pragmatic level. At this time the model requires this knowledge to be fed through the dissipative pipe for the purpose of organizational learning. We begin with an explanation of the model's respective layers.

Morphological Layer

At the morphological, the physical level, we are concerned with various actors and objects of interest to the organization. These agents are collectively termed sources of information. At this stage we are less concerned as to whether the agent can walk on water; rather, we just want to know he can swim. A wide assortment of sources can be found, we can have agents or objects within the control of the organization such as one's manufacturing or human resource systems, those that are owned by one's business partners such as a supplier's or customer's inventory system, or those that belong to the external environment at large such as government publications, and so forth. Data collected can be represented in a variety of forms including visual, auditory, graphic, or text, and can also arrive through various channels such as data transaction systems or through informal routes such as employee discussions or chat rooms or possibly brainstorming sessions.[17] The intelligence community frequently uses acronym guidelines to classify sources of information, like HUMINT, IMINT, MASINT, and SIGINT. These acronyms are actually a useful way to classify sources of signals at the morphological layer. Human intelligence (HUMINT) refers to information gathered from human agents; these may be both internal and external agents of the organization. Imagery intelligence (IMINT) and measurement and signature intelligence (MASINT) represent information gathered through photography and intelligence on an adversary's weapons program, respectively. Signal intelligence (SIGINT) represents information from intercepted electronic communications.

This practice is also used in the private sector. While we may recognize sources of human intelligence, for example, organization employees, as a primary source of knowledge, they are not the only sources. Some organizations develop competitive intelligence programs in order to gain a strategic advantage by gathering information on their competitors' programs and possible future actions. Imagery intelligence, while rare in private enterprises, is used in the handling of blueprints, engineering drawings, and technical schematics. Imagery intelligence is also making headway through the deployment of devices such as video conferencing, biometrics, and other sophisticated image-processing tools used in video mining. The use of SIGINT activities is also becoming more popular with organizations that now routinely gather information by monitoring employee e-mails or other communications. They may also use sophisticated data- and text-mining tools for the sole purpose of scanning huge volumes of data by using techniques like word-search.

At the morphological level, an organization must clearly identify the sources, types, and characteristics of signals it has at its disposal. At the morphological level we have an inordinate number of signal sources. Unless the source of a signal is clearly identified at this layer, the organization will not recognize it as a signal generator. As such, it will not be concerned with its emission. Gathering data with the potential for generating information begins with the decision to be in the information business, which is an organizational concern. Here the presumption is that efficiency in gathering information and effectiveness in acting upon the information gathered is important. At the formative level of the semiotic model, data is expected to be general and has the potential of being unnecessary; it represents a start in data collection that may act as "seeds" that grow information, hence it is *generative*.

Not all data will sprout useful information. The type of data collected is determined through the process of "flagging" any source that fits rather broad, though established, parameters. Sources of this type of data may be in trade or foreign journals, newspapers, lectures, from rumors, or may be something on *Oprah*; it is more critical to begin the process in the semiotic model than to become weighed down overanalyzing the types of data that should be collected. An Arab proverb reminds us, "If you plant no seeds because you are undecided as to whether you want radishes or corn, your yield will be the same," so *where you start* is less important than *that you start*. An example of a "flagging" approach that "refines" data is "parenting" software that captures and then inhibits any access to requests of a browser to visit Internet sites containing predetermined blocks of letters. At this stage it is unimportant as to whether the data collected is relevant to anything beyond the parameters that have caused the data to be captured; we are merely initiating the "staging process." Sources of information may be determined at this stage and, to be effective, should be *divergent*, that is, they should embrace and reflect the ultimate needs of units within the organization whose purposes serve common objectives of the organizational mission.

Empirical

The next level on the semiotic chain involves empirics. Here, data sets from objects are placed in similar classes, that is, we aggregate like sources into manageable portions. Empirics is concerned with studying statistical properties of the objects from the morphological level. Common tasks at the empirical level include the validation and processing of data. In the validation stage, judgments need to be made as to the legitimacy of the data gathered, how much significance a particular data element should be given, and whether the data needs to be cleaned or further processed. The latter are all common statistical exercises. The first phase is validation or error checking. This involves ascertaining that data elements have right values associated with them. For example, it is not reasonably feasible to have a negative sales value. Assume that a store has a limit that is considered the maximum for a sales transaction, for example, $10,000. We create a range that represents $0–10,000. Thus, all items falling in this range are said to be valid for a given transaction. Values outside the range are deemed invalid data because of a negative value or other need that must be verified through analysis. But in the event a transaction is entered incorrectly, for example, $34 instead of $43, the above-mentioned error checking mechanism will not recognize the error since both $43 and $34 are within the specified range. This is where the machines kick in with scanning mechanisms that help to prevent human errors and omissions during data entry.

Once data elements are validated, they must be processed. Here, triangulation is necessary because we look to check the accuracy of a data item by evaluating it from several sources. Triangulation aids in validating data, lest we run the risk of allowing *false data items* to proceed to the next stage of our information development. This can be costly in leading to incorrect decisions based on myth-information as well as representing the potential for lost opportunity costs to the organization. All organizations are economic beings that seek optimization of unlimited wants with scarce resources. Any resources used to the conduct a task are denied to other resource users.

False data items have provided two disturbing examples recently in relation to intelligence regarding the suspected weapons of mass destruction (WMD) program in Iraq.[18] The British intelligence community released two dossiers that detailed the state of Iraq's WMD program. The first one was released in September 2002 and the second in February 2003. The February report made public has become known as the "dodgy dossier."[19] In addition to abundant typographical errors, there are indications the document may have been plagiarized from an American student's thesis. This illustrates an example of poor data validation efforts. In other examples, problems developed for the *New York Times* in 2003, leading to major resignations by the editorial staff,[20] and there is evidence that at least one high-ranking career official in the Homeland Security Department obtained her doctorate and graduate diplomas from an uncertified "diploma mill," indicating that her academic credentials are worthless and that she is likely unsuitable for the sensitive position to which she was appointed.[21]

Measures need to be in place to evaluate and validate information provided by an organization's own employees or agents. Interagency counterintelligence may be required to avoid debacles similar to those experienced at Enron and Arthur Andersen, which can be traced to the fact that no one effectively monitored internal activities that involved abnormal transactions and practices that otherwise would have been reported in an audit. The responsible employees exploited a weakness in validation and error controls and generated or manipulated information and knowledge for their own advantage while literally sacrificing the identity of their organizations. It is unreasonable to suspect that no one knew what was happening. By example, we were hired to investigate the circumstances involving something that appeared to be, on the surface, an atypical success story that occurred at a Chicago advertising firm. It seemed that a middle-level manager of the marketing group was surpassing his target requirements with such consistency that he managed to capture his company's best salesperson award for six straight months. While this was not unusual in itself, the fact that this manager was relatively new to the organization triggered a small covert inquiry into his activities at the behest of upper management. A review of his activity indicated that most of the sales being generated by this manager were to "new" accounts. Because the firm allowed billing terms on new accounts to extend up to 180 days, no validation procedures were required. Additionally, the company counted such new business as sales that were counted toward this manager's bimonthly commissions and bonuses. Our investigation revealed that the majority of these "new" companies *never* existed. By the time the fraud was exposed, the firm had lost money while the manager under investigation had profited and was in the midst of changing jobs when terminated. A simple validation check could have avoided this embarrassment. Businesses are sensitive to matters involving their employees and money. In a separate instance, a brokerage house requested that we do surveillance on a terminated employee who had effectively embezzled $3 million from them. The purpose of the surveillance was not to recover any of the lost funds, but rather to determine if the former employee had spread the word on how he had duped the company. The firm was more concerned with its image than with dollars.

Such employee practices are not restricted to the private sector. Robert Hanssen (FBI) and Aldrich Ames (CIA) deceived their organizations with minimal effort using unsophisticated equipment. The need to validate information "across the board" cannot be overemphasized. We will address other notions of trust and belief in information in the second half of the text. Unless we have appropriate data validation controls in place, the organization will generate only information or knowledge that is suspect.

Once validated and triangulated, we apply statistical analysis to the data items. The most common form in this endeavor is summarization. Summarization in its purest sense is any form of aggregation.[22] A bookstore might want a summarization of individual book sales (morphological objects) that could be useful in projections of total sales (empiric information). Other forms of summarization include the calculation of averages, deviations, and other statistical and mathematical operations on data elements. A term popular among intelligence circles is *collection management*, which is concerned with aggregating data on an object of interest. The level of summarization will vary depending on organizational needs and system design. The greater the level of summarization, the less detail we have on individual transactions. The lower the level of summarization, the more details we have, but it also uses up more system storage capacity. Eventually every transaction will be summarized. It must be emphasized that there is a degree of uncertainty associated with any data inspection. The notion of summarization provides executives quick access to the proverbial snapshot of the big picture; save the details for later.[23] This may facilitate the general *efficiency* required in the decision process since the executive is not overloaded with details, but it does little toward improving the *effectiveness* of the decision-making process. Hiding details can lead to poor decisions, as some potentially important signs will be missed. For example, a project manager receiving weekly update reports may assume everything is on track and moving smoothly based on how he interprets hours worked and tasks completed, because no major plan deviations are perceived. But if the 80–20 rule applies, that is, 20 percent of the workers are doing 80 percent of the work, and the best workers leave the project, problems are likely to occur. Summarization should occur only for information with low value or high uncertainty (entropy). If all workers share the load equally, there is no need for some line-item summary of their tasks. However, if a known discrepancy exists or is anticipated, for example, an impending strike, then delineation helps the manager juggle people or anticipate immediate needs for personnel.

This example presents circumstances in which events emerge from recognized signals. Hiding important signals such as outliers, the extreme edges on either side of a normal distribution curve, through summarization can prevent a manager from addressing a potential problem early on. Unchecked, such problems have a tendency to gain momentum, leading to crisis. The end product of the empirical layer will be localized or internal information. We have made the first stages of evolution from low-level *data* to a higher, fitter form of *information*; we have generated information on groups of entities. Once data on individual objects is aggregated and integrated we may draw connections between disparate entities. This is accomplished at the next level.

Syntactical

The syntactical level is focused on deriving complex and higher-order objects from assimilating and linking incongruent signals while placing data sets in similar categories. At this level, our primary concern is with structuring signals in meaningful sets; common tasks include ensuring referential integrity and defining relationships, according to some grammar. Prior to integrating data, we must ensure referential integrity, that is, validity, by removing the inconsistencies among data stores. For example, we might want all sales amount items to be referred to as *one* variable, thereby establishing referential integrity in that any other variable representing sales is considered invalid. This process is similar to normalizing a database. If a sales amount is referred to as "samount" in one system and "sales amount" in another, we have the reason to aggregate the two data sources. Failures to ensure referential integrity will result in construction of duplicate sequences that result in time-consuming cross-checking for errors. Allowing a system to exist in a state without referential integrity is ultimately costly in terms of systems and personnel. One of the critical reasons why our intelligence agencies fail miserably to communicate and integrate disparate sources of intelligence or to make meaningful connections is the lack of common terms and an accepted universal doctrine.[24] To address some of this concern, in 1952 the three disparate signal intelligence agencies of the military wings were asked to form a joint group under the auspices of the Department of Defense.[25] This kind of merger is common in the private sector. A key reason for the merging of information systems and the rise of enterprise resource planning systems is to address referential problems. Referential integrity represents one of the main reasons for combining twenty-two government agencies under the Department of Homeland Security.

Defining the relationships between the data items is the second crucial task of this phase. One needs to have clearly defined rules or protocol prior to carrying this out. The concept of a *syntagm* is salient here. A *syntagm* can be defined as an ordered combination of interacting signifiers, which forms a comprehendible whole. A sentence in a paragraph can be considered as a syntagm, similarly a paragraph in a chapter. The key thing to note here is the concept of ordered combination. Just tying a bunch of letters and punctuation together cannot be considered a syntagm. But if letters were combined so as to lend a word, syntagm is achieved. One approach to linking or structuring data can be carried out using devices such as triggers, enhancers, or suppressors. Triggers alert the system to the first wave of symptoms or signs of an impending event, which usually needs attention. Enhancers are elements related to events that increase the sensitivity of a trigger, either because of the perceived consequence of an increase in magnitude of some event or by lowering the threshold at which the trigger is activated in an effort to make the trigger more sensitive. Suppressors work in the opposite fashion to curtail the reaction of the trigger. Trigger-alerts may be used at any level of the semiotic model and vary only as to the level of sensitivity required to "trip" the trigger so that an alert is raised. Other approaches to developing syntactics are cause-effect diagrams, association rules, and network analyses. Cause-effect diagrams are visualizations of antecedents and consequences of a phenomenon. For example, we can have a cause-effect diagram that links change in heat temperature to its consequential effect on the amount of energy released by a system. An example of association rules is evident in male purchasing habits in grocery stores. It was deduced that men who bought diapers also purchased milk. Hence, the presence of one is associated with another. Network analysis enables us to map such information flows in an effort to determine trends.

At the end of the syntactical level we have moved information from a localized to a more global form. Evolutional aspects of adaptability have allowed us to make this move. We now view a larger picture of the organization as the result of making connections among local information groups. In our next step, we need to make inferences from this information.

Semantic

Semantics binds definitions to some expression of "reality" within the information system; it provides meaning. Binding here represents the minimal descriptions necessary to distinguish the system (information) from the rest of the immediate setting (environment). A newspaper (environment), for example, represents a collection of bound "systems" related to sports, local or regional topics, entertainment, and so forth. Each binding is an encapsulation of information on some specific presumption or context, and there is generally no overlap between sections. Sometimes a reader might pick up a newspaper, take out the sports section, and discard the rest. This would imply that the reader's interest is in sports. Similarly, it would be unreasonable for a field commander to be concerned with the cost of ammunition while involved in the context of a battle. On the other hand, it would be reasonable for the Government Accounting Office (GAO) to anticipate the costs associated within the context of war at some time prior to an engagement. The semantic level achieves this goal through careful analysis of the components of the relationship in the appropriate context. This requires studying the component objects in their relationship and association as well as the role that the environment plays in regard to these connections. Context, in which the relationship is viewed, plays a crucial role in this interpretation. Up to the syntactical stage we are concerned with the mechanical aspects of compiling and aggregating of signals. At the semantic stage we are concerned with the psychological process of signal interpretation.

Signs have no meaning on their own unless they are interpreted in relation to some context. As noted by Peirce, "Nothing is a sign unless it is interpreted as a sign."[26] A sign signifies something and stands for something other than itself. Much like in the field of semiotics, there are two main models of what constitutes a sign, one by deSaussure and the other by Peirce. deSaussure defined a sign as being composed of a "signifier" and the "signified."[27] The signifier is the material form that the sign takes while the signified is the concept it represents. Again, a stop sign is just a piece of red-painted metal, but it is meant to convey a message when posted at an intersection. As a result, the *sign* is a signification that is attained by associating the signifier with the signified. The signifier is normally thought of to be a more mechanical and physical aspect of a sign while the signified is more psychological and interpretive. Langer notes, "Symbols are not proxy for their objects but are *vehicles for the conception of objects*. . . . In talking *about* things we have conceptions of them, not the things themselves; and *it is the conceptions, not the things, that symbols directly mean*."[28] According to Peirce, a sign has three components—the representamen, an interpretant, and an object. The representamen is the form that the sign takes, the interpretant is the sense made from the sign, and the object is the goal/item to which the sign refers.

Peirce highlighted the process of *semiosis* through which the meaning of a sign arises by interpretation or acting on the representamen. At the semantic stage we are trying to make *sense* of a signal or a collected group of signals. As argued before, anything can be a sign so long as it signifies something to someone. However, signs or signals can make sense only as part of a formal system. Sense is made from signs when they are taken in relation to other signs and the environment. A stop sign standing on a corner of an intersection should convey meaning to approaching drivers because of the relation of the sign to the environment. The same sign hanging in a men's dorm on campus loses some of its meaning because of the environmental change.

Signals by themselves may be arbitrary. deSaussure noted that if the words of languages were to represent definite concepts without ambiguity, we would be able to have equivalent/replacement words in all languages. But there are words that do not translate well between languages. It is likely impossible for a sign to have a truly universal meaning. The arbitrary nature of signs and meaning has been well documented in the literature dating from ancient Greece. Meaning must be gathered from a concept and perception about the environment. Aristotle noted, "(There) can be no natural connection between the sound of any language (words) and the things signified."[29] The semantic stage requires the development of language necessary to gather information from signals. The development of such a language is essential to be able to understand the signals and act on them in a defined manner. If all signs were totally arbitrary, it would be as if all humans would be condemned to communicate from within a tower of *Babel*. Semantics imposes a definition of signs to allow for the possibility of universal understanding. Lévi-Strauss suggested that signs are arbitrary a priori but cease to be arbitrary a posteriori, that is, after the sign has come into a historical existence, it cannot be arbitrarily changed.[30] With time, every sign acquires a history and connotations through use within communities of practice or a sign-users' culture. Elements of these cultures should be regarded as static or dynamic. Static, nonchanging environments are indicated by the occurrence of relationships that have the same outcome regardless of timing. Dynamic, or changing, contexts are more common in today's environment. Timing, as a component, for example, has a major role in dynamic context. Prior to September 11, a "box cutter" was regarded merely as an implement generally restricted in use to warehouse or tradesmen. After September 11, the tool took on a more sinister meaning.

At the semantic stage then, we have moved from the more objective levels of signals (morphological, empirical, and syntactical) to the nonneutral arena. It is essential to understand that while in transit, information and data are to be considered neutral, that is, no interpretation should be ascribed until the information is reviewed using semantics. Semiotics and analysis modify and give meaning to information in search of knowledge, and knowledge is seldom neutral. Realities are constructed in a localized fashion of the semantic stage. These realities establish what will be considered knowledge. As this processes localized information at the empirical level, so too here we have generated localized knowledge. The generation of knowledge from information is salient for organizations today. At the next level we seek to act on this localized knowledge.

Pragmatics

At the final stage of the semiotic model, we are concerned with extracting knowledge. We move out of a defined context to an undefined one. The pragmatic level deals with the reality of the environment, which can be neither bound nor defined. Moreover, at this stage we are also concerned with aggregating semantic knowledge in search of insight.

The pragmatic level seeks a global context in which one views and applies knowledge with an environmental perspective rather than in a local (systemic) and narrowly focused view. Pragmatic knowledge may be considered analogous to tacit knowledge.[31] In the semantic and pragmatic stages, reality is constructed from the signs and the comprehension of what is being signified.[32] Reality is molded from the process of signification, making sense of what is being signified by the signs.

The role of the *interpreting agent or object* is crucial at this stage. Individuals bring to bear a distinct cognitive set of experiences, biases, expectations, and values that affect how a relationship is viewed or analyzed; these traits must be considered. Experience in the context of the investigated domain is important in order to make sense of what is being observed. Bias creates a priori *expectations* of what a given relationship means or what the effects of a given context are or should be. Values, however, can present a stronger mental stigma than bias and can serve to control individual behavior and actions. Because biases may predispose one to certain prejudices about semantics, values should be used to prevent such occurrences from happening.

A major consideration in moving from the semantic to the pragmatic level is making knowledge comprehendible to a wide range of audiences within the environment. Nonaka and Takeuchi discuss this notion in terms of *externalization.*[33] Unless the metaphors, analogies, and symbols used to explicate knowledge have universal comprehension, the transition will be difficult. For example, a marketing department may attempt to convey some sense of knowledge in highly semantic terms (code-jargon) that is easily understood in their particular group. However, if this knowledge needs to be transferred to operations or finance, it may need to be modified or "translated" if their terms are to have significance for the new audience.

The purpose of information processing through the semiotic levels is to derive a basis for actionable knowledge. Actionable knowledge means taking some action based on attained knowledge derived from information. The success of such action is reflected in behavior modifications within the organization. In order for this to occur, the knowledge must be dissipated, or dispersed, throughout the organization.

Dissipation

From the pragmatic level we generate actionable knowledge or insight. Dissipation calls for changing the organizations' behavior based on information that has been synthesized through the generative side of semiotic ladder: in other words, "What do we do now?" Ramaprasad and Ambrose define dissipation as "the transformation of information from the epistemological world of thought to the ontological world of action." The action of dissipation is predicated on the development of some new knowledge that has prompted the action. Actions that are predicated on information alone produce premature consequences, which sometimes produce false-positive results. Several advertising fiascoes reflect this notion, as when Chevrolet, in attempting to secure a Latin American niche, had difficulty marketing a popular North American model, the Nova. While the campaign demographics were likely correct, the fact that, in Spanish, *no va* indicates that something "won't go" would have been captured at the semantic level of the semiotic model. Dissipation will channel "new information" through the organizational system, and concern for a product name in relation to a target market's culture could have been anticipated during this process.

At the semantic level we are concerned with how to transform logical thought or knowledge into physical action. This requires viewing knowledge in the appropriate context and understanding its various constituents. For instance, if at the pragmatic level we generated knowledge that a new scheduling system of humans and machines on the factory floor is needed, we first need to clearly identify a production schedule. One contextual variable may include the need for rescheduling full-time and part-time workers. Each of the contextual variables has implications on the nature of potential actions. For instance, rescheduling full-time union workers is a much more complex task than hiring part-timers.

Once the environment is identified, plausible actions are more likely to be comprehended. Plausible actions are a function of the syntactical connections between the constituents in the environment. To list available options, it is important to view the relationships between all affected parts, to get a holistic view, and to mitigate the effects of what Herbert Simon refers to as bounded rationality.[34] Simply stated, bounded rationality contends that all systems have restrictions imposed on them because of the availability of limited resources. Once selected, courses of actions are identified, however, their effects must be calculated.

During dissipation, the organization selects an action to be implemented. Calculating statistics or running simulations on each action and monitoring probable empirical effects can assist in deciding the best course of action. Common method approaches to this end include the development of what-if scenarios or sensitivity functions analysis.

Changing the behavior of agents based on information is how we virtually create organizations from information. This is crucial, as the generation of insights or knowledge has no value unless it is acted upon. Task objectives include "debriefing" members associated with each level as the effect (success or failure) *of their contribution* to the ultimate decision(s) for action. This facet of the process does more than merely inform; it establishes a bond among members (organizational units) as to their role in information and knowledge creation. Imagine two illustrations of Figure 4.1, placed next to each other. Once the process of information generation is completed, as indicated by the left side of the model, dissipation moves found knowledge down the right side of the model, throughout the organization. This may begin the cycle again as other data associated with actions of knowledge dissipation may produce new data. Ultimately the scope of the effects related to this model is intended to modify the behavior of the organization based on the results produced at the various levels of the generation side of the model. Modification based on knowledge indicates that the information obtained in the process has value to the organization. As noted by Saussure, "The notion of value . . . shows us that it is . . . a mistake to consider a sign as nothing more than the combination of a certain (data . . . or) a certain concept. To think of a sign as nothing more would be to isolate it from the system to which it belongs. It would be to suppose that a start could be made with individual signs, and a system constructed by putting them together. On the contrary, the system as a united whole is the starting point, from which it becomes possible, by a process of analysis, to identify its constituent elements."[35]

On Efficiency and Effectiveness

As we move upward or downward through the semiotic model levels, the notions of efficiency and effectiveness come into play. From the lower levels of the model moving upward, our process is centered on validating, assimilating, and aggregating large quantities of data. The seminal criteria are focused on efficiency. Efficiency of information processing up the first three semiotic levels is important in curtailing the information overload, and we intentionally sacrifice effectiveness for efficiency. At the first two levels of the model, the idea of effectiveness has little bearing because of the mechanical nature of processes used at these levels. Once structured, the validation, processing, and aggregation of data are routine mechanical tasks that seldom change or require attention. Conversely, at the higher two levels of the semiotic chain, we are more concerned with effectiveness than efficiency. Deriving semantic and pragmatic notions effectively is important, as efficient generation of incorrect insights has no value. Decision-makers must be careful in choosing the appropriate context in which to view syntactic information, and time is required to carefully evaluate semantics in order to optimize subsequent forms of knowledge.

Similarly, during the dissipation phase, the role of effectiveness is most crucial at the higher levels. Efficient but ineffective activities do more damage than inefficient though effective actions. Once the decision-making process is complete and objects to be changed are identified, the organization seeks to efficiently induce behavior modification. This occurs at the lower levels of the model where efficiency is most important. Logical action needs to be communicated efficiently to the agents and objects down to the morphological level so as to produce verifiable change.

It is also interesting to note that one cannot skip levels in the semiotic ladder. In learning development, specific objectives are contained in the principal domains related to instructional design, for example, the cognitive domain. Bloom stated that his taxonomy of cognitive objectives according to levels of increased intellectual capacities related to comprehension (lowest level of understanding), application, analysis, synthesis, and finally evaluation (highest level of understanding).[36] Because the capacity of the learner is essential to the tasks associated with higher-level learning, as tasks become more complex, it is important to first establish competency in the lower levels as a basis for learning. Similarly, in order to succeed to the higher, more task-intensive, levels of the semiotic model, previous tasks at the lower levels must be completed. It is a mistake to assume that an analyst can bypass levels within the process for quick, or accurate, answers.

The Semiotic Model in Practice: Case Study 9/11

In the months preceding 9/11[37] the United States accepted a new presidency under conditions that had come close to challenging Constitutional authority. The subsequent party transition in the White House had been less than cordial but included an exchange of information regarding world terrorist activity. Starting in December 2000, the intelligence community indicated that its surveillance activities had monitored unusual spikes in the amounts of communications traffic between known terrorist factions.[38] This traffic was steadily consistent through June, and the CIA in particular was concerned with the possibility of terrorist strikes intended to coincide with either the Fourth of July or perhaps during the president's appearance at the G-8 economic summit scheduled for late July in Genoa, Italy.

There appeared to be little focus on the probabilities associated with strikes directed at domestic targets. This posturing underscores a point made by John Parachini of the Monterey Institute of International Studies, who had repeatedly warned against the weakness in Washington's ability to calculate threat assessments because they rely too often "on what people think terrorists could do . . . [and not] on what they are able to do." [39] Linear thinking of this type impedes any consideration that allows the data process to succeed along the levels of the semiotic model. The following data would have been useful at the morphological level in the development of a semiotic model applied to the unfolding events:

- December 2000–March 2001—Intelligence sources, including the CIA, become aware of increased communications activity among Islamic extremist groups. Such activity is often interpreted as an indicator of impending action.
- February 2001—Arizona flight schools report to the FAA that an Arab student, Hani Hanjour, may have a fraudulent pilot's license and is seeking advanced certification to fly jets. The FAA allows Hanjour's credentials but inform him that he will not be certified. (Hanjour was aboard and may have piloted the plane that struck the Pentagon on September 11.)

Again, at the morphological level, the task merely requires the gathering of data such as that listed above. Frankly, at this stage the focus is on quantity rather than quality of information. But as data filters upward in the model, it will be thinned quickly.

At the empirical level, data has been broadly filtered but not critically evaluated. This stage of appraisal should validate usefulness and give weight to the significance of the data collected as well as determine whether synthesis of the data is likely to provide information. This process establishes "value" to data. Examples from the media indicate the likelihood that some data related to 9/11 may have reached a level similar to the empirical stage of the semiotic model.

- June–July 2001—In a memo to his superiors, an Arizona FBI agent theorizes that al-Qaeda may be training pilots to use planes in terror plots; supervisors defer the memo.
- The Egyptian government tells the CIA that Muslim terrorists may intend to use planes to crash into buildings. This information is based in part on an incident in which an Egyptian airliner is crashed by a hijacker who appeared to be aiming for, but missed, a government structure.
- A member of the Senate Intelligence Committee (SIC) tells CNN in June 2001 that her staff has advised her of the high "probability of a terrorist incident that will occur in the U.S. within the next three months."

At the syntactical stage of our model, the similarity of events would have been noted. Counterterrorist expert Thomas Bradey used information analysis to review suspected failures in U.S. intelligence gathering by the thirteen agencies involved and observed that the failures were less related to the collection of information than to "failures to put (it) together properly."[40] We see a number of activities among agencies that are reactionary in that available intelligence was either held or not channeled through a semiotic system.

- August 2001—The CIA asks Immigration (INS) to place a suspect from the attack on the USS *Cole* (October 2000), Khalid al-Mindhar, on a watch list. This is in response to the FBI informing the Agency of their arrest of Zaccarias Moussaoui, a known Islamic extremist who had been attending flight school training at a Minneapolis center. The INS informs the CIA that al-Mindhar had entered the United States in July and his whereabouts are unknown. (Al-Mindhar is one of the hijackers aboard the plane that crashed into the Pentagon on September 11.)
- Early September 2001—A Minnesota FBI agent writes an analytical memo based on Moussaoui's case theorizing a scenario in which Islamic extremists fly a plane into New York's World Trade Center. The SIC seeks a meeting with Vice President Cheney to address terrorism, but is informed by the chief of staff that it will take six months to prepare before such a meeting can take place.

September 11, 2001—Despite the erratic behavior of four in-flight jets on the East Coast, no information is provided to or by any authority that indicates the possibility of a threat. Following the crash at the first tower, no threat alert is issued. When the second tower is attacked, there is confusion. In a seemingly "unrelated" incident, a third jet crashes forty miles southeast of Pittsburgh. Extrapolation of that flight's course would have indicated that it was pointed in the direction of the U.S. Capitol. The fourth commercial plane makes a wide pass over Washington before banking and, while possibly heading for the White House, crashes into the Pentagon. Only now are the nation's air defenses scrambled.

By late June 2001 there appeared to be a specific "message" building that indicated there should have been some cause for concern in the intelligence community. The channel that carried that message experienced noise, like all channels, but it also contained elements of *certainty* that should have been interpreted as associated with a message. Before we regard the state of uncertainty of the receiver, who should have been receptive to new information, we must regard elements involved with the state of positive certainty, which, in the broad sense, also occupy the channel. This certainty is predicated to a large degree on experience.

The World Trade Center had been a target of religious fanatics in 1993. Subsequent terrorist activities against American interests, albeit overseas, gave no indication that such activities would abate. Individual bombers who strapped themselves with explosives were always a concern of the intelligence community until larger bombs were found in parked cars. Cars near secured buildings were checked until terrorists started driving trucks into their targets, and then barricades were erected. In 2000 a U.S. warship was attacked by a small, simple watercraft outfitted with explosives, and the navy ordered procedural changes. It was apparent that the methods of conveyance used by terrorists were expanding. It should not have been too much of a stretch to consider that someday planes might be used as weapons. The possibility had been presented in U.S. popular fiction.[41]

Under this case's existing information structure, any certainty that might have resulted in a positive actionable event was lost by mid-July 2001. This does not imply that the events of September 11 could have been averted, but the probability for a less reactionary response is certainly higher. The use of military jets to shoot down commercial airliners perceived as threats is not without precedent. In the best-case scenario, one that attempts to evade rather than avoid disaster, scores of lives might have been saved.

In Figure 4.3, the stages of the semiotic model are represented along the x-axis starting with the morphological level (data gathering) at stage 1 and ending with the pragmatic level (beginning of action-events) at stage 5. The y-axis indicates date ranges when data, information, or independent action were taken prior to attaining the pragmatic level.

Data related to September 11 had been coming in to various intelligence centers since the beginning of the year and escalated by the summer. The lack of understanding of any relational basis for this data failed to become apparent until late July, when there is a convergence that affects the major players involved in intelligence gathering and prompts the possibility for a common

Figure 4.3   **Time Line Leading to 9/11**

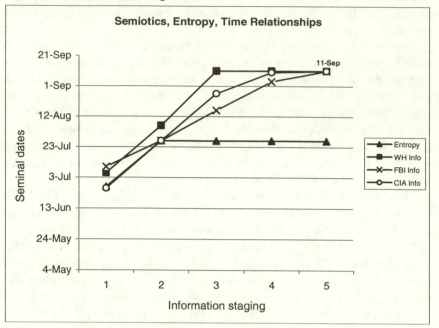

concern. Instead of taking advantage of any joint use of some plan that might have approached the semiotic model, these players continue along independent paths. It is here that any chance for certainty (for decisions) breaks down and the inevitable chance for greater entropy (uncertainty) increases. The principal players converge again on September 11 while conditions of entropy that might have efficiently lowered, in late July, instead maximize.

Conclusion

It should be noted that while other useful semiotic models exist, each is used for a purpose determined by specific boundaries. Agendas are driven and motivated by culture, society, and politics, which involve an intrinsic use of semiotics. Other semiotic systems involve verbal language; parole, the act of speaking, and signifying practices in codes; diachrony, time, history, process, and change; the processes of signification. The transactions involved lie between signifying systems and structures of reference; structures of the signified or the material nature of signs as noted by Robert Hodge and Gunther Kress in their work on social semiotics.[42]

Errors involved with the failure to apply semiotics to decisions may be seen as a type of hubris often apparent in successful organizations. "To the ignorant, the world looks simple."[43] When the organization believes all things to be certain, there is a tendency to dismiss new knowledge regardless of its form or origin. Prior to the events of September 11, a common American expression of reminiscence compared life in the past as easier, possibly more pleasant, because "it was a simpler time." The comparison is, of course, selective, as those "times" were less complex in terms of the general consumption of information. In our argument, complexity, which we discuss further in later chapters, is closely related to uncertainty. Times were not simpler at any given point in the past, but the allusion of certainty was much greater. Following World War II, lines were simply drawn for a Cold War between the two super powers with little regard for the rest of the world; a classic good-guy, bad-guy scenario. But the situation became less simple (more complex) as the time line associated with events indicated a complexity during which the good guys, for example, planted the seeds, in 1953, for the repatriation of an Islamic fundamentalist, Ayatollah, to Iran. Meanwhile, the bad guys were the ones supporting a popular revolutionary who had deposed a self-serving dictator that had kept the population in poverty and ignorance on an island ninety miles south of the United States. By extension, and causation, a case for the destruction of the World Trade Center could be tied to the launching of *Sputnik* in 1957 when "times were simpler."

The semiotic model is workable, that is, is it likely that data can ultimately be transformed to meaningful information as a basis for knowledge upon which actionable events will occur. Many of the processes involved with the model take place daily for individuals, organizations, and governments, but they lack coordination and at times are counterproductive. Sometimes these conditions are connected to the notion of bounded rationality, but more often such conditions are the result of not using what is available. Long after the reader finishes this text, "new" information will come forward in support of data that was available and not used that would have allowed the United States to be far better prepared against terrorist attacks generally and, though unfortunate, the World Trade Center attack specifically.

Amid the confusion and destruction in New York on September 11, there was a haunting, ironic note that underscores the importance in the use of the model we have presented: few if any New York firemen who responded to the attack were "surprised" that the World Trade Center had been targeted for destruction. It appears that their understanding of the probability of the event was deeper than many whose job it is to anticipate or prevent such disasters. The use of the semiotic model could have converted the tacit "feeling" shared by the NYFD into the realm of useful data available to other governmental guardians.

The model presented in this chapter is reliant on understanding the variables associated with the scheme. As with the practical use of any model, the first independent variable governing the successful application of the model is organizational commitment. The second most important variable is time. In the first instance there is no need to begin any process regarding information flow if the organization sees no need for it. On the distaff side, if an organization professes a need and slots the resources for the objectives generally associated with information management, everyone in the organization should be aware of it or the system will be hampered from the start as potential data sources are missing. Einstein viewed time to be a constantly flowing river of which, under normal conditions, we can catch only a fleeting glimpse. So too data and information should be regarded as fleeting and as having a relevant, observable shelf life. The element of time then is closely related with the element of risk in that there is a direct correlation between the amounts of risk to which an organization is willing to expose itself before the time is right for action. Both Enron and Arthur Andersen chose to ignore this relationship.

While we will discuss the spatial aspect of information processing in greater depth in a later chapter, we now turn to the devices used by the semiotic model to assist in the process of synthesizing data-to-information-to-knowledge. The efficient design of devices and units within the organization can greatly augment a business's ability to handle the increased demands resulting from information flow. Failure to consider the need of organizations to engage such systems contributes to notions on the effects, and causes, of chaos.

In the next chapter we review some of the equipment used by organizations to channel information. More important, we address how information channels, whether human or mechanical, should be arranged to maximize both efficiency and effectiveness. At the conclusion of chapter 5, we assess the nature of chaos with the suggestion that if ultimately the condition of chaos cannot be avoided, certainly there are techniques available that can assist the organization to avert it.

5

Spatial Dimension of Information Processing

Coupling, Cohesion, and Chaos

Having introduced the semiotic model to demonstrate how the transformation of data-to-information-to-knowledge occurs, we now draw attention to some of the devices used in communication to deliver information. While our model represents a "best-case" scenario involving the development of information, conditions under which information transfer will take place are not always optimized. We start with the assumption that methods for the conveyance of information are functional, that is, working. By this we expect that no "physical" malfunctions would interrupt the transfer of information so that the only hindrance to information transfer would arise from how signal devices (information processing units) are arranged for the purpose of control. This notion is described in more detail in the study of analytical induction that infers conditional governance between the properties under study. The study considers conditions that are both necessary and sufficient to the task, in our case, the development of useful information. We consider these conditions in terms of *who or what* has control over information as it evolves, and this control is often determined in terms of coupling and cohesion of signal devices discussed later in this chapter.

Those readers who are familiar with the hardware discussed at the beginning of this chapter may wish to skip to the sections dealing with coupling, cohesion, and chaos. Coupling and cohesion relate to how the instruments of communication, including human hierarchies, are "joined" for efficiency and effectiveness. How the communication devices or channels are joined will affect information flow. Inattention to details in the arrangements related to coupling and cohesion may result in unanticipated calamity. The unexpected results of such conditions are often explained as chaos, which is addressed at the conclusion of this chapter.

It is commonly held that organizations represent social knowledge of co-ordination and learning. Less clear, however, is how this representation is defined as a whole and what that representation means. As argued by Kogut and Zander, individuals learn and possess knowledge; the role of the organization is to integrate the disparate pieces of knowledge and consume it to gain strategic advantages.[1] Social knowledge embraces the language and actions considered unique to the organization. It is often represented by what Wenger has described as Communities of Practice.[2] The language of plumbers or the police is different from the language of physicians or lawyers; so too is the social manner in which the language is used. The word *sweat* for example has different meanings in different occupations. The physician knows *sweat* to mean the process by which the body attempts to cool itself by perspiring. A plumber *sweats* a copper tube by heating it prior to fitting and soldering, and additionally refers to condensation that appears around a cold water pipe as *sweat*. The vernacular of police understands *sweating* in terms of waiting out a situation during which there is degree of uncertainty regarding the probable outcomes in a particular event. Meaning in information is conveyed within signals, but the propagation of "sense" in information can be determined in how signaling devices are arranged to carry the message. To this end, in this chapter we discuss both signals and the devices commonly used to carry information. We begin with a brief review of where we are up to this point.

Thus far our approach to organizations of information has followed a functional frame involving definitions from disciplines including evolution, physics, cybernetics, and communication. Additionally, we have used models, for example, the semiotic scale, which is intended to manage data and information flow. This approach is not intended to convey the notion that we are providing a Rosetta stone for all information problems. Such a contention implies that the solution to each problem would be absolutely predictable. Unfortunately, this is not how the world of information works.

In chapter 2, we addressed the notion of entropy, the second law of thermodynamics, which is a measure of instability or uncertainty within a closed system. Entropy is a state within a system and has its greatest effect when maximized. Once achieved, a new state or form of irreversible equilibrium occurs in which the properties of each agent in the system are indistinguishable and inseparable. Maximized entropy provides no chance for the recovery of the component parts in a closed system; a system modified by entropy remains at equilibrium in its new state unless acted upon by an outside agent.

As discussed before, a classic example of entropy involves an ice cube and a glass of water at room temperature. Initially, set side by side, only the molecular structure of the water and the ice distinguishes them and it is clear which is which. If the ice cube is dropped into the glass, changes immediately take place and the effects are attributable to entropy. Slowly the ice becomes less discernible as it dissolves into the water until such time the contents of the glass are indistinguishable. The "organization" of both the ice and the water have been altered and are unrecoverable. Attempts to re-freeze a volume of water that represented the ice cube will never produce the same cube. At maximum entropy the unique properties of the original elements are lost. During the process, however, there is a time when the introduction of some agent may slow the process of entropy so another state of equilibrium is possible, one that would maintain the characteristics of the interacting elements. It would be possible, for example, to modify and monitor the temperature in this experiment so the water would not freeze and the ice would stop melting. In our examples, the agent that will modify such states of equilibrium in organizations is useful information.

There is a relation between entropy and a deterministic system. A computer or an organization may be regarded as a deterministic system, but the information input to the system has specific qualitative dynamic characteristics that lend themselves to entropy. Our contention for modeling information delivery via the semiotic model is intended to keep the effects of entropy in check. As in our ice cube example where temperature modification can check entropy, the proper use of information can have the effect of reducing entropy that otherwise encourages confusion in organizations. Conventional use of information and computers (automated applications) often involve linear, logarithmic, or step-at-a-time approaches. This "step-dependency" involves variables that must be arranged properly in order to progress in the application: in order to succeed to C from A, B must be accomplished. Assuming the results in C fail to reflect the desired intention, quantifiable variables in B are inspected. It may be necessary to tweak the variables associated with B in order to achieve C, and once the desired results are obtained the linear design can continue. But what if the tweaking produced some unintentional, undetected, and immeasurable difference? What may have been thought to represent conditions of sensitivity in which small changes are easily detectable and corrected may, in fact, produce some unforeseen effect. This effect, termed chaos, will be discussed at the conclusion of this chapter, but for now our focus will involve the signals and the devices that carry them. The proper interpretation of what constitutes a signal and a clear understanding of the devices that handle signal transfer is a good first step toward the design of any worthwhile information system.

As noted in the preceding chapter, the semiotic model is grounded in the morphological layer. Here, data is gathered on objects and agents of interest. Measurements are taken on phenomena of interest. Unless we understand the intricacies of how these agents and objects interact with their environment (the organization), we will not be able to organize information optimally. To this end let us first explore the notion of signals and signal devices. We draw on the fields of computer science, electrical engineering, and system architectures to make analogies of how various agents and objects generate signals in the organization. The collections of these devices determine the signal space of the organization. Signal space should be regarded as the morphological space of the organization. Next, we must understand the functions of these devices. Here two items are of interest—how tightly is the inner working of a signal device integrated (cohesion), and how tightly are signaling devices connected (coupling). The cohesiveness and strength of coupling determine the nature of empirical and syntactical layers, respectively. The signal space of the organization will provide us a platform to address the concepts associated with chaos. We assert that an appreciation for chaos theory will help organizations *organize* their information processing capabilities successfully by paying attention to the initial conditions—*morphological*, *empirical*, and *syntactical*.

Signals

As noted in chapter 2, information can be said to be a logical collection of rudimentary elements assimilated in some logical fashion. The rudimentary elements that assimilate information take shape in the form of *signals*. Information represents a commodity that can be interpreted in a variety of ways. But signals, once generated from the source, have a finite life. Signals that traverse through unobstructed space will be present until the signal's life is exhausted. In obstructed space, however, a signal's life is determined by what *devices* it encounters. A device can extend the signal's life through amplification, inhibit a signal if the obstacle is not negotiable, or redirect the intended path of the signal without otherwise affecting it.

Signals, much like risk, have two components: (1) a numerical *probability* (that is, a number between 1 and 0) that something will occur; and (2) an estimated numeric value of the *consequences* that may result. The product of the two numbers is the *numerical risk value* associated with the specific involvement identified. For instance, in financial markets we see stock prices move up or down based on signals sent by actions of an organization. These signals are not only a sign of an action or an impending action but contain information of the expected consequences of the action.

Signal Devices

Organizations are actually laden with signal generators and dissipaters. These can take the form of a person, a machine, or some combination of man-machine devices. Devices can be classified as *physical* or *logical*.[3] Physical devices include singular machines or individuals whereas logical devices are units built as teams and departments. One of the best information storage-and-retrieval devices that an organization possesses is its staff.

An organization's staff consists of the people that make work happen, the folks that consume and generate information, the people who act and think. As humans are social animals, no member of the organization works in isolation. Each one is connected to other staff members (signal devices) either formally (through designations of an organization chart) or informally (through the social networks they work in). Hence, any signal device in an organization can assume two roles: formal and informal. Researchers in sociology and management have long recognized the importance of informal roles that an employee plays in an organization.[4] In their investigations, scholars have ascribed several roles to employees in informal networks—central connectors (people who connect a local group), boundary spanners (people who connect two or more distinct groups), and so forth. We agree. We however feel that a more comprehensive list of signal devices can be found in examining the literature in computer science and electrical engineering.

The following information involves signal transfer devices, or hardware. Those familiar with the function of such devices may wish to skip to the section involving "signal space."

The simplest communication device is called a *repeater.* Its function is to receive a signal from one input source, regenerate it, and then transmit it to another link. Its primary purpose is to act as *an amplifier* for the signal that has to traverse a distant path, which would require time and greater strength than available in the signal's original life. Repeaters are put in between long communication paths connecting two devices; they can receive a signal from either side, regenerate it, and then pass it to the other device. A collision in communication will occur if both devices emit signals for regeneration simultaneously. In such cases, one, or neither, signal survives and must be retransmitted. A repeater has *no comprehension* of what a signal *means*; it just transfers signals without exploring their contents. Moreover, a repeater can handle only one class of signals. Organizations are loaded with *repeaters*, either physical (in computer networks) or with their human counterparts who may be involved as data entry or mail delivery personnel. These individuals are tasked with the delivery of inputs to designated recipients. Mail clerks seldom care about the contents of a letter; they are concerned only with the address of the recipient and delivery time if specified. Data entry personnel also seldom care about the intricacies of the data. Their task is to transfer data from one medium (for example, paper) to another medium (electronic). Organizational repeaters then connect objects between sources and destinations involved in a class of signals. Repeaters can affect signal processing and traversal in several ways. For example: depending on the number of incoming signals from a source, there will be a delay in when these signals reach a destination. Due to the lack of comprehension of what a signal represents, repeaters follow the first-in, first-out rule; there is no mechanism for prioritization or filtering. Repeaters serve only one purpose, that is, regeneration of signals, hence they can be an overhead to organizations and clog up the organization's signal space.

A *hub* is a "multiport repeater" and is therefore also tied to signal processing in organizations. Like a repeater, the hub's function is to serve as an amplifier for signals, however, it is more sophisticated than a normal repeater in that it can receive and relay signals to multiple nodes. As with repeaters, these devices can handle only one class of signals and have no comprehension of contents. Organizational *hubs* can be defined as logical groups consisting of organizational *repeaters*. In the human analogy, an entire mail department of an organization made up of individual mail personnel (repeaters) would represent an organizational hub.

A *bridge* is a device that connects independent networks; it is akin to a bridge that connects land masses separated by water. A bridge accepts signals, buffers (holds) them, and *makes a decision* whether to pass them or not. If the signal is addressed to a network, the bridge is connected to it and the signal is passed in the process of forwarding. Otherwise, if the signal is destined for a local location on the originating network, it will be *filtered* and not passed. It is interesting to note that, if a signal has an external destination, but it is not clear which external network the destination is on or if it is available, the bridge will pass the signal *to all nodes* on which it is connected. This can lead to a *broadcast storm*, sometimes resulting in information overload. Whether a node is a designated recipient or not, the signal will be passed to it, and it is then left to the node to either accept or reject it. This leads to extra effort for the nodes to process the incoming signal. Some bridges have built-in intelligence facilities that allow their routing table to be updated when a recipient node acknowledges that it has received and processed a signal. But bridges have several limitations. They can connect only two networks with similar architecture, and they can cause delays. Delays are due to the fact that they have to process each incoming signal and make decisions to forward. Organizational *human bridges* may be represented as personnel who actively interface between multiple departments or groups such as project or middle-level managers. These individuals are boundary spanners; they connect multiple groups within an organization. These individuals act as connectors between two or more local groups/departments. It is important to note that bridges *must operate on the same architecture*; organizational bridges connect groups that are internal and unique to the organization and they function to bring local signals to other nodes on the network. A bridge must have the ability to detect the correct node to which a transfer of signal is being made. Without this ability, the signal can be transferred to all external members, leading to information overload, and a question of credibility is attached to the signal originator, leading to the "bystander effect" in which all receive the signal but all wait for someone else to act on it. Under such conditions the signal is often simply ignored.

A *router* connects heterogeneous (mixed) networks, in contrast to bridges that connect homogenous networks. Routers have several advantages over bridges, including the fact that they do not produce broadcast storms as they route signals to the designated recipient only. This is because of a routing table that contains the logical addresses for each node and also the routing paths. Routers are also intelligent; they can transfer signals in an efficient manner from a source to a destination, thereby reducing the number of hops (intermediary devices) a signal has to pass through. One might think of a router as an intelligent bridge that works with multiple network architectures. Organizational *routers* are personnel or departments that are connected with the external environment such as government agencies (IRS for tax purposes, SEC for financial statements), vendors (supply chain agreements), customers, competitors, and so on. Much like their electronic counterparts, an organizational router must be able to deliver the *right* information to the *right* node and not generate a *broadcast*. Routers perform a necessary function of interfacing with the external environment and hence are sources of signals that might indicate exogenous concerns.

A *gateway* is a highly intelligent device that connects dissimilar networks, such as LAN (local area network) and WAN (wide area network), or PC and mainframes, by translating different *protocols* used by those different network devices. When a *gateway* receives packets of information from one network, it extracts data from those packets and converts (translates) it into other packets based on a protocol used by the other network. Organizational *gateways* may be regarded as individuals who act like extended hubs both within and outside the organization. These individuals must be able to speak multiple languages in order to communicate with distinct networks. Hence, an individual who speaks both French and Japanese can communicate with an organization's divisions in Paris and Tokyo; moreover, an individual who understands both accounting and marketing terminology can communicate with the two distinct groups in the same or different geographical locations.

Filters remove unwanted noise from the signal of interest. All signals carry "noise" that provides unintentional distortion, which can interfere with transmission. Unintentional examples include "white" or background noises. "White" noise is blank or open space in the signal channel and is similar to wind in a tunnel; it does not necessarily affect anything directly but may require an increase in signal strength to deliver a message efficiently. Background noises may include interference from either outside sources or from other traffic within the same channel. By analogy, if you are speaking to someone next to a construction site, background noise is likely to interfere with your communication. On the other hand, if you have ever attended a meeting where several people try to speak at once, you have experienced some degree of distortion similar to what happens when a number of signals traverse the same space. Filters are capable of reducing some of the distortion associated with information transfer by screening unwanted noises. Other filters have a more direct purpose. Virus detection software is an example of a filter that intentionally seeks known parameters within a signal that may not comply with accepted protocol requirements. During the assurance process of information flow, filters act to insure the integrity of a signal. Filters insure that signals are unimpaired. Whether or not integrity is maintained in the signal belongs solely in the domain and responsibility of the system design and actually has little to do with the signal per se. In 2003 a KLEZ virus affected a number of computers, although patches and fixes were available that might have prevented the problem. Hence the patches, which were to act as filters, were absent due to poor management on the part of organizations. Organizations generally have formal and informal filtering schemes. Middle-level managers are "formal filters." They are tasked with transferring strategic knowledge from the upper level of management to the frontline workers, who are operationally focused. A filter responsibility sometimes includes filtering only information that upper management wants to hear. This can be a mistake. In 2002, one of us (Kevin) conducted research as a visiting research fellow at Accenture's Institute for Strategic Change in Cambridge, Massachusetts, into how a division of a consulting firm gathered information and disseminated it to its members.[5] The group had a formally appointed "gatekeeper" whose role was to check the integrity of information, see how it fit the existing schemas and agendas, and decide whether it should be made part of the group's information repertoire. Gatekeepers such as these are an example of an organizational filter. On the one hand, they can be very valuable in reducing the proliferation of noisy information and unwanted infor-

Figure 5.1 **Signal Space of the Organization**

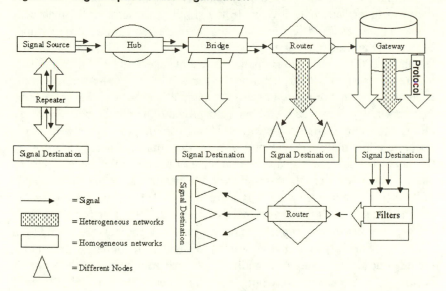

mation going to the group; on the other hand, they may be harmful as there is a possibility of intentionally blocking relevant and genuine signals.

Encoders/decoders are parts of the communication system to prevent security breaches of sensitive information. Signal processing issues involved at this stage may involve techniques as simple as passwords and log-on IDs but should involve either some encoder/decoder schemes or basic encryption. Encryption provides that "keys" be available to both the sender and the receiver of information. This serves to reinforce the irrefutability of data or information transmitted between the origin and recipient. It is important to understand that system designs should have the ability to recognize and authorize not only people but also devices. The importance of such an approach is underlined in Cliff Stoll's *Cuckoo's Egg*, where a few people were attributed with the ability to bring down an entire network.[6] Organizations are laden with encoders and decoders. The most prevalent encoding/decoding scheme is when an expert is trying to relay knowledge to a novice. The expert needs to decode tacit insights and make them explicit in a form that is comprehendible by the novice. Unless both individuals agree on the "rules for encoding/ decoding," sense-making will not occur. The role of a translator is salient here. If a French person wants to talk to a German, either they both have to speak a common language or have a translator perform the communication.

Figure 5.1 provides a visual summary of the devices listed above. As the legend indicates, arrows indicate signals and how they are managed when they encounter particular devices. In the simplest sense, a signal may pass between the source and destination using two cans tied with a piece of string, but the strength of the signal as well as its type will be limited. Plain old telephony (POTS) technology found the use of repeaters helpful as a means to strengthen signals over distance; longer distances required multiple repeaters. The signal relation, however, remained one-on-one, that is, sender-to-receiver, which proved inefficient as bandwidth increased and technology allowed for more signals to be carried along a single pipe. Hubs were introduced to allow multiport transport of signals to multiple destinations using the same channel. The signals were nondiscriminatory of a specific type or class. Bridges served as the first devices in the signal chain that were capable of "decisions" in that they not only received signals but served to determine destination paths within homogeneous networks. Mixed or heterogeneous networks required more sophistication in order to negotiate a path that led to a variety of node types. This was accomplished with routers whose tables included destination addresses indicating signal routing paths. As systems became more expansive, for example, campus networks connecting various departments, efforts to connect the variety of equipment attached to the network was accomplished through the use of protocols established by the gateway. The gateway in turn works as a clearinghouse to dispatch signals to destinations, where they may be routed to specific recipients.

Signal Space Within an Organization

The signal space of the organization is represented by the logical *organization* of signal devices used to aid in the processing of a signal carrying information. How well signal devices are organized has a direct bearing on how well a job will be accomplished and additionally helps preempt or avoid future problems or crises. The organization of signal space comprises two facets: the internal and the external. Each signal device must be internally organized to perform a given task. How well the *internal* design of the equipment is integrated determines the functional efficiency and effectiveness of the device. This refers to the *cohesiveness* of internal functions within the organization. We must also be concerned with external integration of the signal devices, or how they are connected. Here the notion of coupling is important. Coupling determines the degree of interdependence between two or more devices. Optimal signal space is demonstrated by high cohesiveness and loose coupling.

We emphasize a need for a systems review and classification since the concepts of cohesion and coupling represent the initial staging devices or agents in the organizational information environment. Failures to properly identify dependencies at this stage will likely result in unforeseen consequences later. Such consequences lead to a variety of defensive, nonproductive reactions within the social context of the organization. These reactions include *denial* expressed in the refusal to acknowledge any reality associated with failure; *disavowal*, or separation from the problem by acknowledging a degree of reality but downplaying its importance; *fixation*, a rigid commitment to a particular, often exclusive, course of remedial action; *idealization* in ascribing omnipotence to another person, object, or organization; *intellectualization*, elaborate rationalization of an action or thought; *projection*, attributing unacceptable results, actions, or thoughts to others; or *schisms*, a splitting that results in the extreme isolation of different elements and, in the extreme, dichotomization. Each of these is an indicator of impending chaos.

Coupling of Signal Devices: The Analogy to Evolution

In addressing evolution we have found that a species succeeds not because it is the strongest, but because it is capable of adaptation in order to function in the environment. About 4 billion years ago, *life* began on earth, but it was not until around 600 million years ago that these forms displayed the first signs of *evolution*. At that time, for some reason, single-cell organisms began combining to set out on the path that has led to the world we know today. The joining of cells to form early organisms involved both coupling and cohesion in the right combination, which allowed for adaptation.

While devices used in communications have been around for the better part of a century, and though they continue to improve, techniques are still being developed to make them function better in their respective environments. During life's evolution on earth, there have been at least five instances during which almost all life was wiped out; during the earth's lifetime, 99.9 percent of creatures that once lived are now extinct.[7] It is likely that at least two of these instances were the result of some cataclysmic event directly affecting the environment, for example, asteroid collisions and other causes may have been related to how the life forms were "coupled." Coupling indicates how well two units, once connected, work together and whether there is any meaningful product produced as a result of this union. In most failed evolutionary cases, organisms were "coupled" effectively but were unable to generate any identifiable uniqueness, which might have helped sustain them. Such arrangements are more often parasitic than symbiotic, so when the host fails, the coupled organisms fail.

For most of those species the problem was not merely related to coupling, since with the passage of time even the simplest organism would likely have produced some unintentional "new" variants. The problem lay in their inability to conform to the Darwinian concept of adaptation, something in successful species that allows for a closer symmetry with the environment. Here, nature looked at the initial conditions and in most cases found them to be wanting. If we carry this analogy to our semiotic model, information evolves through the semantic level, where meaning is established within the context of what is being examined. This "context" represents the environment. If these information components were taken out of context, they would likely lose their "meaning" and become useless. The adaptation required for the information to survive occurs in the syntactical level as a type of coupling, or joining of context, in meaning similar to the biological notion of the relation between adaptive features and the environment.

Coupling is represented by modules and in the results from signals exchanged between any two modules. Its quality for systems design can be determined by the degree of connectivity between modules and by the quantitative items exchanged. Any system can be broken down into a number of subprograms or modules. Each module is a collection of program statements and can be characterized by the specific function it performs. The term "coupling" is used to gauge the degree of interdependence between any two modules.[8] The goal of a good system design is to minimize the degree of coupling between two modules. By doing so, one can identify interrelationships of program statements and then improve the simplicity and understandability of the structure of the systems. The desirable type of coupling is "loose coupling" that suggests the minimum dependence on the structure of one module by another. Modules with loose coupling are more independent and easier to maintain. An undesirable type of coupling, "tight coupling," implies the opposite. Various types of coupling are possible between modules.

Coupling between agents or modules may be mechanical or social. In the mechanical design it is generally easier to discover deficiencies by running a trace routine to detect errors. A trace routine basically involves sending progressively more complex instructions through coupled devices until they choke, and then trying to find out why. Social coupling involves human players who interact, and tracing problems through their associations can be difficult. Following the first World Trade Center bombing, for example, the coupling among agencies within the Justice Department was so tightly controlled by prosecutors that it was difficult for law enforcement to work effectively. The FBI complained that the U.S. Attorney's Office held up their continuing investigation because of evidentiary snags; the police wanted to do police work but the lawyers wanted to do lawyer's work, which often results in inhibiting the potential of any productive process. In the following paragraphs we outline a variety of coupling arrangements that can exist in an organization, some of which are conducive to the flow of information, others that are not.

Data coupling is the ideal kind of coupling. Information flags or data elements passed from one module to another are the source of coupling. Neither module needs to know the details of the other module's internal function so long as it gets the required data or information flag. This represents the "loosest" type of coupling and exhibits the best quality of systems design. For software engineers it requires a minimum level of interconnection between modules. In social interaction, while agents are coupled, each serves an independent function that contributes to the organization without direct or required dependency on each other. This form of interaction normally occurs when an organization deals with an external entity. Bill payment is a good example. As long as "data" related to your bill arrives to you in a timely manner and your data "payment" is made, no details are required as to how the bill was generated or how funds were allocated to pay the bill.

Stamp coupling is the next desirable kind of coupling. In stamp coupling, data items along with their underlying structure are passed between modules. Here, each module needs to know some degree of details on how the other module functions, as knowledge of the data structure is essential. This interdependence between two such modules characterizes the first instance of a less desirable structure within a system. Here, any change accomplished by one of the modules with regard to the data structure will influence modules that use the same data structure, even though those modules do not use the same data elements. This arrangement also exposes modules to unnecessary amounts of data, which will increase a chance for error when one module fails to recognize the data substructure. A possible remedy for this problem is to *normalize*, that is, make all data consistent, or to pass only necessary data elements. However, a possible side effect of this solution is *bundling*, the practice of collecting fairly unrelated pieces of data into an artificial data structure.[9]

Control coupling presents conditions during which one module literally passes directives or protocols to the other module. As a result, one module controls the behavior of the other. If this is allowed, it requires each module to have an intricate knowledge as to how the other module operates. Atypically, control information is sent from modules in an upper level (superordinate modules) to modules in a lower level (subordinate modules); however, the opposite can be possible and is referred to as an *inversion of authority*. In such cases, subordinate modules have to know the intentions of the superordinate modules.[10] In the social context, any command and control organization is familiar with the notion of coupling. Control information is communicated through a series of directives, but field conditions may dictate alternative actions not covered by procedures. Here, some authority is temporarily surrendered in an action that may be represented delegation. Surrender of all authority would lead to anarchy.

Common coupling assumes that two modules are using the same global data area for a variety of reasons. While modules may be coupled, their interaction involves a need to simultaneously interact with a distinct piece of data. As a general rule, the more people who have access to modify or interact with a common repository, the greater is the chance for it to become unstructured. This results in a highly unstructured data area that increases the chance of error as neither module is aware as to whom, when, and why data has been accessed and for what purpose. In worst-case scenarios, one module may defectively modify data or introduce a virus to the global data, which then affects the second module. On the mechanical side, common coupling can often be traced to the laziness of designers. In the social context, problems of common coupling occur when separate agents are allowed to place their own spin on information so that it appears in the best interest of the agent and not the organization. Commonly this condition is often mistakenly represented in the saying "the right hand doesn't know what the left hand is doing" and might be corrected if the proper reference were cited: "One hand washes the other and both hands wash the face." Sharing of common repositories always involves sensitivities associated with trust and, to varying degrees, authority. Problems associated with this relation begin when the issues of sensitivity for one process become confused with the other. Under the current conditions that exist between various law enforcement agencies and the Justice Department, it would not be difficult to provide examples indicating these types of problems. For the sake of brevity, we employ examples using regressive models to emphasize this point.[11]

Assume that an agency, regardless of structure, seeks to collect data that will be synthesized into some form of information. Because the intelligence "source" is of interest to the agency, it deploys three units to investigate the source. Each unit has a unique function that is regarded as important to the investigation. In our illustration we will posit a crime scene as the source for our intelligence gathering, and the agency units dispatched to the source include (A) a preliminary investigator, (B) a detective who has special knowledge regarding the type of crime being investigated, and (C) an evidence technician. The function-in-common for each unit involves securing the scene from contamination, gathering evidence, and documenting the steps involved during the respective stages of their investigations so it is possible to accurately reconstruct the scene at a later date. The investigation may proceed under two possible sets of conditions. In the first instance, the actors representing the units are highly suspicious of the others and genuinely feel that their contribution to the investigation deserves higher consideration by agency authorities. Each actor subscribes to a belief that their effort alone is sufficient to determine the facts for a possible case and that the other unit activities are largely superfluous to the most important matters, which will determine the case. These conditions characterize a hierarchical regression model that will represent conditions of ordered entry, ad hoc use of data or information, and restricted access to the other actors. Ordered entry suggests that each unit will have initial access to the intelligence source in some successive manner. *A* will enter and retrieve data that will not be known to *B* or *C*. *B* and *C* will then follow suit. Anything gleaned will be used, with little exception, exclusively by the unit that collected the data and only for purposes that unit deems important. Access to the data collected by the respective units will be restricted and therefore immune to conditions of time dependency, which may affect the other units. The agency, meanwhile, reports that each of its respective units has completed its responsibilities and expects to pursue the matter under investigation without realizing that their options have already been compromised in respect to choice-action processes. The second model presented represents circumstances of a general regression process. Under this model, the units may converge on the intelligence source at the same time, and conditions are conducive to immediate exchange interaction. Any explanation of data is common to all, and each unit is encouraged to share in their expertise. In this situation, analysis begins immediately. Discovery of data is immediately shared (open), and objectivity is maintained through of the influence of the interaction. Upon the completion of their respective tasks, each unit documents its findings, which include supplemental inputs from the other participants. These results are archived and commonly available to the agency through unrestricted channels. The agency reports that each of its respective units has completed its responsibilities and expects to pursue the matter under investigation with clear options in its choice-action processes. In both of the above cases, access to a common crime scene will cause one agency to point fingers at the other due to lack of trust or credit given to its findings.

Content coupling represents the worst type of coupling and has the "tightest" relationship between two modules. Here, one module is compelled to know the inside workings of the other. The fact that one module must explicitly know the other's implementation and content practically defeats the purpose of having separate modules. Here, Heisenberg's Uncertainty Principle, the notion that interaction between the observer and the observed changes both, comes into play. In this case the subservient role of one device compels modification as dictated by another; the dominant device is required to feed correcting information to stress conformity. If organizations or their management practice micromanagement, they demonstrate the concepts of content coupling. Content coupling is counterproductive in that it defeats any possibility for creativity and produces unnecessary redundancy.

Cohesiveness of Signal Devices

Cohesion represents another way to evaluate the quality of systems design, this time in terms of efficiency. The term *cohesion* refers to the measure of the strength of associations of all activities *within a module*. The significance of the concept of cohesion in software engineering is that it allows one to recognize the functional ability of the module. Good system design can be accomplished by maximizing the degree of cohesion.

The idea of cohesion was originated by Larry Constantine and further developed by others as a reliable measure of the maintainability of a module.[12] A highly cohesive module can be maintained easily since the elements of the module are strongly related to each other. Elements comprising the individual modules are discouraged through design, from building dependent relations to other modules within the system. This otherwise would lead to "tight" coupling between modules. This fact ties the notion of cohesion and coupling together; highly cohesive modules result in "loosely" coupled modules. By taking advantage of this relationship, designers can minimize the degree of coupling by maximizing the degree of cohesion. As with coupling, various types of cohesion can be found within a module.

Functional cohesion represents the best type of cohesion. All activities in a module relate to a singularity; the execution of the same single function. When direction is provided, a module carries out one job without regard to other activities within the system. This leads to the best maintainability and provides the best coupling among modules. A real-world example of functional cohesion might involve certain military or quasi-military specialists who are trained for maximum efficiency to perform as a team (two or more) with a specific mission and objective in mind. The purpose for such a design is simply stated: "Failure is not an option."

Sequential cohesion represents the next most desirable type of cohesion. The activities in sequential cohesion are not related to a single function, but they are related to each other through the data rather than through the task assignment. This is similar to the work-flow of an assembly line: the first activity uses the input data, and the second activity uses the output of the first activity as its input; the output of the second activity then becomes input for the third activity, and so on. A sequentially cohesive module generally has good coupling and is easy to maintain because it is easy to monitor. However, its reusability is slightly lower than a functional cohesive module since it may be designed for activities that will not generally be useful together in other task functions. In business, if a check is written, processed, and accepted, there is no need for any of the entities at any stage to understand the intricacies of any process other than their own.

Communicational cohesion is similar to sequential cohesion in a way the activities within a module are related to (input and output) data flow. The distinction is in the sequence of executions; specific order does not matter in communicational cohesion. Communicational cohesion is applicable when designers combine functions that work on the same data into one module. This can be avoided, however, by splitting the tasks assigned to the module. Students of professional sports in general and of American football in particular know that when a quarterback throws a pass, he is not throwing to an intended receiver but rather to a "spot" where the receiver is expected to be. If each member of the team does his part the play will succeed, and if not, problems of some sort are likely to occur.

Procedural cohesion represents a design that is the most difficult to maintain. Procedural cohesion is identifiable when the activities within a module are related to each other only because of their order of execution so the emphasis of the task is more connected to a procedure and not a single function. In a procedural cohesion, the data that a module sends and the data that the module receives may not even be related because a procedural cohesive module passes only partial results. Major personal computer manufacturers assemble machines with the materials available; it is not necessary that all the video or Ethernet cards be from the same subvendor as long as a completed machine that fits certain specs is produced. The associations of the activities in procedural cohesion are that of the one's daily work-flowchart. The activities are related only in that they might happen in that order during the particular day. This cohesion might occur because of wrong factoring or overfactoring. A possible remedy for this is to try different factoring again.

Temporal cohesion is represented in a module where activities are related by time. The associations of the activities can be found in the fact that they can be performed at the same point of time. Temporally cohesive modules are difficult to reuse, either in this system or in others, since their activities are so specifically defined by time. Temporal cohesion can, for example, be designed to have modules for initialization or termination processes only. At NASA, a number of specific instructions are relayed to provide information prior to a launch. Based on the information received, a mission may either be allowed to continue or be scrapped because convergent temporal indicators fall or fail to conform to specific guidelines for launch.

Logical cohesion is characterized when activities in a module are hardly related to each other. The activities in a logically cohesive module fall into the same general category but are distinguished by variety. Overall, this makes a module difficult to understand and maintain, since some activities may share common lines of code while others may not. At Chernobyl, prior to the meltdown there, any number of activities were occurring and were interpreted as unrelated when, in fact, they were. Decisions affecting the entire plant became impossible to monitor effectively because too many of them were being made independently. If those decisions were correct, logical decisions, the disaster might have been averted. However, while the objective of everyone was the same, the results indicated that a better form of cohesion was in order.

Coincidental cohesion represents the worst of the cohesion types. The activities in a coincidentally cohesive module are not related at all. Additionally, activities lack commonality with relation to data flow or through flows of control. This architecture is rare but appears from time to time when a system lacks design or new people attempt to continue a design without regard for what has already been accomplished. As the name implies, any connection between the task and the effort is purely coincidental. This is found in organizations when politics overrides purpose and creates such a condition by placing incompetent people in sensitive positions.

Chaos and Signal Devices

Chaos is the result of small changes in as little as one variable within a system, which invariably leads to big changes affecting everything. This can be understood through the nonlinear analysis of systems in which particular attention is given to initial conditions and the relationship of the variable involved. Edward Lorenz, employing nonlinear dynamics on weather patterns, proposed that storms developing on the American coastlines could be attributed to a butterfly flapping its wings somewhere in Asia.[13] His models demonstrated outcomes that held a keen dependency on initial conditions.

Small variations in initial conditions result in huge, dynamic transformations in concluding events. That is to say that there was no nail and, therefore, the kingdom was lost. Problems associated with chaos can often be traced to a total disregard of early information related to an event. In the world of supply chains, a well-studied similar notion is produced by the *bullwhip effect*.[14] The basic tenet here is that a small disruption in information flow will cause increasing magnitudes of uncertainty in the system. Here the notions of chaos and entropy converge.

Chaos theory suggests that there is the possibility that small, usually undetected variations in the initial conditions of a system may result in totally unexpected outcomes. Gollub and Solomon wrote:

A chaotic system is defined as one that shows insensitivity to initial conditions. That is, any uncertainty in the initial state of the given system, no matter how small, will lead to rapidly growing errors in any effort to predict future behavior: the system will become chaotic. Its behavior can be predicted only if the initial conditions are known to an infinite degree of accuracy, which, of course, is impossible.[15]

Because initial conditions determine all consequences, there appears more of a need, when inspecting dynamical systems, to focus on what is happening initially. The correct approach to information must embrace the logic of evolution as well as aspects of nonlinear functions. The notion of evolution *expects* change if things are to improve. This is contrary to the popular view of deterministic systems that aims to determine the future from an initial state and governing laws. The assumption is that a system can be broken down into smaller parts to be studied independently, then reassembled to make a new whole so that what applies at the unit level is expected to apply to the system. This is dangerous thinking. During "reengineering," one may encounter unique governing laws that apply to subsystems but not to the whole. The governing laws may in themselves change from subsystem to subsystem or between subsystem and the whole. In the traditional deterministic notion, the governing laws are assumed to be static and applicable to both the whole and the subsystems. This is rarely true.

Chaos occurs because of natural changes among variables and should be considered as an alternative to what is expected. Products of both adaptive evolution and chaos processes generate new "forms" that take on a life of their own. Conventional deterministic and predictive methods, on the other hand, generally produce only habitual routines. The proper approach in an analysis of these processes requires a logical standard, such as a semiotic model, that addresses nonlinearity in information as an evolutionary process leading to actionable knowledge.

Revisiting the ice-to-water example used in the entropy discussion, we wish to focus on an important aspect related to chaos theory—*critical points*. A critical point is an event or time period during which a small change produces large consequences. By example, the instant heated water turns to steam is a critical point. Within the semiotic model used to analyze data, each level represents a *critical* point in the processing of information in organizations, small changes either for the positive or negative will have large effects on the future stages. An organization cannot have good cohesion in signal devices unless they are properly calibrated, or sensitive to the data being examined. Consider an example—if an organization does not have appropriate signal device management in place, and specifically, if it has not calibrated all sources of signals it must be aware of, poor cohesiveness and coupling will occur, a first-order and second-order effect. Following this, poor sense-making will occur at the semantic level (third-order effect), and finally poor actions will result (fourth-order effect). Each effect magnifies the following one, and in the end the actions calibrated will completely miss the original point of data collection. As we stressed in chapter 4, the semiotic model is cyclical. Once the pragmatic stage has been reached, knowledge must be funneled back down to the morphological layer. Hence, critical points at all stages will affect subsequent stages. Then it is not surprising that most organizations have superior data management techniques, adequate empirical capabilities, average syntactical capabilities, and poor semantic and pragmatic capabilities.[16] The developments in the fields of information systems and computer science were fueled by the need to gather data and process it locally. Each department has its own data processing needs and rules; this is a facet of the empirical layer. Only later did cross-department data analysis begin lending to the syntactical stage. Recently we have seen a surge in the interest in knowledge management that addresses the semantic and pragmatic layers of our model. Each layer builds on the one below. Hence, the critical points must be managed adequately.

Chaotic systems are *aperiodic*—systems that almost repeat themselves but never succeed. Consequently there is no steady state. This is because such systems have a high sensitivity to initial conditions. Few would refute the adage that "an ounce of prevention is worth a pound of cure," yet the practice of intervention in areas as sensitive as crisis management is all but absent. Crisis impact is measured in terms of scope of effect on organizations and ultimately by their ability to contain the conditions of crisis before they ruin the company. We maintain that such conditions are capable of being detected either in advance or in such close proximity to their occurrence that they may be defused before they are allowed to bear their full potential. The appreciation and study of initial conditions is the science of chaos.

Conclusion

Our purpose in emphasizing the architecture of signal devices is to underscore and ground our conceptualization of the morphological, empirical, and syntactical layers of our semiotic model. Unless signal devices are organized appropriately, the initial conditions will cause disruptions in later stages of the semiotic model—semantic and pragmatic. The semantic layer, which is concerned with the generation of meaning, will be dysfunctional if a faulty syntactical or morphological layer is in existence. This anomaly may occur if information is unavailable, mishandled, or misinterpreted. For a business this may represent missed opportunities as the result of misreading cues or warnings, which are included in the information and indicate impending crisis.

All signals are generated from one or more organizational devices, those aggregated teams or departments mentioned earlier. To efficiently and effectively *evade* crisis, an organization must *organize* its signal generating and dissipating devices in such a manner as to direct impending crisis signals to salient responders. Clearly for our purposes, we assume that the *right* decision-maker is capable of comprehending signals and acting upon them, a topic we will address later. However, history has shown that in many cases, crisis signals are defeated well before they have the opportunity to reach the appropriate responder, or they become lost (for example, continuously traversing) in an organization's *logical* space so that they become useless. Again, if the devices are properly configured, this is less likely to occur.

But even with the correct equipment and personnel in place, attention to initial conditions on which future actions will be predicated is critical in order to prevent conditions leading to chaos. We contend that the proper sequence of devices or agents is a good first step in defeating the advent of the unexpected. To accomplish this task, organizations must rely on new methods in handling information flow. Some solutions rest with technology, but far more belong to the realm of the decision-makers. The successful combination of these sources requires an interaction, which leads to a unique condition with which most organizations are forced to contend, yet few may be ready to accept in the new information age since such circumstances require focus on the conditions of emergence and complexity.

6

Temporal Dimension of Information Processing

Emergence

In the previous chapter we discussed how systems are joined for the purpose of efficiency and effectiveness and demonstrated that results are often affected by the dependent relationship of such an arrangement. This introduces the notion of complexity in systems and organizations. Complexity relates directly to how the numbers of layers in systems, though represented as separate entities, are *mutually dependent.* Failure to appreciate this interdependence, often the result of "high walls" in organizations, contributes to the hindrance of information flow in organizations. Though complexity will be addressed more fully in the next chapter, aspects of both complexity and emergence affecting stored information in organizational memory during temporal processing will be discussed in this chapter.

In the new age of information, more attention is being given to ideas associated with the concepts of emergence and complexity. Emergence refers to components of a system that are so basic they are the called "building blocks" that appear, or emerge, at the most fundamental levels in organizations or systems. They are unique in that they possess the qualities of self-replication and consequently display a high degree of adaptability to the system in which they appear. Emergent conditions require study as they may affect organizations in ways that produce unanticipated conditions. In general terms, for example, the culmination of a number of emergent components that appeared during the late 1950s and 1960s in America included the activities of those involved in civil rights issues, the conflict in Vietnam, and the impact of drug use on society; each represented phenomena that eventually transformed not only cultural attitudes but also the hierarchy of a government that ignored the conditions of emergence. A consequence of ignoring emergent information is that it transforms existing hierarchies.

Organizations are complex beasts, and there should be some regard as to how they assume this nature. In the context of this book, the terms *organization* and *system* may be used interchangeably, although a system reference generally refers to a part within the organization. Pondy and Mitroff,[1] in a classic paper, characterized organizations as being on level 8 of Boulding's 9-level scale of complexity.[2] Moreover, research into organizations, mainly empirically focused studies, assumes a complexity of level 1 to 3, subscribing to the notion that organizations behave as static and mechanical systems. As an old joke goes—Three men—a physicist, an engineer, and an economist—were stuck on a desert island with only one can of food. They had to decide on how to open the can. The physicist suggested that the can be placed in a position that would maximize the sun's heat on it, resulting in the lid popping off. The engineer remarked that by using the trees, he could devise an instrument that would open the can. Then they turned to the economist. He remarked, "Let's *assume* we have a can opener." Assumptions establish the basis of investigations into organizations; however, they reduce the nature of investigation to futile simplicities that bear little similarity to reality. In this chapter, we begin our discussion into temporality and emergence while revisiting some thoughts on chaotic systems. All of these are more appreciative of the reality that organizations are complex, adaptive systems. Organizations make interpretations and adapt to their environment through the processing of information.

Richard Daft and Karl Weick, in their work on interpretation systems, proposed three activities to the overall learning process organizations experience —scanning, interpretation, and learning.[3] The process of scanning has been addressed in the previous chapter in our discussion on signals and signal devices. These involve the sources of information that are scanned and from which data is collected. Once collected, data must be interpreted and made sense of, and useful information will be archived as part of the temporal process. This process involves an important stage in temporality that occurs during the semantic stage of the semiotic process. Organizations have memories, and results from their cognitive systems can be seen as behaviors, standard operating procedures (SOPs), mental models, and so on.[4] These determine how new data is evaluated, assimilated, and accommodated in the organization. Once sense is made from the data, actions are conducted (or one does not act). The process of learning from actions then kicks in. Learning is the result of a process within the overall interpretation cycle, that is, *feedback*. Feedback represents a critical stage in information processing and learning since feedback is the basis on which adaptation in organizations is determined; if the use of feedback in an organization is poor or nonexistent, an organization is unlikely to modify its behavior. Failure to learn will result in mistakes being repeated. We will address this issue as our discussion on emergence and temporal information processing begins.

Top-Down Designs

In the previous chapter we touched on the possibility of problems resulting from the effects of chaos as a condition brought about because of inattention to a system's initial conditions. Chaos is a result, not necessarily a cause. While it is possible for chaos to beget chaos, unchecked preliminary conditions in an initial instance develops an unexpected causal relation that determines a result, which is unstable, hyperdynamic, complex, and unpredictable; this is chaos. Yet local rules exist within the context of chaos, and these rules can be programmed. It is possible to generate a simulated plant or weather patterns on a computer screen by instructing the machine to follow an unabated application intended to replicate fractal designs that become increasingly more complex until distinct, often elaborate, patterns emerge. Often these patterns are surprisingly lifelike. Failed information systems often exhibit similar developing patterns when the conditions are chaotic but, unfortunately, these conditions are realized only when the unpredictable consequences become apparent, that is, the failed system breakdowns.

The *Challenger* disaster reflects a continuing failed information policy by NASA, which routinely neglected important initial conditions that not only pointed to the possibility of disaster but also resulted in unexpected tragedy because of neglect. The stifling policies of federal agencies likely contributed to several conditions that allowed the attacks on the World Trade Center in 2001. In these and similar circumstances that produced chaotic results, the problem rests with procedures determined through top-down designs. Top-down designs are the products of executives who attempt to cover all contingencies with sweeping, unmanageable directives. Such conditions compel strict adherence to specific procedures as a matter of complete accountability while ignoring the variety of other concerns that may occur. The Chernobyl disaster provides an example in which attempting to adhere to a number of procedures exacerbated conditions until they were out of control.

We argue that this approach is deterministic and replete with embedded flaws because it is contrary to natural order. Organizations, society, and organisms are multifaceted entities that derive meaning and successes through interaction based on information. Entities are determined by boundary limitations and influence, size, and how well and how often they work together within a given system. The ability for entities to work together depends on information. The exchange of useful information that develops into success strengthens the ties between entities. Reinforced successes lead to stability while failure produces some level of instability. In business, as in nature, only adaptable entities may be expected to survive.

As with success in other fields, success attracts attention and generates emulation. This is common in traditional economic situations. For instance, without excessive barriers to entry, the monopolist cannot expect to enjoy abnormal profits in an industry for too long. New firms will study the activities of the monopoly and try to mimic them in the hopes of entering the industry and capturing a share of the market. In chaos theory, *strange attractors* act like gravity to draw elements in proximity toward them in an effort to achieve stability. Similarly, stable elements within the organizational system attract less stable elements, which attempt to *mimic* normalization and adaptability in an often ill-fated effort to maintain their existence. By way of analogy, in sports, teams will attempt to copy whatever strategy served to allow the current champion to succeed in an effort to replicate success in the name of variation. Consequently, in American football, teams modify their routines to incorporate the "west coast" or "run and shoot" offenses, or perhaps they will adapt some variation of a successful defense. Such attempts are rarely successful. In business, organizations attempt to "compensate" strategies to fit current successful trends that may include reengineering, diversity, or copying certain methods. Because such approaches may be regarded as experimental they are not necessarily adaptive, although such modifications may be regarded as partly experimental, partly adaptive. Experiments are trials that seek to "find" one or many solutions during the process of investigation, while adaptive changes represent the solution as part of a process. In this sense, top-down processes may be regarded as "experimental" in the sense that organizations generally have an idea of what they hope to accomplish but often find themselves experimenting in order to find the right way in which to implement their ideas. Adaptation is more closely related to a bottom-up process.

Emergence: Bottom-Up Design

In dissecting an entirety, be it an organism, machine, or organization, one ultimately encounters the basic "building blocks" that represent an entity's foundations. At this basic level there exists a type of entirety that functions as a component for the next higher level within a system. Components that interact within the system establish a pattern that is recognized as organization. The interaction of these components is facilitated by "information" exchanges. Without this exchange there is little chance for interaction, and without interaction there is a poor chance for development or adaptation by the organization or organism. For example, if purchasing suddenly modified its routines so as to impact inventory levels and failed to communicate this information to manufacturing, a production problem would likely occur.

The concept of emergence holds that the components that determine some higher-order system (an entirety) may not be reduced into parts or subsystems. In our earlier discussion on chaos we witnessed unanticipated events that can be traced back to initial conditions. In emergence, we look initially to the interaction of a system's basic components with an understanding that their success in establishing patterns of organization will enhance their own ability to stabilize and regenerate. Crystal formations present a good example of this emergent concept.

Simply stated, concepts involving emergence employ a bottom-to-top structure that focuses on discovery and is sensitive to the conditions under which any investigation is conducted. Emergence involves constant questioning and self-critiquing to the extent that while the investigator seeks evidence of value in information, he or she simultaneously seeks evidence that may negate the value in information discovered. That which remains is likely to indicate the presence of an emergent condition that bears attention. In this sense the activity is self-policing and self-correcting.

In contrast, traditional approaches to data and information analysis are structured in terms of theory or hypothesis testing and have a tendency to restrict useful analysis because of the methodology used in the investigation. Emergent techniques attempt to develop theory to fit the situation under investigation. The adequacy of an emergent approach can be judged by the fact that it fits the situation under investigation and that it works.[5] Traditional methods of information gathering, for example, tend to be more "shotgun" in their approach so that data is collected and forwarded to another authority for cleansing and dissemination. This technique, atypically empirical, is time-consuming and subject to interruption along this type of information chain. Emergent approaches investigate information immediately and classify it against conditions of existing hypotheses that fit the situation under investigation. If the information appears to be of value, theories are developed that apply to that situation. On at least two occasions prior to the 2001 attack on the World Trade Center, federal agents used emergent techniques to develop theories involving religious fundamentalist terrorists that might use commercial airlines to attack domestic targets in the United States; one of these theories, developed in July, went so far as to suggest that the intended target would be the World Trade Center.

Application of the emergent approach to the organizational design requires a change in methods, but the flexibility associated with an emergent system can make any transition almost seamless. Emergence emphasizes that it is important for organizations to experiment with alternatives as a part of their culture. Experimentation affords exposure for systems that may eventually become dominant to the organization and allows them to develop the repertory from which to draw. This suggestion is consistent with current and related literature, which underscores the adage that "practice makes perfect."[6] The effect of the change requires little modification in current practices while the results produced may significantly increase organizational capabilities. But change is rarely the result of a unilateral effort. Rather, change results from multiple causes and multiple contributors whose interaction should be thought of in terms of "feedback" loops among participants rather than a series of individually contributing lines.[7] As a matter of policy, guidelines of association must be established in order to understand how the looping effect will work. High walls have to be removed.

Emergent systems are heuristic in character in that their internal parameters can be modified when necessary, through feedback. Feedback loops can serve as guides to discovery, which in turn assist to minimize the work associated with problem-solving. An emergent system that employs flexible and dynamic processing has the capacity for exaptability not found in traditional information and management models.

The trait for exaptability, common to nature's successful species, is the ability to develop new functions or the utilization of a structure or feature for a function other than that for which it was developed.[8] Gould offers the following definition of exaptation: "a feature, now useful to an organism that did not arise as an adaptation for its present role, but was subsequently co-opted for its current function and features that now enhance *fitness*, but were not built by natural selection for their current role."[9] Whether in nature or organizations, fitness is the ability to attain goals efficiently and effectively. An organization's ability to adopt these traits reflects directly on the organization's information-sharing policy between the group's respective subunits. This notion is consistent with Prigogine, who saw an organization's ability to adapt as a method of making it robust against perturbations from the outside world.[10] The emerging problem results not from the *volume* of data received, as addressed earlier, but rather from how that data is managed by personnel.

For the better part of the last couple of centuries, organizations have been established and run along paths dependent on hierarchical structures: the top-down approach. When the Industrial Revolution began in the eighteenth century, this was a reasonable approach since the groups that provided the jobs also provided the rules, and during a less complex time the rules were easier to administer. In a sense, these organizations mimicked the patriarchal models already in place in many Western societies. While reserving any value judgment on whether this practice was fair or just, this form of organization was perpetuated through the twentieth century and is still representative of many businesses today. But lessons from recent history indicate that the company line may not always be best for either businesses or employers. During the late 1960s Detroit carmakers missed the information provided by foreign competitors, which indicated that when a better quality, economic alternative became available, consumers would take note. The Kodak Company regarded digital imaging as a gimmick and failed to respond to or acknowledge the possibility of this threat to its market share. Such a conclusion and subsequent company strategies were based on top-down decisions with little regard for information that opposed these decisions. Had either company surveyed the buying habits of its employees, they might have discovered trends indicating that these top-down decisions should be revisited based on information and feedback.

With emergence, that which is the basis for building determines both the form and function of a system and its hierarchy. For example, an ant colony, its constituents, and behavior are composed of and dependent on ants, and as such it succeeds. Similarly, the brain, its neural networks, synapses, dendrites, and activity will be predicated on signals established by the organism's RNA sequence within a DNA model. In each instance, like a growing crystal, qualities unique to the system's adaptive, nonreducible instruction subsets provide the basis for adaptation and possible evolution to a more complex system. In organizations, like the different ants in a colony, we see a variety of the right people who develop a business's core competencies and help establish the identity of the organization. In each instance, we see that what occurs at "the bottom" is largely responsible for providing the definition of the system under investigation. The ants in the colony are not aware they define the colony any more than dedicated workers who are just doing their jobs are consciously aware that they are defining their organizations. Yet each affects the capacity for adaptation within their respective system and may in time contribute to another plateau in the system's evolution. Stanley Salthe who, in comparing biological and social phenomena to complex systems considered evolution to be the result of *a margin of error* in a developmental process, advanced this notion.[11] His theory employs hierarchy theory, information theory, and semiotics and focuses on the premise that without the *capacity* for development, there is no foundation for evolution.

At the heart of emergence is the notion of *design* that is predicated on the contention that machines and systems should be seen as living entities. The idea is not new, and variations on the theme appear in a number of popular fiction pieces ranging from the *Arabian Nights* to the works of the prolific writer Isaac Asimov. While the concept may seem simple, that is, if a machine is seen as "alive," it would require certain maintenance and care, an energy source, and generally be "guided" by its creator, the application of the concept was limited to machines that were created to serve a specific purpose, usually some form of service. In 1940, however, John von Neumann considered the development of a machine that might be capable of duplicating itself; for him, life was to be premised in its most fundamental capacity, the capacity to reproduce.[12]

Information and Cellular Automaton

Von Neumann's concept of a "living machine" involved the idea of *cellular automaton*, wherein a machine could (a) replicate itself and (b) deliver the instructions for subsequent replication to a "clone." Cellular automata describe discrete dynamic systems in which behavior is absolutely determined in terms of a local relation. This concept, while simple in comparison, mirrored an important attribute in DNA and living replication and has some interesting implications concerning information and emergence. While the idea of self-replication by a machine-as-organism was interesting in itself, the notion of how such a creation might impact a system's environment created a new set of questions with relevance to organizations, organisms, and information.

Continuing on this idea, von Neumann developed a large grid to represent a simplified environment in which both space and time were represented as discrete entities. In the grid, *space* was represented by each of the squares or cells on the grid and each cell contained bits of information, which may be, for example, rules. *Time* would advance like seconds on a clock, as an indicator of when change within the system might take place. While change could occur with each tick, it was not requisite with the changes in time. However, when changes did happen, the effect was simultaneous and everything represented on the grid was changed. The hierarchy of the grid was itself altered without the need for programming instructions that would have normally been required to "order" such change.

Cells containing information and in closest proximity to the emergent cells were affected to a greater extent than those that were farther away; cells that contained no information were initially unaffected. What is interesting in this model is that *each cell must react* in accordance to its neighbor's information. As cells cluster, they form simple patterns, which combine to become more complex. The ability to repeat this complex activity indicates that stability existed among the cells and within the environment. If this stability were absent, the patterns would not develop. Here, the information bits contained in each cell represented (1) the initial conditions that will ultimately determine how the system reacted within the environment, critical to avoiding chaos, and (2) the building blocks that would compete or cooperate for adaptability, during an "evolutionary" process as the system was created.

As cells collect, they display a tendency toward diversity; once created, they are distinct from other cells in the grid. But an interpolated commonness exists in the information pool that attracts certain neighboring cells to each other. Initially, two cells that combine to form a new "block" will have an effect on the entire grid because this activity has modified the environmental hierarchy. Note that the hierarchical change was not directed from a higher level; rather higher levels have been affected because of the creation of a new level upon the grid. Subsequently, when other new levels emerge, the hierarchy is forced to reorganize further. This model also simulates biological symbiosis and cellular reproduction.

Traditional approaches to the idea of hierarchical change presume that decision-makers at the top are responsible for guiding the behaviors of their charges through policies and procedures that demonstrate the intentions of the organization. While from a managerial standpoint this appears reasonable, from an organizational standpoint the nontrivial aspects of emergence in information indicate that there are more concerns that need to be addressed but are often neglected. NASA projects often reflect changes in their organizational order because of inattention to bottom-up emergent information that is ignored. Recent problems at NASA indicate an organizational culture that is unwilling to learn from past mistakes, and the problem is endemic. In 1990 the excitement over the much anticipated launching of the Hubble space telescope was dampened when, upon reaching orbit, it appeared to have problems with the lenses and communications equipment. Although many of these problems had been brought up in quality control meetings with engineers, management seemed more concerned with launch deadlines than mission objectives. While most of these malfunctions were corrected through activities involving cost overruns, subsequent reports indicated, "NASA had a risk prone culture, a weak Quality Control department and problems with (internal) communications."[13] One might reasonably expect that since the *Challenger* disaster of 1986, after which it was clear that emergent information cautioned against a launch, extraordinary steps would have been taken to avoid preventable accidents, but the Hubble experience indicated that little had been learned in the NASA organization. In 2003, when the *Columbia* space shuttle broke apart, this contention was brutally reinforced. Some of the problems from an information standpoint had to do with the fact that the "complexity and coupling of the ships and the (NASA organizational) system was intense."[14] Such tight coupling virtually eliminates the possibility for creativity by any of the system's participants because the rationale is that the system "knows" more. It also severely inhibits the possibility for constructive or beneficial learning in organizations that fail to understand how emergent information can impact their work.

Temporal Information Processing

Organizational learning has been broadly classified as following one of a handful of approaches, most of which are deterministic and none of which are mutually exclusive because they deal with many of the same qualitative concerns. Such concerns include the organizational ability to adapt, knowledge creation, and management issues involving the cognitive role of individuals within an organization; some communities of practice approaches, which regard the influence of organizational culture on learning; and the proper guides for placing value in information and knowledge.

In general, all organizations are concerned with learning as a method to modify behavior in reaction to environmental demands. What is not always regarded is that modification will eventually work to change the state of the organizational system. Pawlowsky suggests that perspectives related to organizational learning may represent at least two paradigms, one that considers the analysis of information in order to eliminate false assumptions so that "knowledge" can be added to an organizational base, and another that allows for varied interpretations and continual interaction in an effort to develop a construction of meaning value for the organization.[15] We concur and believe that these notions are expressed in association with information expressed as either *temporal* or *spatial*.

In an earlier chapter we reviewed informational aspects of spatial and temporal information flow. *Temporal information* resides in an organization's memory or is stored because it has direct relevance to the entity's being. In this sense, information that is spatial represents the sum of an organization's experiences and will be constantly used as a criteria for considering whether new information is useful. *Spatial information* is "new" information that, as the name implies, arrives from multiple sources over time. Somewhere in between there must be the opportunity to synthesize temporal information, which occurs during the semantic level of the semiotic model. Information perceived to be useful is archived for reference in learning. Learning represents the transfer of information from a source to the learner and is considered to be effective when the learner demonstrates use of the information through behavior such as on a task assignment. Because newly collected information that is intended for archiving may change aspects of the organization's memory repertoire, temporal information may be thought to be coupled with time to a lesser degree than spatial information.

If problems develop in the information spatial-temporal relation, they are more likely to occur during the spatial phase because it involves information gathering. For organizations, important information is highly quantifiable, understood in terms of a fixed relation to what is salient for the organization and contains attributes of particular interest. The degree of interest ascribes value to such information. While an organization may have some idea of what it wants to look for in new information, the sheer volume of new data received from the outside sources can be overwhelming. This reality involves the notion that spatial information is often received from conflicting or unreliable sources that make it imperfect in the sense that it is *uncertain*. Because there is this possibility for conflict in information, there is also competition for what represents information in the best interest of the organization and for what organizational members will learn. Remember, in our entropy example of ice melting into water where a new state of equilibrium was achieved, the atoms have not changed, but the system as a whole has demonstrated a transition. Empirically, the atoms are behaving in a different way. Similarly, any organizational transition that is possible, as the result of spatial information being accepted into the mainstream, must be analyzed employing specific standards such as the semiotic model in which semantics (meaning) and pragmatics (actionable events) are driven by useful information that is intended to affect behavior through learning.

In discussions of time, in relation to information that arrives in organizations, there is first the issue as to whether a notion of time should be considered as subjective or objective; we contend it is both. In the objective sense, although it is a man-made, relational concept, time fits the math of the universe and has always existed, though our measurements may be considered transient against the bigger picture posed in time and space. In this sense, time is an absolute, quantitative, and linear function that may be measured for reference; its status is immutable and unaffected by man. But then how does one explain that the Hundred Years War (1337–1453) lasted 112 years? Because time can also be subjective, and from this perspective time is a criterion for measuring events, less invariant than objective time, and indicates such things as deadlines, holidays, and seasonal changes or boundaries of social and organizational change. Merchants now put up Christmas decorations just after Halloween, or the organization implements new directives that it expects to be in force within the terms of a specified period. Subjectively, time is seen to be socially constructed and relative.[16] In this sense, time, rather than being merely a measurement of duration, gains meaning when it is combined with reference to social occasions, for example, New Year's, and the more personal the occasion, the more relative to the individual, for example, birthdays. This can be a dangerous proposition in that there is an implication that culture and social time has a way of superseding natural time. From this perspective, approaching deadlines dissolve in the face of chronological time, which may indicate that scheduled completion dates were unrealistic.

The concept of time, emergence, and useful information are bound because of an immediate relation that is both subjective and objective. Like with von Neumann's grid, an emergent information bit that succeeds to become useful possesses "attractors" (similar to the notion in chaos theory), which compels adaptability to similar information bits within the information system. Information that is not adaptable otherwise degenerates and destabilizes. The building process of emergent information is related in a temporal sense in that both the system and its hierarchy will begin to change in the objective sense, whether or not the information is immediately recognized. Such events impacted the fate of the *Concorde*. Despite a half dozen previous similar incidents involving runway debris that caused tire explosions and subsequent structural damage, including dangerous fuel leaks, to the plane, Air France took no corrective steps to consider what consequences might occur. Most of these instances were regarded as "close calls," that is, instances when the aircraft was severely damaged but there were no injuries.[17] On the twenty-fifth of July 2000, a *Concorde* taking off from Paris experienced the same conditions but crashed, killing over one hundred including passengers, crew, and bystanders. In this instance, the emergent information described the susceptibility of the plane because of tires that failed if they encountered runway debris. At the second such similar instance, the temporal aspect of the emergent information shifted from the objective to the subjective because, having occurred twice, without remedy, the chances for a third event were increasing. Because of the organization's inattention to emergent information, conditions within a system that might have been controlled assumed fateful consequences. While Air France considered a hierarchy dedicated to supersonic flight and speed of delivery, the system developed its own priorities, which disregarded safety as a crucial consideration in the equation.

The notion of emergence and timing also plays into how organizations and individuals learn. Like people, organizations are subject to an unfortunate tendency associated with learning, which suggests that the first way one learns to accomplish some task affects subsequent attempts at relearning the same or similar task from a different perspective. People who are exposed to desktop and productivity software changes provide a good example. Especially if a person is proficient in, say a Corel product, often they show a huge reluctance to embrace Microsoft products that provide the same basic features with no higher learning curve.

In organizations, it has been said, "It's not the change that kills you, it's the transition."[18] Often, conditions related to change involve inappropriate timing, inattention to emergent information, or little regard for training in the effects of change. When a new boss takes over a division and begins implementing directives without regard to existing conditions, there are bound to be problems. These problems involve the fact that some form of temporal information is likely available but not being used. If information is not used, it is worthless. This process follows notions associated with Hebbian learning in the design of networks.

Hebbian learning balances network information related to topics under investigation so that outputs reflect some relation to inputs in an otherwise unsupervised process. If payroll information is input, one would not expect inventory information to be part of the output. Unfortunately, Hebbian learning can be "forced" to reflect a predetermined and desired response that serves to modify what otherwise would be reflected in output. Ideally, relevant information at the emergent level could be detected and its subsequent adaptation and importance would be tracked while nonadaptive information would fall by the wayside. Unchecked, however, the results of this process may result in "false positive" readings, especially if the design is associated with the concept of "self-fulfilling prophecies" during which the designer massages input with the intent to produce only particular results. For example, we are all aware of situations in which a job posting is distributed when, in fact, the job has already been filled from the "inside." Under such conditions, designers or managers look for predetermined results from the process, which defeats the *first rule of information* in that it must be unique and unexpected. Any data that is received and already known is not unique; it is not information.

The idea of emergent information structuring a hierarchy of systems comes into play again. All complex adaptive systems anticipate the future.[19] We discuss the concept of complexity in the next chapter, but for now it is important to know that notions of chaos, emergence, information, and complexity are all intertwined. As we have seen, emergent information has the effect of changing the basic hierarchy of a system, and those changes compound to eventually impact the entire organization hierarchy. Successful emergent information adapts the organization by contributing and preparing the organization for future changes. If the organization turns a blind eye to the emergent information, such information will not be used and it becomes useless. Nevertheless, the system will change and it is likely to suffer for ignoring emergent information. Ignoring information occurs consciously and unconsciously. In the first instance, there is a direct and intentional effort to disregard information received. This may occur when new information is interpreted as either not fitting certain criteria or being otherwise incredulous. A consequence of inhibiting information flow is its effect on learning.

Learning

Learning at the conscious level requires exposure to new information sources. Several cognitive theories on learning begin with the notion that reception on the part of the learner of new information is the start to learning. Repetition of something newly learned is the best way to develop expertise of the learned content. This, of course, requires conscious effort on the part of the learner. But if the learner is repeatedly exposed to a policy that includes the restriction of information flow, a different type of lesson is learned. Unconsciously, learners are less likely to value, want, or need anything that represents new information because the known learning culture in which they exist ascribes no value, want, or need to new information. Everyone who drives a car has experienced this kind of unconscious learning, especially if they drive prescribed routes to and from work, for example. What has been "learned" through repetition allows the driver to set themselves on "autopilot" while the conscious mind is busy with other thoughts, a tune on the radio, or a conversation with a passenger. The conscious mind may not kick in again until the routine, in this case driving home, is completed or other stimuli, for example, a detour, forces an act of conscious focus. In the case of the detour, which represents emergent information, the conscious mind is forced to take note of a variation to a learned pattern, that is, the usual route home. Failure of the conscious mind to learn from the emergent information will impede the task at hand, in this case driving home. Properly used, emergent information is incorporated into the system's memory. The system's memory is the basis for learning, although factors related to how agency, unit, or cell members act can affect whether or not the memory is used effectively.

In human behavior, environmental conditions can contribute to an individual's behavior being affected in terms of cognitive dissonance. Cognitive dissonance involves a behavior modification on the part of an individual in an attempt to favorably interpret or rationalize behavior.[20] In organizations, while agents, protective of their immediate environment, often employ activities related to cognitive dissonance, the properties of emergence do not allow for such "modifications." Rather, the bottom-up approach of emergence corrects only when there is a threat to an otherwise successful adaptive change in progress. One computer model provides an example of this application in comparing adaptation within a system. Given a simple set of three "rules," a computer generated a simulation representing a flock of birds in "migratory" flight.[21] The rules, as in nature, determine how environmental boundaries determine the chances for adaptability. It would be unreasonable, for example, to presume emergent information might provide a way to defeat gravity under conditions of standard temperature and pressure. In the bird model, the minimal rules included that the birds maintain a minimum distance from objects, that they attempt to match the velocity with other birds in close proximity, and that they move toward a preconceived point or center of the flock.

The results of the animation determined the success of bottom-up development within a system as "birds" randomly set to positions on the screen invariably "flocked" together, negotiated obstacles, or sometimes broke into subflocks that rejoined when circumstance deemed necessary. While there is an argument that the instructions "tacitly" determined the bird's activities, it does not address the variety of the environments presented and how the "birds" managed to "learn" to react to changes presented in the environment. Conventional system/organization designs attempt to cover every contingency in global, top-down specifications in an attempt to define the environment and how agents within the system should act. The rules provided by the "birds" simulation of Craig Reynolds provided the conditions for natural tendencies that determined the actions of the "birds" through "learning" in much the same way that Adam Smith's notion of an invisible hand "tends to pull supply into balance with demand."[22]

History provides an interesting example from the early days of NASA in which the top-down approach by an organization exposed its vulnerability while the actions of a principle agent, functioning solely on emergent information, saved a mission. When the automated controls of the vehicle carrying America's first man in space, John Glenn, malfunctioned, he assumed manual control. Ground control was aware that Glenn's chances of survival rested with his skills alone, as there was insufficient fuel for the pilot to make any corrections in his trajectory and sensors indicated that a required "landing pack" that was attached to the craft appeared to have been lost. Glenn was not informed of this until after his successful landing, and he was furious. In this instance, Perrow notes, "The rationalization of the system, the province of designers and managers, replaced the operator." [23]

This presents the concern on how organizations perceive what it means to learn. Today, three general categories involving organizational learning prevail, but each owes its existence to the scores of people who have contributed to the concept. Traditional learning in organizations resides within some "knowledge base," which serves as an explicit information source for current practices. Typically this knowledge base is a compilation of past practices, often codified in some manner, for example, policy manuals, routines, procedures, and so forth, so as to be easily disseminated. However, this is not the best circumstance for adaptability, learning, or otherwise, or response to a dynamic environment because such an approach is generally slow to react to change. A reaction exception of this blasé style may occur if the organization is publicly "shaken" into response by extraordinary events. A slow-moving federal bureaucracy *appeared* to quickly mobilize for immediate action following the events of September 11. Two years later, we find that while the hierarchical architecture was reshuffled and the legislature has taken an opportunity to expand federal authority, little has been done to expand the ability for agencies to gather and share information related to a common interest. Consider one aspect, the terrorist watch list. Two years after the events of 9/11, various law enforcement agencies still work from different terrorist watch lists, and what is even more strange is that the Department of Homeland Security has publicly acknowledged this gap in security and promised to have a centralized list by January 1, 2004. These actions are ridiculous, as any terrorist now has been given a deadline as to when they can beat the system and enter the country.

A second method of organizational learning involves "knowledge creation" on the part of the organization, which actively seeks the contribution of individuals to enhance a "knowledge base." The organization may actively seek to convert an individual's tacit knowledge to explicit knowledge.[24] Organizations that attempt activities involving drawing on the knowledge of their employees also believe that learning is a necessary condition of organizational policy in which cooperation is a matter of communication and information sharing.[25] Use and development of teams involved in knowledge management within an organization are typical in this style to learning. The concept of an organization's absorptive capacity is salient here.[26] Wesley Cohen and Daniel Levinthal define absorptive capacity as the organization's prior knowledge that enables it to recognize the value of new information, assimilate and accommodate it, and generate requisite actions. Unless an organization has adequate absorptive capacity, it will fail to process new knowledge and innovation; however, just having the absorptive capacity without capabilities on how to deploy it is also useless.

Recently, as more attention has been given to the emergent concept, organizations are combining the best practices of the above two approaches with a method that considers the cognitive abilities of the participants in knowledge management tasks. This approach is common and often productive in university research. In such research, individuals representing specific disciplines bring a variety of interpretive and cognitive experience to focus on a topic. The cognitive experience of the group (collective cognition) represents the reality of the cause being examined, and the group interpretation is expected to impact the existing organizational knowledge base. In this sense, both spatial and temporal information are manipulated in a near-simultaneous fashion so that critical information may be disseminated quickly. Here the semiotic model is useful since it is designed to transfer data to actionable knowledge in one unified process. The actionable knowledge involves dissipation of newly created knowledge through the system that serves as a method for checks and balance to insure that other new sources of information are not in immediate conflict with the created knowledge activity. Any modification of the organization's knowledge base as a result of this exercise may be construed as organizational learning. Once an organization has experienced such modifications, its ability to process more difficult material related to the issue under investigation is facilitated because the organizational muscle-memory has been exercised and is stronger. Again, it is critical that information leading to knowledge be used, that is, acted upon, otherwise it has no value to the organization.

A considerable amount of literature involving emergence and learning has been devoted to "closed" systems, whether that system is represented by a flock of birds in a computer animation, an economic model, or an organism. In human physiology, for example, how an "idea" is created in the brain can be mapped in terms of stimulation and neural connectors, but the associations that produce the "idea" are still vague. The answer is related to an interaction of connected agents within the brain, which draw on past experience or existing knowledge repertoires for a basis in perception. How information is perceived is key to this equation. Some savants, for example, process information in a unique way that, at times, defies normal cognitive processes; some can reproduce complicated musical arrangements after one hearing, though they are not trained in music; others can instantaneously perform complicated math routines, but none are "creative." The illustration indicates that humans have the ability to mimic patterns depending on how they are able to process input. An Australian group has experimented on subjects using procedures intended to block the brain's cognitive functions. These investigations have produced some interesting results, including a subject's ability to demonstrate fluency in mathematics and recall, which they were unable to demonstrate before the experiments. As a result of some of the experiments, subjects were able to multiply a five-digit number by another five-digit number and render a correct answer almost instantly.[27] While not completely understood, the tests seem to indicate that generally accepted cognitive approaches to learning may inhibit the brain's potential. Otherwise, most of the people who are normally capable of demonstrating such "tricks" are called savants, not geniuses.

It has been said that the world of humans is composed of a majority of normal people and a few geniuses. The geniuses have the ability to transpose events that are observed, but not seen, by others into expressive thought and actions and to represent such transpositions in the fields of literature, music, science, politics, and philosophy. In the human social structure the works of genius find some bond with large segments of the population who, while unable to produce such works, draw a sense of connection to those works. An interesting notion exists that may assist in explaining this connection. The notion may also give some indication as to the process of how emergent information seeks to adapt its environment for the purpose of its own continued growth. Perhaps it is worth considering other aspects that affect learning that do not generally appear in teaching textbooks. One such aspect involves the transfer of ideas as information.

The Emergent Mind: Mnemons

What and how we learn may be in part hardwired in the brain. In the late 1970s and mid-1980s, author Richard Dawkins suggested the possibility of a genetic connection to explain the way in which "ideas" are transferred.[28] In theory, the same "connectivity" argument can be applied to emergent information systems and how they evolve. The notion of idea transfer begins with the "meme" which Dawkins defines as a "unit of information residing in the brain."[29] Individuals store tons of information in their brains every day, but whether such information is useful or not depends on the ability and sometimes the conditions used to recall any or all of the information.

But each individual's information base is unique to the extent that it is highly unlikely that any two people would have the identical idea in the reservoir of their respective information base. Certainly, while Bell was working on his telephone or the Wright brothers were developing a flying machine, others had similar notions of communication or flight, but those "ideas" were not exactly the same. More important, once the creative ideas were expressed in actions, others "picked up" on the inventive ideas for the purpose of enhancing or mimicking the original designs. Once this process is initiated, such activities can proceed quickly. To accomplish the transfer of ideas, nonliteral abstract representations of stored information determine the basis for the transfer; two people with the "same" idea means two people have abstracted a common set of qualities so the ideas-in-memory are of the same kind, so some common element resides within the abstraction of the particular idea.[30] Once the condition for memory abstractions, or *mnemons,* exists, replication of an idea may proceed. This process involves the notion of "sameness" residing inherently in the brains of those who find that exposure to an idea-abstraction fits with their own perception of an "idea." An idea could be represented in beliefs regarding "gun control." Certainly, a variety of meanings are required to cover all ideas concerning whether or not "gun control" is necessary, and most of these ideas are tied to preconceived beliefs. What is important here is the "idea-abstract" has common elements that carry some mutual meaning or "sameness" in each incident when "gun control" is mentioned. Successful marketing people employ this notion all the time. If you have ever watched a program, movie, or commercial that seemed to have little value to you, chances are you were not part of the intended target audience. Whether you attend a movie that has a love-interest theme or is from slasher genre, chances are the trailers for upcoming movies will be geared toward a similar story line as the featured film. The marketing people expect you to want to see the same type of movie you are about to view; they are using "attractors" to coax interests in "sameness."

Propaganda, the mother of modern marketing, employs similar techniques in its methods. When Hitler addressed the German people prior to the 1932 elections, he asserted that there were those who charged him as the man who would eliminate the scores of political self-interest groups, each aspiring for representation in the Reichstag. In response to this accusation, Hitler boldly admitted, indeed, that it was his intention since the multiparty system was dividing and undermining the potential strength of a unified German people, an ideal he had already preached in his writing.[31] Voters had not heard that spin before, and while Hitler did not win the election, he garnered enough votes so his party would be firmly entrenched in government matters. Something he had said struck the chord of "sameness" in his audience, so that a large segment of the German public was consciously willing to vote away their freedom of choice.

In an earlier discussion involving information processing, the point was made that transfer of meaning in information is not a prerequisite for successful signal transfer of the information. In the semiotic model, the two lowest levels receive and classify signals without regard to meaning before semantics come into play. In emergence and as a condition of mnemonics, "sameness" is the attractor that provides the condition for adaptation. This is the antithesis of the saying "opposites attract," when in reality it is more a condition of "self seeking sameness."

Successful art and literature present examples of idea transfer and replication of idea-abstractions in practice. In the 1960s and 1970s music produced by the Beatles had a universal appeal, which was attributed to a number of factors including pentameter, content, simplicity, and fad. But what the group had accomplished was a successful demonstration involving the notion of "transfer" of the abstract, using their media to present mnemons, which were popularly accepted because they struck a familiar chord in a wide audience.

It is important to note that hundreds of musical groups presented their works and to some degree also experienced success in transferring ideas to audiences with similar interests in expression, but few had the staying power to adapt to the degree of the Beatles.

This illustration demonstrates the nature of competition rather than cooperation in terms of a characteristic that exists between interacting mnemons.[32] It also characterizes the relation between emergent information sources within the same system (for example, world of music). Any expressions unsuitable for adaptation will eventually go by the wayside and do not affect the hierarchy of any system.

Conclusion

Our approach to organizations of information has involved us with a variety of disciplines and theory including evolution, cybernetics, physics, engineering, philosophy, and communication. This direction is not intended to make the field of information seem particularly confusing, rather it shows at once the range and direction one might take in an endeavor to understand some of the collective notions that determine when information processes are successful. It also demonstrates the notion that difficult subjects are often illustrated in terms of borrowed examples grounded in scientific reference. This may present a problem according to Barney Glaser, who notes, "If you judge grounded theory by the criteria you have learned to use for hypothesis testing research you will likely misjudge it, perhaps badly."[33] This is because the criteria for research in a chosen field are generally limited in scope to things that make sense in that particular field. It is rare indeed that the methodology used for a dissertation would attempt to drive home some point that alluded to the fact that everyone else in the field may have been using the wrong approaches all along. However, this is exactly what produces innovation and, in information, unless something unique is conveyed by the message, the effort to communicate real information is lost.

Information in organizations comes from a variety of sources and is often conflicting, and yet all received information affects learning processes associated with organizations and individuals. It is beneficial for organizations to develop methods to manage both existing and newly received information input. One effective approach is to deal with information in terms of time that considers the most recent information received (spatial) in direct relation to archived information (temporal) that is often represented in terms of "organizational memory" or the organization's "knowledge base."

As previously noted, the semiotic model presents a valuable tool for accomplishing this task. As information is received, it can be immediately guided through the model in order to determine relevance through meaning (semantics). Meaningful information, that is, information of value to the organization, can then be channeled to decision-makers for the purpose of action, including dissemination through the organization. It is important to recognize that use of the model allows for the insightful interpretation of new information and is not merely "pushing" it forward without reflection. This scrutiny assists in uncovering characteristics in information that may be described as "emergent." Emergence in information systems is critical because of the patterns that develop. If patterns emerge in information there is every indication that the information basis for the patterns are recurrent and self-replicating, indicating they require attention because they have exhibited the tendency for adaptation within the environment. Because adaptation is an indicator of strength, emergent information patterns form the building blocks upon which other contingencies will arise. Ultimately, some of these contingencies will result in changes in an organization's hierarchy.

By example, emergent information related to the attacks of September 11 represented itself throughout a number of agencies charged with insuring the domestic tranquility of the nation. Prior to the attacks, the CIA had been informed by foreign intelligence that fundamentalist fanatics were using commercial aircraft as weapons. The FBI had been informed by Immigration that known terrorists had entered the United States, but that their whereabouts were unknown. Regional FBI offices were informed by flight schools of unusual requests for training by Middle Eastern students who were concerned with portions but not complete instructions related to flying commercial airliners. Based on conjecture, at least two agents prepared hypothetical reports involving domestic flights being used as weapons against U.S. targets. One of these reports indicated the target to be the World Trade Center.

Each of these information reports represented emergent knowledge that would impact an information system and ultimately rearrange the hierarchy of a number of organizations. Each of these reports went unheeded. As a result of "nonaction" by agencies or bureaus that were supposed to be interconnected, there was no contingency plan for conditions that were least likely to occur (probability) but which would have a tremendous impact (consequences) on our nation. Inattention to initial conditions produced conditions tantamount to chaos. But chaos may have been averted, or at least diverted, if more attention would have been paid to information that was emergent.

In our discussion on learning, there is a tendency to equate individual learning to organizational learning, which is viable if one considers the associated cognitive aspects related to teams in organizations. However, organizational learning is not just the sum total of individual learning. An organization can learn independent of specific individuals, however, not independent of all individuals.[34] Individuals in an organization may take it upon themselves to learn new skills, approaches, and actions; this in turn will shape their mental model on how the organization should operate. While good, this is incomplete in terms of the organization. Skill acquisition of individuals within the organization may mean something to the individual, but not to the organization. Even organizations that subsidize the continued education of their employees rarely take advantage of the results of the very benefit they provide. Unless these individuals actually help shape the organization's mental model, the organization per se will not learn. The reverse is also true: when an organization learns and modifies its behavior, there will be individuals who hold on to past ways and means of task accomplishment and do not incorporate new learning into their mental models.

From topics discussed thus far we see that information failures related to crisis events are often due to a number of consistent factors. Initially we are concerned with the effective life of information and the possible effects of entropy as a measure of uncertainty within signals. After reviewing information dependencies and forms, we addressed how information can be affected during processing. We then discussed a variety of arrangements involving how information is handled and the importance of "coupling" in system designs and organizations. It is here that we find that even effectively delivered information can be impeded because of the ways in which an organization is structured. Additionally, we find that if initial conditions are ignored or taken for granted, it is possible that the system will experience unintended consequences, sometimes referred to as chaos. To help stave off the advent of chaos, we have suggested that organizations employ methods that integrate both temporal and spatial information processing. Once such standards have been integrated into an information system, we have stressed the importance of seeking and recognizing the development of emergent information, which, if missed, can be responsible for effectively altering, through a process of adaptation, the hierarchy of an organizational system. It is important to consider how the components of organization and information are layered. The proper arrangement can facilitate decision-making and facilitate information-to-knowledge processes. The wrong arrangement can enhance the chances for crisis in organizations. Both conditions are related to information processes and the notion of complexity, the topic of the next chapter.

7

Information Processing, Complexity, and Crises

In the previous chapters we looked at devices that carry signals and considered a variety of ways in which they were connected. We have also considered how dependencies of information relate to transfer, conditions that may lead to chaotic behavior and the importance of emergence information and its impact on organizational hierarchies. In this chapter we look into how organizations *process* signals. Specifically, we will examine signals that indicate impending organizational crises. To a large extent, these observations are related to an organization's ability to adapt to environmental changes because of characteristics associated with complexity. Complexity involves a concept in which a number of agents are interacting with one another, *consciously or not*, in a variety of ways.[1] We have discussed how adaptive emergent information may unintentionally, that is, not by design, modify organizational structure, and here we find that the cumulative actions of agents can assist or impede an organization's ability for adaptive reorganization.

The practice of adaptive reorganization is a common process that takes place spontaneously in nature, business, and information systems in such a way that it may be taken for granted or otherwise unobserved. While most systems may be intentionally manipulated, often things happen without a guiding hand for direction from a decision-maker or manager. Although the feds may lower interest rates in an effort to stimulate the economy, there is no guarantee that consumer spending will increase. It is the interaction of everything comprising the "market" that will decide whether economy will take off. The guiding powers of Western Europe accepted German occupation and annexation of the sovereign nations in 1938 in the name of appeasement in order to avoid a major military conflict. Yet within a year virtually all of Europe was engaged in a war that would shortly engulf the world.

Mitchell Waldrop notes that the critical mass of plutonium is just barely stable before it enters into a chain reaction leading to a nuclear explosion.[2] It is this notion of "barely stable" that affects all systems, and it is the way information can be handled that determines if a system is capable of controlling a situation or whether the situation will control the system. In each previous example, the state of the conditions represented was critically tied to complexity. Because complexity involves the interaction of a variety of agents within the system, if the relation between agents working on the same task is too tightly coupled, information, regardless of its source, is likely to be interpreted the same way by all agents and have no impact on the system. By example, after the first World Trade Center bombing, the Justice Department was tightly coupled and controlling over other agencies with which it was working. Consequently, information important to, for example, the FBI may have had little effect on the investigation if the same information was seen as inconsequential by the Justice Department. This can drive the system toward crisis.

The traditional definition of crisis is an unanticipated occurrence of such magnitude that it alters the strategic or tactical plan for an organization. Crisis is regarded as anything that causes scarce resources to be diverted from existing operations and functions.[3] This includes aspects of either destruction or disruption of perceived routines because of events that have been represented, in extremes, by fire or natural disaster, the physical loss, or loss in capacity of key personnel, or as something as unexpected as a sudden surge in demand for product that exceeds production capacity. It is important to note that crises can be both positive (sudden increase in product demand) and negative (natural disasters). Crisis impact is measured in terms of scope of effect on organizations and ultimately by their ability to contain the conditions of crisis before they ruin the company. We maintain that such conditions are capable of being detected either in advance or in such close proximity to their occurrence they may be defused before they are allowed to bear their full potential. As asserted by Ian Mitroff, all crises are predicated by warning signs.[4] Hence this begs the question, why can not crises be averted or evaded?

It is our contention that many of the issues associated with crisis aversion have roots in how well an organization processes, transfers, and manages signals. We have seen in previous chapters that tightly ordered (coupled) systems can virtually "choke" any possibility for information integration or dispersion because of a tendency to act as a self-contained closed system. At the other end of the spectrum, we have discussed chaos where order dissolves and information becomes freely dispersed, but with such randomness that its significance is lost. In between these conditions is the organization, and how it is arranged can enhance or impede information usefulness. Both information in signals and organizations are complex in that they represent the result of interaction between varieties of agencies, all ostensibly working together. If this is not the case, weaknesses develop within the system, and the chances for requisite adaptation to the changing environment are lessened. Because organizations and information both develop along dynamic states, there is a perpetual change in these states, sometimes pushing for order and sometimes pushing for chaos. In order to understand this process, we take this opportunity to consider conditions that determine complexity.

Complexity and TAO: Phase Transition of Information

Earlier we spoke of information in terms of it being temporal and spatial, the former representing archived information in organizations constituting a "memory" and the latter representing incoming information from varied sources that required synthesizing. Spatial information then may be thought of as "residing" in a location while temporal information may be considered in more fluid or free-flowing terms before it is captured and classified. We make this point to raise a similar distinction that has been noted between chaos and complexity. "Chaos" is often used to indicate an irregularity in time while "complexity" implies some irregularity in space.[5] This is important because there are a number of information irregularities related to chaos that can often be associated with complexity. And because complexity indicates an arrangement of sensitive dependencies, it is easily linked to chaos, which, as we have mentioned, is usually predicated on unobserved initial conditions that produce unanticipated results.

Nietzsche observed, "When chaos and order are in conflict, chaos must win because it is better organized."[6] Order is a function of complexity in which information is tightly compacted and resistant to modification, while in chaos, information exists in a far less restrictive arena. The success of any venture that involves tight constraints on information can be like a game of chance, hinging on precise interaction between varieties of agents that are expected to make the one correct and common call to produce a winning hand. This is a difficult proposition and is tantamount to hitting the same number on a roulette wheel five times on successive spins. Less restricted information flow in chaos allows for greater variation, for a short time, from the information provided. Chris Langton has suggested that a phase may exist in informational space (within signal space) that presents a buffer between perceived order and chaos; he refers to this locus as a "phase space in information."[7] This phase exists, according to Langton, precisely at the "edge of chaos."[8] In order to get a better feel of how this "phase space" might operate we use an analogy from Oriental philosophy.

Consider the Taoist symbol for harmony, Yin-Yang (sometimes called the

Figure 7.1   **Yin-Yang**

tai-chi symbol) that is conventionally represented in a static state as a circle partitioned by an "S" curve through its center dividing a dark side from a light side (Figure 7.1). Each side represents principles that are in opposition to the other side. Each side contains some element of the other. All things are created under the principle of Yang but are completed through the influence and principles associated with Yin; no principle dominates. The symmetry presented is deceiving because inside the circle, there is a constant and cyclical ebb and flow as the sides move back and forth, in opposition but in the pursuit of the harmony that is portrayed in the static symbol. Under the notion of "presence of absence," it is important to know that no phenomenon is ever devoid of its opposite state, that is, each state contains a little of its opposite. The Tao philosophy emphasizes an exchange of controlling principles that are constantly changing and rearranging conditions, and it is these changes that will subsequently impact the universe. In a similar fashion, information at the "edge of chaos" interactively passes between agents within a system in such a manner that it has the effect of "transforming" the system as it approaches and recedes from order to chaos. Chaos, in some senses, may be seen as a consequence of complexity, although it is not deterministically bound. Transformation from ordered systems to chaotic ones represents a prerequisite for the *emergent* conditions addressed in the last chapter and may be described as "phase transition." [9]

In discussing entropy (chapter 2) we used the example of ice dissolving in water to illustrate a state of equilibrium achieved when entropy is maximized. In the example, while it is apparent, because no other agents were introduced during the process, the molecular structure of the system, that is, hydrogen and oxygen had not changed; the molecules themselves were *behaving* differently than when they were first introduced to each other. According to Langton the conditions for "computation," that is, transmission, storage, or modification of information, is strongest "in the vicinity of phase transition" since the phase represents conditions in which the system is not as tightly constrained as it might be under conditions of absolute order, nor is it as loose as it might be under conditions of chaos.[10] Ordered systems display the tendency to internalize or hold onto information without any regard for sharing it with other parts of the system, while chaotic systems release and scatter information without concern for direction so that it dissipates randomly and without purpose. These tendencies are characteristic to levels of complexity in both system states. While in phase transition then, as in the representation of the Oriental notion of Yin-Yang, there is the opportunity for information to influence the dynamics of the system, and changes will occur. In a metaphysical sense, information is synthesized and dissipated, and the universes are affected either positively or negatively. In much the same way, the semiotic model presented earlier manages information that impacts a smaller "universe," the organization. The computation (storing, retrieving, dissipating) of information has the ability to contribute to the complexity in both the organization and the information used, which presents an interesting question. Is complexity the result of organization hierarchy or information systems?

Which Came First?

Our discussion thus far has addressed the actions of complexity on information within a system as well as how the system may be affected to produce an ordered, chaotic, or crisis-prone profile. The question becomes, "Is it the complexity of the system that determines the direction in which a system profile is headed, or does information (or lack thereof) compel greater complexity on even the simplest systems?" While complexity is dependent on sensitivity involving the activity of agents within any system, viewing the activities in isolation is of little value. It is quite likely that among the agents within a system, some are very good at what they do while others are marginally successful or poor at what they do. Overall, the system may appear to "function," but at what expense? A vehicle that is fine-tuned and running at maximum efficiency may appear to be functioning properly until the operator discovers the brakes to be inoperable. Here, the efficiency of the engine, fuel, and electrical system may suddenly and unexpectedly become dependent on the efficiency of the brakes in a system design layered with dependencies. Because all issues related to complexity have to do with layering effects, we must first investigate the system structure to find how it manages information.

Thus far we have addressed some of the equipment that relays information (chapter 5) and interaction of information dependencies (chapter 3). Further investigation should include an examination for the quality of adaptation, the ability to change, among the layers within the system or organization. Change is inevitable, but not so the inclination or ability to adapt; that is, while change is persistent, organizations often resist it. This notion involves complexity when the organization expects that it is capable of adaptation only to discover that because of breakdowns among interdependent parts, an anticipated change is not fully realized. In nature the inability to adapt leaves a species at a distinct, sometimes fatal, disadvantage. The same is true in organizations that fail to respond or adapt. In order to effect change, which is a response to the environment, the system or organization involved must at least be aware that internal existing conditions are also in flux and that they also may require modification before successful system adaptation will occur. Whether or not change will occur is a separate issue: for now we must first be concerned with internal matters that suggest the possibility for adaptation.

Sequence Dependencies as Complexity Restraints

Certain types of input may be considered as constraining to systems or organizations[11] as, for example, when the volume of input exceeds the capacity to accept the information load. In conventional systems, output is directly related to input, that is, if the input is rich, the outputs are expected to be robust and outputs at one level often serve as inputs at another level. In complex systems, while input from the environment is of critical concern, one aspect of input that is often overlooked is from internal sources, *hierarchical* information sources, and these have a profound effect on the system's efficiency. They determine the conditions of "dependence" within the interdependent complex system. If, for example, the genetic makeup of an organism includes cellular information of inherent genetic flaws or propensities regardless of an organism's regimen, the likelihood of the organism succumbing to traits associated with the flaw are greater than if this weakness did not exist. This is consistent with Herbert Simon's notion of bounded rationality.[12] An organizational agent may have access to vital information, but if their hands are tied by conditions of sanction or restraint related to hierarchical controls, such information can be lost to the organization as a whole. This is a condition of "higher-level constraints."[13] John Holland, the father of genetic algorithms, refers to a similar notion in terms of "constrained generative procedures" or *cgp*.[14] Under either condition, the "laws of nature" associated with the organization restrict the freedom of interdependent agents within a complex system. Although the hierarchy of an organization should provide the methods for making complexity (a creation of their own design) manageable,[15] we often observe that conditions of information leading to crisis are *observable*, but organizational complexity obviates any constructive use of information. In the events involving September 11, it appeared that several retirement-conscious law enforcement managers were more concerned with maintaining the status quo than in releasing information that would otherwise rock the boat. Unfortunately, that information later proved vital to assembling the time line associated with the attacks on the World Trade Center. The resulting interaction of failures can work to defeat other interdependent schemes, otherwise deemed reliable, to produce a cascading effect sufficiently strong enough to produce the failure of an entire system.[16]

Following the blackout along the central and northeast United States in the fall of 2003, power experts were quoted as saying the "system's sorry shape appears to have been a surprise only to the unwitting consumers who relied on it."[17] The potential for failure within the system was brought to the attention of the White House just after September 11 by the National Research Council, which stated that even without terrorist threats, our power grids were in desperate need of updating. The fault is within an antiquated system, but efforts to correct the situation have been compounded by the complexity of steps required to begin a fix. These steps included dealing with environmentalist groups, lobbyists, landowners, and legislators in an effort to secure a safe resource on which the population may depend.

Complex Relations and Crisis Aversion

In today's uncertain economic times, the impact of organizational crises is stronger than ever.[18] Current events have been so impacted by the concept of crisis that management now regards it in terms of policy rather than as some afterthought under the heading of exceptions. The repercussions from the September 11 attacks on the World Trade Center and the Pentagon have taken their toll at a number of levels, from personal grief to the slowdown in the economy; it also provides a new dimension to the public sector's concern with crisis. The domain of large-scale organizational crisis has been addressed conceptually and empirically in the literature.[19] Because of the multifaceted nature of the phenomena, much of the related literature is dispersed among fields of psychology, sociology, international politics, and information technology.[20] For organizations, crisis may be defined as an organizationally based disaster, which causes extensive damage, social and economical disruption, and involves multiple stakeholders.[21] Today we are discovering that the scope and impact of crisis has the ability to produce a bold ripple effect that forces a reshaping of attitudes and realities among all organizational and social processes.

Organizational crises can be represented in many forms: hostile takeovers, product tampering, copyright infringement, security breaches, malicious rumors, national disasters, workplace bombing or destruction, terrorist attacks, sexual harassment, counterfeiting, etc.[22] They are polymorphous phenomena, and they bring to light the complexity of relationships between the component parts of an organization in its immediate and distant environments.[23] Because of the broad, dimensional nature of crisis, definitions of crises are abundant and vary across the different disciplines. One example that covers the most bases succinctly says: "An organizational crisis is a low-probability, high-impact event that threatens the viability of the organization and is characterized by ambiguity of cause, effect, and means of resolution, as well as by a belief that decisions must be made swiftly." [24]

Organizations are grappling with how exactly to prepare, or prevent, any situation that may lead to crises. The issue of crisis preparation has been well addressed in the literature, but much of it is focused on crisis management once some disaster has already occurred. These approaches are ad hoc and generally result in finger-pointing rather than learning anything about crisis aversion. More attention should be given to how crises may be prevented from occurring. History tells us that signals appear well before the final triggering event that predicates disaster. For example, prior to the *Challenger* disaster, a series of key memos related to structural weaknesses within the craft's design failed to make it to important NASA decision-makers. This is an example of "higher level constraints" built into the complexity of the system hierarchy that encourages the crisis process. Those memos explicitly stated problems related to design flaws, which, if unchecked, went so far as to describe the *Challenger* in terms of a disaster waiting to happen. It is interesting to note that the same problems that plagued NASA during the *Challenger* era reappeared recently and resulted in the *Columbia* disaster.

Investigations into the *Exxon Valdez* incident also demonstrate how the crisis might have been prevented if early warning signals had not been ignored.[25] Exxon had a contingency plan, but it was not implemented during the signaling stages indicating an impending disaster. The resulting oil spill caused devastation to a large ecosystem and cost the company millions more than would have been required to effect intervention at the initial stages of the crisis. At Chernobyl, not only were early warning signs ignored, but organizational pressures also served to speed the process toward disaster.[26] Despite the call for continued power from the Soviet reactors, personnel were engaged in testing at the facility that would generate wild, uncorrectable swings in the system, which ultimately exploded and spread toxic radioactive particles into the atmosphere. These examples as well as many others indicate to us that the case for preparation, while important, is not sufficiently addressed by academics and practitioners. Factors outside of any contingency plan play an important role during the development of situations leading to disasters. Our contention involves the use of signaling techniques to address circumstances not normally associated with most crisis models.

Signals and Crises

Signals of impending crises should be considered as *weak triggers* pointing to some final event. We argue that these triggers are either enhanced or suppressed by characteristics of complexity within the organization. The early detection of signals and their efficient processing is not merely crucial, it is pivotal to preventing crisis. Early signal detection can lead to one of two outcomes; if detected early enough, appropriate resources can be brought to bear to prevent or deter the crisis. If detected in advance of crisis, the forewarned organization can be put on a state of alert or readiness. Organizations should come to expect and understand ". . . that anytime you're not in a crisis, you are instead in a pre-crisis, or prodromal, mode."[27] This idea is important because for organizations to think otherwise is to leave them vulnerable.

Organizations are complex systems that thrive on information; they do not function well under conditions of ambiguity. But the signals pointing to the possibility of crisis *may originate from any of these sources.* Optimal processing of these signals and the subsequent dissipation of resultant information to effect component behavior is key to impeding or, more desirably, defeating crisis. While many crisis management essays focus on issues after the fact, it is our intention to provide points indicating that the focus of plans to prevent crisis is better observed at a *precrisis-to-learning phase* early in the program.

Crisis has been defined as complicated, and invariably it is the system and not the migration of events toward crisis that proves complex. Preble built on previous definitions of crisis by adding elements of natural disasters as well as acknowledging the element of surprise, the need for quick response, the threat to high-priority goals, and the presence of stress.[28] Other features in anticipation of disaster may always be added, possibly addressed, if one assumes that crisis is "always preceded by warning signs."[29] Several of these aspects may combine under a single heading of a factor less addressed in crisis: *chaos*. In a perfect world, where perfect order prevails, these elements or contentions surrounding crisis theory are valid. The world is not perfect, however, and with time, unmonitored complexity leads us to believe that chaos is the destiny of all things.[30]

The "C" Words

Crisis management can be studied from four key vantage points sometimes referred to as the "four Cs": causes, consequences, caution, and coping. It is worth observing that such traditional approaches do not include a "fifth C" for *creativity*, which we will address later. *Causes* include immediate failures that triggered the crisis and the environmental conditions that allowed failures to occur. *Consequences* are immediate and long-term effects. *Caution* represents planning efforts taken to minimize the effects of the crisis, while *coping* deals with postcrisis measures taken in response to the event. Some researchers assert that crises can be recurrent and nonpreventable, hence most crisis management literature deals solely with tactical decisions and actions at the pivotal point of the emergency period in disasters. For these reasons we have elected to address aversion.

The collection of "C words" we have chosen to use include chaos, complexity, calamity, and creativity. The first three are used by an organization when things degrade to the point where they cannot or will not be repaired; the last is underused because prior to crisis it is overlooked for lack of "fit," and following a crisis organizations are anxious to get back to the status quo, which may have been part of the problem to begin with. Each of these words has its place in planning contingency programs, but often the words are transposed or used in the context of defense by management to explain, or lay blame, on activity leading to failure. Crisis for an organization becomes uniquely subjective in one sense, that is, how it affects the operations of the organization. A review of case studies, however, indicates that crisis is generally framed on a temporal platform when, as a result of oversight during a phase, matters cascade out of control, resulting in calamity. The compounding of little failures, unchecked, leads to instability within any system. Promulgated instability supports crisis.

In dealing with a crisis, management will attempt to identify or anticipate potential "flashpoints" or incidents that may signal the advent of crises in an effort to develop actions and measures intended to *prevent an incident from evolving* into a crisis, (while) minimizing the effects or disruption from a crisis that could not have been prevented.[31] As stated by Pearson and Clair, "Crisis management *effectiveness* is evidenced when potential crises are averted or when key stakeholders believe that the success outcomes of short and long-range impacts of crises outweigh the failure outcomes."[32]

Following these observations of stages in a crisis, researchers have proposed dealing with crises in terms of prevention, preparation, and reaction. The model is sound but addresses the overall scheme of crisis when we believe it can be used in a strategy for early containment. *Prevention* entails reducing to a mini-

Figure 7.2 **Crisis Management Model**

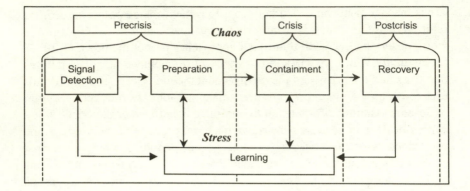

mum the *various triggers* of a crisis, while *preparation* consists of implementing procedures and plans to minimize the impact of an impending crisis, and last, reacting involves minimizing the damage of a crisis.[33] Mitroff proposed a five-staged model for crisis management (see Figure 7.2): signal detection, preparation, containment, recovery, and learning.[34] We have added the elements of chaos and stress to the model and believe that more consideration should be given to the signal detection phase. There are always precursors to a crisis. Referring to the case of the *Challenger* disaster, a number of memos emphatically stated that unless the O-ring was rectified, a tragedy was guaranteed to occur. Interestingly, one of the memos began with the word, *"Help."*[35] At Chernobyl, a series of demands was placed on the system during the execution of critical testing, which caused the operators to ignore the most fundamental rules of safety. Once signals are identified and comprehended, the organization must begin to prepare for a crisis. Such preparation can be in one of two modes. If signals are detected *early enough* and appropriate resources can be brought to bear, crises can be avoided.[36] The alternative is more drastic; efforts can be undertaken to mitigate the effects of a crisis by securing valuables, moving to a safer location, and undertaking protective measures. The possibility that signals may not be detected (or are detected, but the crisis is not preventable) reflects a weakness in the crisis contingency plan, which forces actions toward containment. Since much of the literature dwells on containment, we chose to address organizational complexity as an inhibitor to the success of defeating crisis.

If we accept the idea that regardless of initiating events, three distinguishing features can characterize crises—*occurrence, scope* of impact, and *time* pressure[37]—we begin to understand the importance of early signal detection. Because crisis conditions are regarded as the exception to the rule (per-

Figure 7.3 **Probability-to-Consequence Aspect (PCA)**

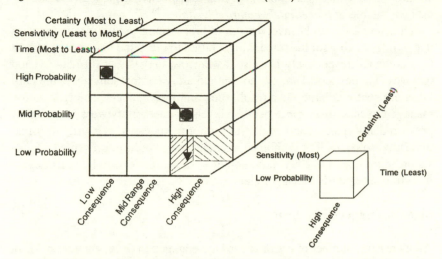

ceived-stability), organizations have a tendency to minimize crisis in terms of phase reaction. Karl Weick characterizes crises as low-probability/high-consequence events that threaten the most fundamental goals of an organization (Figure 7.3).[38] This is a condition of organizational complexity that is always concerned with the consequences of threat and is most often concerned with high-probability events. Decision-making within the organization is predicated on this posture. Oddly, it is rarely the high-probability events that lead to crisis. If the probability were so high that every nuclear reactor *would produce* a meltdown leading to a "China syndrome," there would be no nuclear reactors. (The "China syndrome" suggests that the meltdown of a nuclear reactor's core would produce a mass so dense that it would literally be able to pass through the earth, for example, and figuratively, from the United States "to China.") If it were highly probable some sort of air strike would fell the World Trade Center, contingencies for defense might have been in place. Decision-making in crisis situations becomes a function of time and because there is often little regard for low-probability/high-threat possibilities, stress, often related to conditions requiring multitasking, is added to the equation and the chance for poor decisions comes into play. The time pressure component *often differentiates* crises from other scenarios by degrees of sensitivity.

Fink emphasizes that if the real cause of a crisis cannot be identified and eliminated, the crisis will lie dormant and eventually cycle back, hitting the organization in the future.[39] Greater complexity within an organization raises the risk of the possibility for the latent scheme in crisis. Complexity often belies a structure using intricate plans involving a complex interaction "of unfamiliar sequences, or *unplanned and unexpected sequences* that are either *not* visible or *immediately comprehensible.*"[40]

A current case study involves the failure among public safety agencies that, while looking for the same things, failed to grasp the importance of data they collected respectively because, as Perrow suggests, it formed a vision that was (1) unexpected and (2) not immediately comprehensible to the public safety sector at large. As a result, the combined agencies-as-organization managed to cease *in purpose* because levels of uncertainty were so high they prevented any chance for meaningful semiotic processes (primarily information flow) to occur. The combined agencies may not have prevented the crisis of September 11, 2001, but another system might have included signal detection safeguards to trigger alerts on data "anomalies."

Signals, Triggers, and Learning

An increasing number of organizations are engaged in developing products or services that require extraordinary attention to avoiding major errors that could lead to destruction of the organization and or hurt the public at large.[41] This type of attention may be reasonable because it serves to protect the organization. But if the methods used are predictable, they are also vulnerable. Logically, if you anticipate a problem, that problem should not occur. The problems that do eventually cause crisis situations are usually not predictable. We suggest that such schemes be designed to include as much emphasis on early signal detection as possible. Deterministic, predictable assumptions are common in an ordered environment and are generally thought out in ways that leave little chance of uncertainty. But uncertainty involves a wide range of variety and it is likely that not all contingencies will be covered. Today's vital organizations are both complex and uncertain. One way to increase the probability of detecting early signals that may require attention is to design sensitive triggers.

Triggers are the first wave of symptoms or signs of an impending crisis. Shrivastava defines them as "a specific event that is identifiable *in time and place* and *traceable* to specific man-made causes." [42] Failure by the organization to respond to a triggered event can have grave consequences in potential crisis situations when they otherwise might prevent a situation from escalating or increasing in magnitude.[43] Dealing with triggers can lead to isolation and containment of crises. But which signal trips the trigger so that the day may be saved?

If the organization has no regard for the nature of triggers and what they may represent, triggers serve little purpose. Triggers serve as *relays* in the fact that they communicate other signals. The key significance lies in how the trigger is designed and relies on what signals engage them. If a trigger design is not specific enough, the relayed message may reach too many or sometimes the "wrong" stakeholder, who may not be the correct person to interpret the information in the signal. Different stakeholders deal with triggers in spontaneous and varying ways; they may solve some problems but while doing so create new problems and make the situation worse, leading to poor decision-making.[44] This describes a system with little or no trigger mechanism, where the signal is merely received and circulated. But detection and managing crisis is heavily dependent on institutional or organizational memory.[45] People can "sense" triggers to deal with situations from previous experience. This brings us back to game theory.

Signals in games (discussed in the following chapter) influence play and are either direct or inverted (Figure 7.4).[46] Direct signals rely on convention, are strategic in nature, and have little to do with the rules, as the game remains the same. Inverted signaling, also strategic, sends false or incomplete messages in an effort to mislead. This is often a tactic used in games, where a player wishes to convey weakness in order to set up an attack that may be less obvious. In games of chance this is called "bluffing." In chess, the first three to five moves of the game are direct, indicating strategy but presenting no immediate threat; in organizations, a direct signal would have few if any triggers. A queen's gambit (offering the strongest piece on the board to your opponent for some other perceived advantage), however, might be interpreted as inverted because it serves as an ambiguous signal, making it more difficult for an opponent to infer the outcome based on the next few moves. At the organizational level, the *indirect signal* is released as a condition of triggering and is determined by the sensitivity level that engages the trigger. Once the threshold is reached, the signal is released; otherwise it cannot be released.

The purpose of the inverted signal released by triggering is focus. Direct signals are universally distributed for general consumption. The inverted signal relays messages to "signal agents" for review. Based on the consequence-to-probability review, the signal agent disseminates other signals, some of which will be generally distributed and some of which will hit other triggers. The design of the inverted signal is not intended to confound the players; it is intended to make them weigh action at early stages of potential crisis situations. A signal from a trigger always calls for a response and that response may be to either take action or not. The rules of the game do not allow acts of omission, that is, nonaction merely for the sake of indifference. A report on response is issued to the signal agent without prejudice. This allows the agent to understand that the triggered signal may have been a false alarm, but alerts both the agent and the responder to a record in the event the same type of triggered signal is issued again. Prior to the events leading to 9/11, such a system would have alerted the system to an "anomaly" after a second report

Figure 7.4 **A Signal Processing Model**

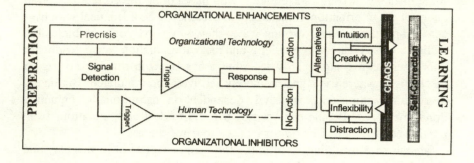

of perceived irregularities at domestic flight schools. A second triggered signal of the same type requires the responder to initiate action.

Once an action is initiated, it is again subject to a probability-consequence review that allows the decision-maker to expect and prepare for the stress associated with other constraints, such as time. A resolution determined at this phase will either be framed constructively through alternatives or, ineffectively, lead to the first encounter with chaos. Intuition based on experience affords the decision-maker the best middle ground for subsequent activities that are determined by sensitivity. If a chaotic system shows sensitivity to initial conditions, *any uncertainty in the initial state* of the given system, no matter how small, will lead to rapidly growing errors in any effort to predict future behavior. But chaos is often linked to irregularities associated with *time*, while complexity is more likely related to irregularities in *space*,[47] and such posturing does not take into account the condition of self-organizing systems because of adaptation. These systems "react to changes in the environment . . . (making) them robust against perturbations from the outside world."[48] Their strengths derive from a design dependent on hierarchical technology over human involvement in the management of technical processes. Humans have a way of avoiding complexity while organizational hierarchy anticipates and self-corrects within complexity. In our model, the consequences of chaos merely afford an opportunity in time for learning when uncertainty is so apparent that current concepts on how to address a problem are freely abandoned. At this phase creativity that in its simplest sense is looking at old problems in a new way is allowed. Use of the word "allowed" is intentional. Our signal detection effects model indicates organizational enhancers at the top and inhibitors at the bottom. Despite having the most creative people, an organization that refuses to acknowledge and promote creativity will not only stagnate but, in the face of crisis, be likely to compound errors because they are inhibiting any possibility for creativity.

Conclusion

Successful use of signaling and the techniques described in this chapter can enhance an organization's ability to learn how to manage crisis. Human cognition follows different levels of understanding, which eventually allows us to make judgments; these serve as the basis for creativity in thinking. In our model we emphasize *the management* of the progression of signals, triggers, distribution of information, actions, and choices leading to learning as a viable condition before crisis manifests itself. The objective is learning, and through learning it is possible to avert some or all of the conditions that can lead to crisis. One inspiration for the model comes from Eleanor Roosevelt, who said, "Learn from others' mistakes. You don't have *the time* to make them all yourself."

It is essential that organizations develop strategies to deal with the issues of complexity in information and hierarchy if they expect to be able to address the reality of crisis issues. Of course, the first step toward developing such a strategy is to recognize the need. In the next chapter we suggest the use of existing theory involving how games are played in order to understand that the players within an organization sometimes thwart even the best intentions of the organization. Recent failures within organizations have been traced to organizational players who sometime represent separate states within the system; many of these states have an agenda that is separate from that of the organization. Employing a vigilant approach assists us in discovering possible weaknesses or inhibitors that otherwise impede information flow and successful signal transfer.

8

Barriers to Optimal
Information Processing

Reliable information, as we have argued, determines viability within the organization and can establish creditability outside the organization, while unreliable information can destroy an organization, as was the case with Enron. In this chapter we will discuss the notion of game theory and how it applies under a variety of conditions that exist among organizational players. The purpose of this discussion is to help make the reader aware of common conditions that may serve to impede optimal information flow before such conditions can impact the organization.

The ability for the organization to sustain itself depends on how information, the lifeblood of the organizational system, is managed. Like an organism must balance its metabolism, the organization must have the ability to handle the infusion of information as well as some method for the evacuation of waste. As an imbalance in this relation causes problems for the organism, so too can the inability to track and manage information become detrimental to the organization. Unless an organism can adequately process the various inputs, sufficient energy will not be generated, hindering the organism's ability to perform tasks. In organisms and organizations, this condition can become terminal. For example, the mere shuffling of information within an organization does little to fortify or enhance organizational health; a suffocating organism internally recycles the same materials until the nutrients are expended and then expires.

Informational input represents some of the vital nutrients that feed the organization in order for it to maintain its existence. This information might be represented in the form of financial or production data and will certainly involve information on the competition. Some data and information will relate to conditions of preservation, safety, and contingency planning. Some information should be categorized as essential and archived for reference while much of the information received on a daily basis is disposable. Organisms expel waste and by-products as a necessary function in order to get rid of unused inputs or by-product residuals resulting from consumption. Similarly, organizations must have appropriate mechanisms to dispense of old information in order to make room for the new as part of a "circulatory" information cycle. All organizations have a finite amount of resources, hence, unless some things are expelled, there will no room for new.

In this chapter we will discuss the difficulties organizations face while conducting information processing tasks. Much like their living counterparts, organizations can succumb to certain *ailments* that prevent them from optimally processing information. If ignored, this condition will lead to further complications (see chaos, chapter 5). While this may appear to be a "balancing act" (and to some degree it is) the reasons for seeking harmony in information processing within an organization is more directly related to game theory.

The Need to Understand Games

The theory of games stems from the work of John von Neumann (1903–1957), a brilliant MIT scientist whose works form the cornerstone in the fields of economics and social sciences. Games consist of four ingredients— *players*, *rules*, *payoffs*, and *strategies*. Briefly, each game needs to have two or more players. The rules dictate what actions can be taken. Each player invokes their strategies (or actions) in order to attain their objective. Each strategy is associated with some payoff. Moreover, it is the interaction of player strategies that contributes to the ultimate payoff. Here, we are involved with games that are not predicated on chance, for example, gambling, but rather in which players face off in direct competition bounded by specific rules. Examples include most board games (chess, checkers, etc.) or sports that are "organized" by the convention of leagues or conferences.

In the National Football League (NFL), for example, a typical game involves *rules* that determine the limits or conditions under which a contest may be take place. Such rules include that the playing field be 100 yards long, 53.5 yards wide. The field length terminates at an end zone on either side, each ten yards long. An NFL contest involves advancing or defending the movement of a ball to the end zone by either of two teams consisting of eleven men *(players)*. The goal of each team is to reach the end zone of the opponent in order to score points. To accomplish this, a principal objective, according to the rules, involves maintaining possession of the ball *(strategy)* for a series of four "downs" (attempts) during which the team in possession of the ball must advance at least ten yards. If this objective is accomplished the possession team is allowed four more downs to accomplish the same task. A team capable of advancing a minimum of 2.55 yards per down will eventually reach the end zone and score *(payoff)* at which time the other team is afforded the same opportunity.

Rules determine the conditions under which the game should be played in order to provide "equity" to both sides while providing an advantage to neither. *Strategies,* however, may involve one side deliberately breaking the rules in order to gain some advantage. In the waning moments of a close NFL contest, an offensive player may deliberately feign an injury in order to stop the clock for a "time-out: injury." This allows his team more time, which would have otherwise ticked off the clock, to prepare for their next play. While the game purist may recognize this tactic as a violation of "ethics," if there is some loophole that provides the potential for advantage in the game, someone will consider using it.

The most popular games are often those predicated on a simple set of rules but which are capable of producing an infinite variety of arrangements (i.e., chess). While practice at any game makes the player better, because of learned routines, the best players are those who have the ability to associate pattern recognition with the available options afforded by the rules. This ability allows the player an opportunity to improve his tactical position during the course of play based on (1) knowledge of the game and (2) the perception involving what is transpiring, which will determine decisions. In game theory the best solutions minimize the maximum damage an opponent can do, and that damage can come either as the result of mistakes or of being matched against a superior opponent.

This idea becomes more complex in the context of information processing, where there are actually several games being played in organizations. In all organizations, employees *(players)* are tasked with activities. Most of these activities involve the use of information. Organizations often assume their employees work in the best interest of the firm, and while this may be generally true, there are times when the tactics used by some of the players do not fit within the *rules* of the organization. While the *payoffs* will vary depending on how information is valued and used, organizations present opponents of whom the player may not be fully aware. This notion is consistent with our discussions of complexity in the previous chapter.

Other "opponents" who may appear in this "game" actually involve conditions of access to scarce resources such as time, money, and effort, while a major goal for the organization is to get tasks done with the minimal amount of resources. This is generally not clearly stated in the rules. The individual player may find himself vying for the set of resources, possibly in direct competition with other unknown players seeking the same resources. Under such conditions, upper-level constraints impede the condition for adequate information before the game begins. Processing is sacrificed as the player makes decisions to optimize task completion, though the resources required to complete the task may be inadequate. While supervisors may lay out the conditions of the game, it is often employees at some lower level, with minimal authority, who are required to complete the task. Resource requests from these lower-pay-grade employees are rarely successful; hence they must suffice with the resources at hand.

Additionally, the "opponents" to information processing in our game may include the mental or emotional state of those assigned to the tasks. As we will discuss later in the chapter, an individual's mental models (schemas) or cognitive frames of reference are initially challenged by the information at hand. If such information is contrary to the player's conventional perception of a situation, the player's ability to make decisions will be affected. But it is the player's perception, not necessarily the existing circumstances, which will determine decisions. The classic illustration of this case involves von Neumann's *Prisoner's Dilemma.* In this example, two prisoners are separated after being arrested for a crime in which it is suspected they have participated. Each prisoner is given the opportunity to "roll over" on the other, that is, implicate the other's involvement in the crime. The incentive for such participation is immunity from prosecution or some reduced sentence. Though the conditions of this situation hold that if neither prisoner "cooperates" both will go free for lack of evidence, invariably, one or both prisoners "defect" because the "known" conditions of promised conditions outweigh the unknown conditions associated with whether either prisoner can trust the other to not talk.

At the group level, games become more complex with the introduction of multiplayers. Now individuals not only compete for resources (external and/ or internal) but also against other individuals. Most of the time, however, such games result in the group taking no action or otherwise poor actions based on the information, resulting in inefficient consequences. Often, despite indications that competitive tasks involved in the game will never reach fruition, none of the participants can be expected to "pull the plug" for fear of being labeled a whistleblower.[1] In the long run, project managers would meet, each hoping for the next one to call their project off, and in the end millions of dollars are wasted on failed efforts because of the constraints built into the organization hierarchy that encourage such activities.

Information processing can be looked at as a two-stage game. In order to win the game (process and act on the information effectively and efficiently), both parts of the game must be played appropriately. The first part of the game is the signal detection phase. Here we are concerned with appropriate mechanisms that will help us recognize that "something" has signaled an impending event (or crisis). We are also concerned with what barriers might prevent us from recognizing these signals. Once a signal is recognized, we continue to the second stage, which involves *actions*. Given a signal, what is the appropriate action to be undertaken? For example, we might draw on data uncovered while interviewing managers who had continued to invest in runaway projects. A runaway project can be defined as an endeavor that takes on a life of its own and continues to consume resources without ever reaching its desired objective. This is praxis and is evident in projects that demonstrate persistent failures despite evidence of negative feedback—"escalation of commitment."[2] Individuals continue to invest in failed courses of action no matter how convincing the information may be telling them to quit. Many times organizational members take *no action* in the face of conflicting information. Either they go through phases of dissonance or do not have the ability or capabilities required for conducting actions. We also find cases where the *wrong* action is taken intentionally.

Once an organization goes through a round of the signal processing game, you would hope that they learn from these experiences and bolster their ability to recognize and act on signals in the future. However, this ability to go through signal resolutions and cycle back learned lessons is found in only a handful of organizations. Most go through amnesia and make the same mistakes multiple times. There are also times when the extensive reliance on past memories or information will result in creativity being stifled and poor decisions. While the past informs our experience, it should not be allowed to unconditionally determine future actions.

Prior to even considering how information can be processed, we need to discuss how information items can be found, or perceived. Instrumental in this process is the search of the information space by an individual in the organization. Searching can be considered akin to scanning. Aguilar defines it as "an exposure to and perception of information."[3] Aguilar proposed a continuum of scanning modes based on the extent to which the area of interest is known beforehand, ranging from formal (or problemistic) search, in which a problem is known and directs the information acquisition activity in a preprogrammed way, to undirected viewing, an exploratory activity in which the problem has not been identified. Scanning can be both problem- and information-triggered. We can classify scanning based on frequency activities: irregular (ad hoc), regular (periodically updated), and continuous.[4] The use of these concepts in research allocation decisions requires an initial judgment about process characteristics (for example, "How frequently should one scan?") rather than managerial concerns (for example, "What problem are we concerned with and what are its characteristics?"). The result of the scanning process will be a set of information items.

We will now discuss some of the barriers and outcomes of information processing games. We begin at the individual and then move to groups. It is interesting to note, if any of the *issues* mentioned below are managed effectively in the organization, they will remain a small *barrier* or can be eradicated. If not managed, they will become an *outcome* of information processing.

The Attention Deficit

Nobel laureate Herbert Simon noted, "What information consumes is rather obvious: it consumes the attention of its recipients. Hence a wealth of information creates a poverty of attention and a need to allocate that attention efficiently among the overabundance of information sources that might consume it."[5] Most individuals and organizations are poor attention managers. As noted by Davenport and Beck in *The Attention Economy*, most suffer from organizational ADD (attention deficit disorder).[6] Organizational ADD results in increased chances of missing key information, a lack of focus, and an inability to hold another's attention. The current information revolution we are passing through only intensifies the issue. We are inundated with more information than ever, from a wide assortment of sources at frequent or near-pervasive intervals. This leads to a higher chance of being distracted and less room for focusing. One critical reason for falling prey to attention deficit is simultaneous multitasking. In the current times of downsizing (or rightsizing), employees in organizations have been asked to do more with less. On average each project manager handles four to five concurrently running projects with varying complexities and requirements. Hence each project gets only a slice of the manager's attention. As one project manager of a midsized software consulting firm in Chicago noted: "With the recent downsizing . . . those of us who are left have to carry much higher loads in terms of projects, hence I am time starved . . . as a result of which, I do not give each project enough attention."

What complicates this problem is the fact that the manager does not have reasonable alternatives. Either the manager must voice an opinion stating that the number of projects or endeavors cannot be managed adequately (which is not a very nice thing to do considering the fact that many of his peers are out of a job) or delegate the job of giving the project attention to one of his subordinates. As we witnessed, in the software engineering world, such delegation goes to the senior business systems analyst or software engineer—*passing the buck.* Unfortunately, these individuals get too caught up in the development phases and microdetails of the project to pay attention to any of macrovariables such as Gantt charts, costs, and so forth. Moreover they are not sufficiently trained in project management methodologies to catch abnormalities and identify signs in projects. This kind of behavior can be seen in most industries. Often the delegation duties from higher authorities is given to people at the front lines who could care less about the macropicture, since their incentives and remuneration are tied to the microdetails.

The Information Overload

An extension to suffering from attention deficit is falling prey to the information overload syndrome. Any manager is susceptible. Take the case of a project manager for a consulting firm based in Austin, Texas. On average his daily e-mail reaches around 250 messages coupled with two-dozen voicemails. Surprisingly enough, most of them have to do with the projects he is responsible for. In conjunction with executing his daily tasks at the company, seldom does he get through all information bytes received on the day. Hence, like most managers he employs a filtering tool that sifts through his inbox and sorts messages based on relevance and source. This implies that many messages are either not read or experience delayed reading. In fact, messages from the "frontline" members of the project team are attended to last, as the manager's first responsibility is to his fellow project managers and his supervisor. Messages from the front lines are often the first indicators that a project is in trouble. By ignoring these messages or delaying attending to them, managers fall prey to the overload syndrome, lending themselves vulnerable to an impeding crisis.

The quantity, pervasiveness, and ubiquitous nature of information will continue to increase in an exponential fashion. Hence, what occurs is the act of *satisficing*.[7] Simply put, since it is not possible to cost-effectively evaluate all possible information before calibrating a decision, one will evaluate just enough so as to make a reasonable decision. This calls for being selective about the information one views and processes. Many times the manager will conduct conscious actions to seek out that information that is more in line with their mental model about the world and will act under the conditions of cognitive dissonance.

The Overconfidence Trap

Cognitive dissonance is often found tied to overconfidence and represents a condition in which a person intentionally adjusts behavior in order to make sense of the environment. Most managers admit that one reason why they failed to detect and process information adequately is because of innate chauvinism regarding their abilities. The overconfidence trap was first proposed by Hammond and colleagues.[8] Consider the following statement made by a seasoned executive": I have been at this organization for over ten years and have managed [well] over 100 projects. . . . I think no project plan can account for my experiences in running projects. . . . Which should I rely on, an excel sheet or my [gut] feelings to call the shots? . . . Computer tools are meant to aid me in my decision, not overturn or force me into a decision."

Most individuals do not like to view all available information. Many times it is not because they can not, but because they simply do not want to. So-called "experts" do not view all information before making decisions; they rely extensively on heuristics and shortcuts.[9] Many times this leads them to ignore facts that convincingly show that a crisis is on the horizon. For example, consider the following. There was immense evidence and knowledge that al-Qaeda was going to strike the United States. Not to mention, it could have been easily predicted that such an attack would be upon the tallest buildings in the United States. The World Trade Center had attracted terrorist interest before 9/11. Yet the arrogance and inability of the United States intelligence forces to adequately recognize and act on the threat continued till it was too late.

Each of the above three conditions prevent organizations from detecting signals in information. Other types of problems can occur either during signal detection or after the signal has been received. The later problems are usually associated with an organization's attitude toward information.

The History Trap

In previous chapters we have discussed the need for an organization to have a repertoire or memory. Without such a mechanism in place, the organization will not be able to learn and is apt to repeat mistakes from its past. While needed, sometimes histories may cause us to miss clues and to act poorly. What is even more troublesome is the reliance one has on *others'* history. Children will never learn adequately *if they do not make mistakes* and learn by conducting actions. Merely telling them how to act is not sufficient; they must actually calibrate the acts, make mistakes, and learn from them. Individuals have a tendency to accept and take for granted information memories in organizations. Many do not question the information or its context and merely apply it. It is necessary for individuals to sometimes think independently of past lessons learned. Unless the old information is purged in a timely fashion, organizational change becomes difficult. Organizational routines and practices get institutionalized and banded, which makes any efforts for futuristic change and thinking outside of the box impossible. As such, one will ignore information, based on the presumption that it did not lead to an outcome in the past, so why should it now? Extensive reliance on the past inhibits motivation and creative thinking. If everything were given to you, why would you have to think? As the old adage goes, necessity is the mother of invention. Many times individuals in organizations try to answer questions based exclusively on the knowledge resources they possess. Hence, any problem definition is fitted to the solutions at hand. Old is not always gold in terms of organizational knowledge.

Organizations operate in a dynamic and fiercely competitive environment. Organizational knowledge, much like computer hardware, hence has a high rate of depreciation. Lessons learned from endeavors conducted five or ten years ago, while important, need to be qualified. The macrolessons, if captured, would suffice without every little microdetail. We all know that in most cases yesterday's knowledge has little if any specific bearing on redesigning the future. It may help us get through the future in an operational sense, but will not help in redesigning or charting the future. Tversky and Kahneman in the 1970s, as well as others have suggested that people often see order where it does not exist or attribute serendipitous fortune to ability largely because the notion of uncertainty is ignored. Subsequent choices by such individuals are largely based on preconception and prior knowledge without regard to either reassessment or the laws of probability. Tversky suggests people have a tendency to take the most familiar, easiest accessible path to a predictive solution under conditions in which some, though perhaps not the best, alternatives are readily *available*. Subsequently, probability becomes subjective, and an individual relates to new situations that are *representative*, that is, similar to those of past experience. As an example, U.S. terrorist experts would not anticipate the use of conventional transportation devices as weapons, as when a small watercraft was used to attack the USS *Cole* or when commercial jetliners were used against the World Trade Center because experience indicated it had never been done before. Each of these conditions reflects directly on the capacity of human judgment, and each gives rise to the need for more effective tools and techniques during times of impending crisis.

Designing or charting the future will call for new uninhibited creativity. Unless the old is purged or challenged, no one will question its existence. Hence many times myths become corporate knowledge, because over time they get instilled in practices and procedures sometime in history and no one seeks to question their relevance for today. One of the key reasons individuals rely on the past extensively is that it is less risky than rethinking and revaluating information. Moreover, it is also less costly in terms of cognitive effort.

The Trap of Conforming Evidence

The conforming evidence trap is a variant of the self-justification theory, wherein decision-makers seek out information that only justifies and solidifies their initial judgments. Under such conditions, conflicting information is ignored because, as Simon and Garfunkel once reminded us, people hear "only what they want to hear and disregard the rest." The presence of conforming evidence is especially pervasive when a decision-maker has to make a case for or against something and the audience is hostile. Here an individual will use segments or a portion of information available to preserve and project their own mental state or model. Any information that challenges their opinions, thoughts, frames, and votes on an issue will be disregarded and given little or no weight. Moreover, the individual will find ways to rationalize not accounting for conflicting individual items. This is where statistics come into the picture. Statistics can be tweaked and used convincingly to support any decision. Consider the controversy over the claim that Iraq had weapons of mass destruction. It is interesting to note that even though the intelligence report stating the claim that Iraq had sought to buy yellowcake-grade uranium from Niger was unfounded, it merited inclusion in the State of the Union address.[10] What is even more interesting is the fact that the report was known to have been questionable several months before the president's speech. This is a classic case of conforming evidence; one will seek out and use only that information that supports the case. The case of choosing information that benefits one's current position is not peculiar to individuals; organizations do it on a regular basis. In the classic book on strategy *Competing for the Future*, Hamel and Prahalad elaborate on how such preservation of one's current position has led companies to lose their competitive edge.[11] Polaroid lost its edge to digital imaging, Swiss watchmakers fell prey to the agile Japanese, and the car companies in Detroit lost ground to the more fuel-efficient competitors in Asia. It is much easier to justify the present rather than deal with the reality of information and make changes to the present.

Cognitive dissonance describes the discord between behaviors and beliefs that motivate people to seek some ground of consistency that reduces or eliminates the conflict.[12] People seek information that confirms their choice and depreciate encountered information that opposes it. They are occasionally at odds when new information threatens or changes current beliefs. Perhaps a more common term for such behavior is *rationalization*. Based on experiential references and certain cognitive processes, it is often hard for someone to admit, for example, they are wrong about anything they have perceived as having "thought out." In crisis situations that this can be dangerous. At Chernobyl, technicians chose to ignore certain safety directives despite clear indications of impending disaster.[13] Evidence indicates that NASA intentionally launched *Challenger* although there was the high probability that structural weaknesses in the craft would lead to dire consequences.

Decision-makers often attempt to restructure information prior to a choice in order to make the *leading alternative* dominate, or nearly dominate, all other options.[14] This might be accomplished, for example, by devaluing the importance of attributes in which the leading alternative is inferior. A major concern involving America's 2003 involvement in Iraq is, while there may have been several options to achieving some form of stability in the Middle East, the inevitability of war was the only one that was seriously considered by our administration. As an oversimplification, this disregards the fact that war is a recognized extension of diplomacy.

Finger-Pointing

When things go wrong, the finger-pointing game will begin. This is ongoing in the case of the current weapons of mass destruction controversy, with the American intelligence community blaming the British for faulty reporting and the British accusing the Americans of taking things out of context. Within (or between) organizations, the fallout leads to considerable confusion and an associated lack of trust. Prospect theory states that individuals are risk-seeking when choosing between two losing options, but are risk-averse when choosing between winning options.[15] Currently, and as a direct result of earlier finger-pointing related to the release of questionable information, the intelligence related to the weapons of mass destruction possessed by Syria has also come under scrutiny.[16] During some research, we spoke to a manager who was blamed for continuing a project well after it was determined that it was going to be a failure. He remarked: "The reason why I did not stop the project in August is . . . I was only presented with a statement . . . that showed us being (successfully) on target."

When we viewed the statement, it was clear to us that the manager did not view it in total: The project summary had a series of footnotes put together by a senior software engineer notifying him about the need to shell out an additional fifty thousand dollars for unplanned expenses. Of course, an additional issue here is the asymmetry of information: the subordinate may not have wanted to display problems prominently because of the consequences for him or herself—*keeping with the status quo.*

Maintaining the Status Quo

Peter's Inversion, an extension of the Peter Principle, suggests that "internal consistency is valued more highly than efficiency."[17] Decision-makers have strong biases toward making judgments that meet the status quo rather than go against it. Going against the status quo means opening ourselves up to criticism and risking damage to our egos. We rationalize our decisions to meet the common norms since it is a much safer route than going against them. Thus managers opt to let information slide rather than admit they made a mistake. Not surprisingly, in organizations in which the notion of failing on an assignment was heavily shunned, managers were less likely to admit their fault. Moreover, we can see the evidence for the "mum" effect, where for those projects or endeavors seemingly going under, none of the project members would want to whistle-blow on the project manager and speak out.[18] Individuals are hesitant to speak out for a number of reasons. In our work on identifying why members of information technology and software projects did not speak out, we came across an interesting statement: "If the economy was in better shape . . . many of us would have left . . . as half of the projects we work on are viewed down on . . . if I speak out . . . I will be on the street, [XYZ] is a much better place right now."

Blowing the whistle, an ethical dilemma, is an action that will invariably cause harm to the individual. Sometimes the result ends up in lengthy court battles, loss of job, or overall stigma. While "the thin blue line" is often described as a "keep your mouth shut and keep any problems in-house" unwritten practice of police officers, similar conditions exist in every workplace. Recently, the *New York Times* was forced to do some serious housecleaning that resulted from the intentional and suspect practices of one of its journalists. The problem had been recognized but it had also been ignored. If individuals do not speak out in the organization, and most projects fail, eventually the organization will suffer damage. Mancur Olson ascribes this behavior as the *Logic of Collective Action;* even though it may be in the organization's best interest for an individual to carry out an action (blow the whistle or go against the status quo), they will not conduct such action, as it is not in the individual's best interest.[19] Moreover, going with the status quo affords the opportunity for one to delay facing the facts, that is, acknowledging a mistake or failure has occurred and that the information at hand is pointing in an opposite rather than the planned direction. This normally happens when one has a particular milestone in mind. For instance, in most organizations there is an annual merit review, which decides bonuses, promotions, tenure, and so on. We found that a project manager is more likely to keep spending on a runaway project in the last quarter of the year rather than let his current year's review be affected. They would rather write off the expense as part of the new fiscal year and still keep their bonuses of the current year unaffected. This is why in most organizations people play the making-the-numbers game. Charging sales to accounts at the end of year and then receiving the returned goods in the new year is a good way to bolster the bottom line. Decision-makers continue to invest in failing courses of action, even though losses continue to mount, due to the perception, "We have already invested in it, so let us follow through on it." Moreover, since many managers are evaluated on the percentage of projects completed (not on the number of projects terminated due to being unprofitable), they view termination of an endeavor as a big negative. Further damage is done when information is intentionally altered or misinterpreted.

Power and Harmonious Battles

Power battles arises, between two or more decision-makers when each of them have equal power and status in the organization and want to protect their agendas at all costs. Management of information turns into a battle of power rather than an objective analysis. Decisions are seldom made in the best interests of the organization; they are made to protect the egos of the decision-makers. What transpires is a blaming and document-moving game. Each decision-maker sends an analysis to their counterpart, who seldom pays any attention to the details of analysis, and instead sends it back with more analysis aimed at fulfilling their own ego. Hence in essence what we have is constant moving of documents exemplifying each other's ego. Each one feels that the other ones' analysis is based on their ego rather than on hard facts. This continues until we have outside intervention into the project or the resources run dry. Members involved in the power battles are always adversaries.

The opposite of the power battle trap involves situations in which each individual has respect for their peers and will not harm egos by telling others they are on a wrong course of action. Like the story of the emperor and his new clothes, no one wants to admit the truth. An outcome of falling into such a trap is that project leaders have a series of harmonious "feel good" meetings that promote a sense of false security. This behavior reinforces the other's action to stay on the wrong track. Moreover, it also leads to a variant of the bystander effect, in which one manager waits for a peer to bring up the thought of axing the project and relies on them to take charge of project termination. As one manager put it: "I was waiting for Jack to call the shot . . . you know he is a year senior to me and I respect his judgment on such matters."

Paranoia

As damaging as any aspect of attention deficit is uncertainty. Here, members of the group are worried about their perception, or lack thereof, regarding individual mental models involved in a project. Consequently, in the group not all are focused on the information at hand. Information that needs the attention of the group as a whole is missed or neglected and not acted upon.

A classic example involves the intelligence community and information available prior to 9/11. Each of the departments was focused on the specific information they had and each acted on it independent of the rest of the organizations. As such, each was only able to put a piece of the puzzle in place, missing the real threat. Each agency cautiously protected their own information and then calibrated actions or called shots based on incomplete information, resulting in a colossal failure for the organization as a whole. Such attitudes are not restricted to government agencies. In the case of product development in most software companies, two independent yet important groups govern the success of product development efforts. These are the software developers, who build the products, and the marketing personnel who determine what should be built based on the analysis of customer needs. It is not uncommon to find that conflicts arise when the two groups try to achieve the goal of better product development. The software engineers know their product, its features, its limitations, and enhancements. The marketers know their customers. The goal of the marketing personnel is to make the customer happy at almost all costs. The goal of the system or software engineer is to ensure that the system is up and running in the most efficient and effective manner. What happens frequently is the following—the marketing folks promise a product to the customer that is difficult if not impossible to calibrate if the system's integrity is to be maintained. The software engineers become angered and get on the bandwagon—the product cannot be built. In the end, after a long debate and standoff, a product is delivered to the customer, which is not 100 percent of what the marketer promised, and the information systems of the software engineering firm are compromised in terms of integrity due to the new product. In the end everyone looses—a classic outcome when the right hand knows not what the left is doing.

Information Asymmetries

A special kind of effect occurs when players from different organizational ranks are involved in the game. Agency theory deals with the relationship between one who delegates work (the principal) and the one who performs the work (the agent).[20] Agents will choose to execute decisions that maximize their own self-interest at the expense of the principal due to information asymmetry. This is not uncommon in organizations. The higher one is on the organizational chart, the less detailed the information gets. Executives all want the "big picture."[21] They do not want to get bogged down with details. But this allows for a lot of the details to be hidden despite the fact they may represent valuable information. Often agents acting on behalf of principals will manipulate information, which serves their end so long as it goes undetected and keeps everyone momentarily happy. While the Enron debacle provides an excellent example of such practices, it is far from being the only such instance in which similar activities are "tolerated." Public sector agencies and utility companies often present facts and figures in support of their policies and actions while they wait for the next unanticipated breakdown in a system over which they have very little control. In August 2003, for example, large parts of the northeast U.S. and Canada suffered a daylong power outage that caught the utilities companies completely by surprise. Despite the obligatory public relations front that was presented, there was no consensus on why the outage occurred.

Similar results from an opposite approach occur when management "destines" some project for success regardless of whether or not the activity has any real value. This is often the result of hubris, a feeling or state in which any entity feels it is omnipotent and can do no wrong. Detroit's lack of response to foreign imports during the 1960s provides a good example of an industry mentality that was attempting to perpetuate the myth that the consumer "could have any color they wanted as long as it was black."

Mental Aberrations

It is interesting to note that when knowledge and error flow *from the same mental sources*, only success can tell the one from the other.[22] Far from being rooted in irrational or maladaptive tendencies, recurrent error forms have their origins in otherwise useful psychological processes.[23] Reason defines error as a generic term to encompass all those occasions in which a planned sequence of mental or physical activities fails to achieve its intended outcome or when these failures cannot be attributed to the intervention of some chance agency.[24] Errors are sometimes referred to as slips and lapses, or mistakes. The former results from some failure in the execution and/or storage stage of an action sequence, regardless as to whether or not the plan that guided them was adequate enough to achieve an objective. Such errors can be variable or constant. Variable errors cannot be predicted because they are random, but they may be detected during real-time surveillance. Constant errors on the other hand are systematic deviations from the expected norm or target. Consider the following illustration: if a signal for an impending terrorist attack states that airplanes might be used as weapons, not being cautious about who boards an airplane with what in their possession is a form of constant error if this signal leads to no action to avert the threat. However, variable errors occur when one acts on a signal and gets multiple outcomes with no pattern. This happens when one tries to buy stocks based on past market trends and future expectations. On occasion one will make money, but it is also possible to lose money or break even. In this case, the pattern of errors is very difficult to trace back to any definite path or action. Mistakes can be defined as deficiencies or failures in the judgmental and/or inferential processes involved in the selection of an objective or in the specification of the means to achieve the objective, irrespective of whether or not the actions directed by the decision-scheme run according to plan. By nature, mistakes are also far harder to detect.

For the human mind, consciousness is specifically attuned to detecting departures in action from intentions,[25] but mistakes can pass unnoticed during lengthy "conscious" periods.[26] Walking down a flight of stairs is something that occurs naturally for most after a certain age. But if one concentrates on such an activity, that is, focuses on the motor response while engaged in the same activity, the task becomes more difficult, awkward, and possibly dangerous. This is the result of processing the same information in different ways; unconsciously and consciously. The same type of experience can happen in organizations that "consciously" rationalize that matters are under control because the organizational chart indicates there is a department that handles such matters. The truth is, sometimes this works and sometimes it does not. Methods for compensating or obviating possible problems associated with such practices are available but require organizational buy-in. Still, defective decisions based on misinformation and poor judgment sometimes lead to successful outcomes. We must acknowledge that chance and the stupidity of the enemy can sometimes give a silk-purse ending to a command decision worth less than a sow's ear.[27] Understandably, the Janis observation explains the exception, not the rule.

Illusions are "dreams" and may be regarded, more precisely, as "any species of error which counterfeits the form of immediate, self-evident, or intuitive knowledge, whether as sense perception or otherwise."[28] Philosophers and psychologists have been aware of how the impressions associated with illusion impact beliefs and decisions. Illusions *present* false or spurious "knowledge" of the first order that present the opportunity for action based on subjective conjecture.[29] Untethered, this can lead to *fallacies,* false or spurious knowledge of the second order as represented in myths. Both dissonance and illusion affect cognitive processes by distorting fact. This affords an opportunity for activities that support a failed course of action or activities that are conducted that serve no purpose; the Greek word is *praxis.* Experts have the annoying habit of relying on viewing current conditions only in terms of past experience. While a use of regression models is helpful, future conditions can never be predicated solely on the basis of past experience.

Moreover, a critical mistake committed by organizations is to stifle the collection of informal signals. Many of the signals associated with an organization can be gathered through formal channels; however, a select few signals must emerge from the informal tracks. These can take the form of signals found in gossip[30] or unstructured surveillance of the competitive marketplace through competitive intelligence techniques,[31] among others. Many have a tendency to view these as illusionary signals and disregard them. This is not advisable considering the fact that the most valuable signals are those that reduce uncertainty within a system. Hence, the more counterintuitive information a signal provides, the better; these are more apt to emerge from informal tracks where there is less stifling and filtering through rigid organizational mechanisms.

Conclusion

The best way to approach a problem is to realize the problem exists in the first place. In this chapter we have addressed a number of issues related to conditions that commonly impede the activities associated with properly processing signals and therefore impede information. One approach that aids in overcoming barriers to optimal signal processing is to consider the signal environment in terms of game theory. Game theory forces active participants to take a deeper look at the relations within the "game" and the general context of a situation or problem at hand. Game theory requires that all players be identified and that strategies be developed in order to reach a successful outcome in the game. Such strategies might include a form of critical path analysis in which dependencies are established. Game theory assumes that strategies will be employed but that no player is capable of comprehending all the strategies that may be available. This is crucial in the effort to avoid the deterministic approaches that do not allow for options in the game.

A second important aspect to obviating possible barriers to signals and information includes knowing the personnel involved in the projects as well as possible upper-level restraints that may unintentionally inhibit information flow. The former is a function of management while the latter should include everyone involved in the project. After several problems with security at an investment firm, despite the existence of routine contingency plans, it was finally decided to involve the people who participated in the day-in, day-out operations of the organization's operations. Employees were asked, "If you were given the task of defeating our security, what would you do?" Within a week, management had not only suggestions but solutions to problems that had been plaguing them for years. The reason these solutions had never come forth was simple; nobody asked! In a sense, many of the problems that existed actually served as a form of "job security," since if the problem could not be resolved according to the organization's plans, it would likely persist and have to be attended to by people who intrinsically knew they had a better solution but lacked the authority to push their ideas.

In our next chapter we seek solutions that will help organizations attain conditions intended to optimize information processing. Thus far we have included a variety of theory-based notions that help understand why information fails to achieve its intended purpose. We now explore methods to integrate these theories into practices, based on an ad hoc approach for optimal information processing.

9

Setting Up the Organization for Optimal Information Processing

Having reacquainted you with most of the conditions that combine to affect information flow in organizations, we now consider organizational models (structure and hierarchy) and discuss how these arrangements may serve to enhance or impede information flow. Many organizational design charts are displayed with the assumption that by demonstrating the organization in some graphic form, how information will be dispersed becomes apparent and automatic. Experience often shows otherwise. There will be those who argue that some information belongs solely in the realm of the upper ends of organizational charts where it may be dispersed on a strict "needs to know" basis. Such critics should, however, be aware that any "privileged" information they receive would be skewed toward a bias of those who present it, and it should be no surprise that these presenters are most often also represented at the higher regions of the organizational charts. This can result in an incestuous arrangement that ultimately proves damaging to the entire organization. The product in such arrangements, especially when new problems are addressed in an old manner, often reflects on Janis's notion of "groupthink" rather than on anything useful. In this chapter we will contrast two organizations facing the same challenge, and review possible reasons why they have elected to set priorities in a different fashion since their structure indicates they will likely produce different information although they are seeking quite similar results.

In previous chapters we addressed concepts that affect, transform, distort, or otherwise alter information. Because problems associated with delivery and interpretation of information in organizations are directly related to the systems in place, the reader may presume that the answer to the efficient use of information rests in proper structuring of the information system. While that would be a good start, most systems affected by information problems are already in place and would require at least some degree of restructuring, if not a complete overhaul. To determine the degree to which changes may be required, a good place to start is by interpreting the hierarchy of the organization. Generally, conventional charts that represent the organization's breakdown represent specific dependencies. While this may seem fundamental, relations of coupling and cohesiveness must be considered to understand whether the efficient use of information can be accomplished. Despite their best intentions, it should not come as a surprise that organizations are often designed to impede information flow, and it this reality that is the focus of this chapter. Once, the observation that "lack of preparation on your part does not constitute an emergency on my part" might have sufficed to address deficiencies that pointed to shortfalls related to information flow. But today, failures in organizational design that restrict or stop information flow should be regarded as intentional since the tools and knowledge to accomplish such tasks are available.

This chapter will be more applied than theoretical in nature and focus on creating the necessary architecture in order to process information optimally in organizations. To begin, we combine an overlay of a conventional "feedback" model with semiotics. An implication in feedback is that the "output" product should serve as "input" for further development within the system. We have addressed how "spatial" information, continuous from a variety of sources, is received for synthesis and that "temporal" knowledge derived from these information sources can serve to broaden the collective memory of an organization. Building on this basic approach, we will present a comparative example between existing organizational structures and illustrate contrasting styles involving the use of similar information. While the hierarchy of the "systems" presented clearly demonstrates elements of organization, their respective organization also reflects priorities that will serve to either facilitate or impede information flow for reasons previously discussed. First, we should review how semiotics overlaps the basic information processing framework.

Information Processing Framework

In order to better map the chapter, we should discuss the components of information processing. Figure 9.1 depicts a basic block diagram of any system. Information processing in organizations should be studied by looking at each component of this basic block diagram. The feedback model fits with the notion of semiotics as the input box deals with items at the *morphological* layer. Here we are simply concerned with the *gathering* of information,

Figure 9.1 **Information Processing Framework**

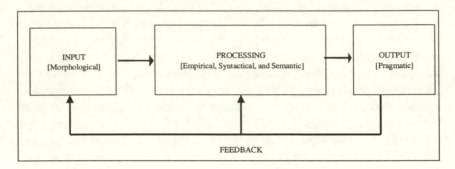

which will be processed. The processing box deals with issues of *empirics,* *syntactics, and semantics.* Inputs are synthesized into logical or physical outputs at this point. The output box is concerned with the applicability or usefulness of the processed information. Useful information includes anything that may act as the basis for a decision or action intended to modify some organizational behavior. At this stage, information has gone through *pragmatic* classification and *semantic* interpretation of meaning and has therefore acquired value. If the information had not been classified or yielded no meaning, the output would reflect that the suspect information had no value but could be recycled once more against the possibility that something was missed. At this stage the process is representative of Miller's 1960 TOTE (test-operate-test-exit) concept in which the process is repeated until value is eventually achieved or the initial data source is abandoned.[1] The newer input is then presented in the form of an information modification, that is, the recycled information source includes some of the original data that has been "seen through new eyes." Positive feedback reinforces existing input and process activities, while negative feedback looks to alter activities.

Einstein once remarked that everything should be made as simple as possible, but not simpler. It is our contention that simplicity is the best way to solve any problem. The accompanying diagram has been in use since the beginnings of cybernetics but is largely ignored today in favor of more complex representations of information processing in organizations. Yet all the tools and technologies available to the organization are likely already in place and can be mapped to fit within the context of one or more diagram boxes. At the most basic level, analysis using fundamental "feedback" observations should reveal information of value. One consequence resulting from the feedback cycle is that information should contribute to processes associated with learning. But to benefit from what might be learned, any cognitive researcher worth his salt will state that you must have a receptive learner. If there is something to be learned, for example, via new information, nothing will be accomplished if an organization persists in relying on old system approaches that will not tolerate and do not support innovation. The best-designed systems have a way of miring when the focus on discovery is overshadowed by political agendas. The question has often arisen about what might happen to medical funding if certain diseases were in fact found to be curable. On the distaff side, despite the socially (and medically) correct observation that all smokers should quit inhaling cigarettes, the reality is that if every smoker in the United States broke the habit tomorrow, the shift and effect in tax consequences alone would be devastating to the economy. Think about it. The question then becomes whether the politics of the organization supports real learning development since the paradigm involved might place a much greater emphasis on information technologies, knowledge management, and the personnel who accomplish those tasks. If the existing information processes related to the organization's structure are merely repeated without regard to environmental influences, nothing will change internally.

Einstein also observed, "The significant problems we face cannot be solved at the same level of thinking we were at when we created them." However, the realities are that external pressures will eventually supplant shortsighted organizations that fail to heed these words and they will never see it coming. Then one predictor on whether an organization will become amenable or receptive to necessary changes might include its own organizational chart or hierarchy structure. By example, new considerations since 9/11 have stressed the need for information gathering and sharing between government organizations at all levels, which is a very good idea. There is little doubt that since public safety falls squarely on the shoulders of local authorities, the first line to open should involve effective information flow and the most efficient resources to accomplish such tasks. However, in reviewing the organization of the Department of Homeland Security (DHS), one might have difficulty connecting the dots regarding how this essential job is to be accomplished. This is a classic problem of who needs information versus who gets it.

Quantitative or Qualitative?

An adage states, *"Not everything that counts can be counted, and not everything that can be counted counts"*; think about that. More often than not, great weight is given to qualitative studies because they tend to analyze social reality through variables that can be coded to determine whether they infer significance in a study; that is, they can be counted. Too often, however, the results of this method of analysis can produce an unexplained answer without explaining the "why" as to the specifics involved in a situation. Unfortunately, decision-makers are often impressed with the objectivity of qualitative reports without regard to the fact that they are based on similarly objective assumptions regarding social realities. The fact that it can be statistically established that more children die in southern California as the result of swimming pool accidents than from handgun accidents might suggest that pools be banned. Decision-makers are often biased toward qualitative studies, however, since such processes produce some sort of quick result and frankly, people are impressed with numbers-studies; they produce *"what can be counted."* What is missed, however, is that results from such studies will provide only inferences that "represent" rather than actually depict a form of social reality.

Often, those who are new to research shy away from qualitative approaches because of the math and choose instead to study phenomena using a quantitative approach only to find that this choice can be far more complex because *"not everything that counts can be counted."* There is a need for organizations to first understand that information processing requires qualitative analysis before quantitative techniques are used. But an understanding of the dynamics of a condition, situation, or phenomenon requires deeper analysis. Few in businesses or research will deny the need for a better mousetrap to capture the essence, use, and function of information in this day of data overload, and toward this end it must be *action, not words, that determines the truth* or the possibility for success lies elsewhere. Too often organizations are far more inclined to "talk the talk" while appearing demonstrably powerless to "walk the walk."

By example, organizations in the public sector that compute their budget requests on a "use it or lose it" basis show patterns that lack creativity because it is easier to replace an office chair with a new one if funds have been allocated for replacement rather than consider whether a chair is really needed or, better still, possibly find a better use of such funds in the name of efficiency. In this sense, it is easier for the organization to restrict its thinking along the lines that pertain to previously existing conditions rather than be creative despite the fact that *"not everything that can be counted counts."* Analogies to this type of "quantitative" behavior also exist in the private sector which, when scrutinized, invite any number of "qualitative" questions, especially when changes to the organizational environment require novel approaches to unique situations; rationality of this sort never optimizes conditions.

Two and a half years ago the federal government launched an initiative in the guise of homeland security to marshal twenty-some agencies under the umbrella of a single magistrate with a single purpose. The chart below indicates their initial design (see Figure 9.2).

Figure 9.2   **Organizational Chart for the Department of Homeland Security**

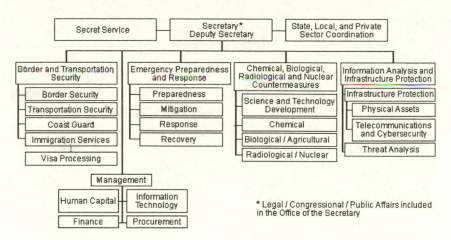

Source: The White House.

By contrast, Europe's Interpol addresses many of the same concerns but for a number of members from a variety of countries (see Figure 9.3). More important, the Interpol hierarchy has been around longer than DHS and it might have occurred to someone that it could have been useful to do some "benchmarking" before beginning to structure the new organization. In comparing the structures of the respective organizations, some interesting contrasts are evident. While some are related to "cultural" differences, that is, the ranking importance of particular resources and services based on past experiences, the Homeland Security structure appears a ready candidate to be affected by conditions related to emergence, complexity, and chaos.

For example, one initial distinction places technology, intelligence, and information as an integral part of each of their principal divisions in the Interpol model. The DHS model relegates similar functions to an analysis section charged with threat analysis that might be better served under the emergency preparedness section. A note on the DHS chart indicates that legal regard and influence over the activities conducted by each subordinate group is tied directly to the secretary, Tom Ridge. The note also indicates that congressional and Public Affairs are to be tied to the secretarial level of authority. Public Affairs gave us the colored alert warnings system that has proven popular, not so much as an effective or reliable information source, but more as a source for popular jokes. Congressional ties include budgetary matters, which are more likely related to "pork" than necessity or require-

Figure 9.3   **Organizational Chart for Europol**

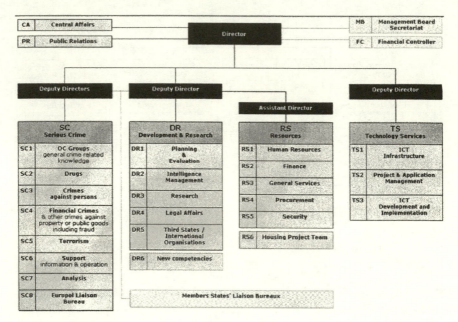

Source: Europol.

ments of the subagencies. This of course presents problems associated with tight coupling as reflected in both the events leading to and the aftermath of the attacks on the World Trade Center in both 1993 and September 11, 2001.

On March 3, 2003, Baltimore mayor Martin O'Malley was named the new chairman of the U.S. Conference of Mayors' Homeland Security Task Force.[2] This appointment coincided with the beginning of the Iraqi war. With the nation on high alert, O'Malley, supported by New York senator Hillary Clinton, stated, "Even a year and a half after 9/11, there is still no federal money in place to support America's cities." Six months earlier, on the anniversary of 9/11, O'Malley presented seven points he believed essential for Homeland Security to be a functioning system.[3] Number one on his list was for every metropolitan area to have its own local intelligence network to allow police from every jurisdiction to share information "instantly and routinely." This point may have been lost to the federal designers of the DHS hierarchy. Getting back to our DHS chart, for example, there is no provision for addressing this point. The tie of "state, local, and private coordination" is a myth parading itself as organization without regard to what is required for this type of coordination. Additionally, this type of "arrangement" with the feds generally means, "You do it." Within the Europol chart, there is a provision for a Liaison Bureau that works in conjunction with focused terrorism, information analysis, and operations groups. Similar consideration is not provided in the DHS model.

While we might press on the perceived inadequacy of the DHS model in comparison to the operational model developed by Europol, the example is merely intended to demonstrate how an organizational structure may unintentionally hinder results. The "organization" of the organization is then critical before information processes can be expected to succeed.

Organizational learning, as with learning for individuals, is accomplished in two basic ways, either as a response to the environment, for example, a conditioned response, or as a result of experience. Additionally, learning is reinforced through repeated use of new information, which serves to strengthen memory. Einstein once said that he was not so sure he was that much smarter than others; he just had a knack for staying with problems longer. Effective learning, in the main, is accomplished more as the result of repeated exercise than from mere exposure. This point is missed on organizations that assume "training" alone fulfills certain needs. Certainly, training is a positive step toward learning but the general consensus in learning theory is if something "learned" is not "used" within two weeks of the initial exposure, most of the learning associated with the topic will be lost. Too often, managers accept a training program under the assumption that what is being presented will be immediately and continually applied toward some application. This is simply not true. Yet, using learned material not only affords individuals the opportunity to become more proficient at the task, there is a residual probability that the user will develop something new, possibly useful, from their endeavors. This residual is sometimes referred to as creativity.

The act of creativity should not be construed as originality, though there are times the terms are used interchangeably. The semiotic model is a *creative* tool intended to produce actionable knowledge from a variety of synthesized data. The implementation of the concepts related to the model would be *original* to the organization, but any activity generated from the process demonstrates the *creative* use of information. Creativity involves approaching a problem from a new or different perspective. In crisis management, for example, traditional contingency theory deals more with recovery than prevention. A creative approach to crisis management might involve techniques that would assist an organization to evade crisis.

Virtual Information Centers

As we have argued, the crisis management literature and practice is flooded with advice on "how to" restore an organization or a system back to some sense of normality *after* a crisis has occurred. This is mostly a facet of management thinking that crisis is a part of operations and hence cannot be prevented. We argue to the contrary, that crises can be evaded if not mitigated. Given this *truth*, why can we not prevent or evade a crisis rather than react and restore following crisis conditions? A key reason for this failure is the lack of adequate signal processing abilities in organizations. Unless an organization has an efficient and effective infrastructure to process signals, warning signs will go unchecked, be ignored, and otherwise become an unused resource intended to evade crises.

To this end, the development of *virtual crisis centers* for organizations should be established. These centers are akin to *monitoring* stations found in industrial plants and other manufacturing centers. They can be regarded as the dashboard of a car, which indicates key vitals during the operation of the machine. Our contention is that having such a center will help an organization monitor the necessary signals generated and dissipated from within and around the organization in order to sense impending crisis. Once detected, the center can be used to evade or in some cases even curtail the effects of the crisis. If signal detection does not work, the center can be used to restore the organization.

We ground our discussion of what it takes to build such a crisis center from past work related to failures in intelligence leading to the disaster of 9/11. As explicated in the study of 9/11 failures, information (signals) available well before the event could have prevented the crisis if our government authorities had processed them efficiently and effectively. This did not occur for a number of reasons.

- Information was segmented and held by various groups trying to work on the same problem independently. Information was gathered but not shared. There was no lateral movement of information.
- There was no use of an *organizational repertoire or memory base* from which to adequately gauge how the past would influence the future. The World Trade Center had, for over a decade, held the attention of a number of terrorist factions; if there were going to be any attacks, the Twin Towers should have been on everyone's "most popular" list.
- To be useful, information must be used and should succeed to knowledge. This never happened, as information was held and not acted upon.

These three aspects of information processing are critical in the management of signals. An organization must be able to generate *decisions* from informational signals, must be able to move decisions and information across a variety of channels, and must be able *learn* from its past. In order to achieve these goals, a well-managed symbiotic information center is needed, which brings these dimensions together: a *virtual crisis center.*

The word *virtual* emphasizes its remoteness from the physical organization. This idea is advantageous for a number of reasons. First, since 9/11 a valid reason for off-site control centers is safety for personnel and data. A remote site as an auxiliary or redundant archive means less chance of loss of resources in the event of a direct attack on a more high-profile office building or locale. Second, at the remote site the division of labor is more focused on the task of information flow and knowledge management. Frankly, the corporate headquarters has too many unrelated distractions. Third, and most important, the remote access center provides accessibility to key information because it serves to funnel and channel data with the intention of providing a real-time, reliable product on which every authorized person may depend. Use of such a center may have prevented more than a few awkward moments. CNN reported, in a recent series of events, that efforts regarding the oversight of governing interests toward an effort to stabilize the regions of Iraq and Afghanistan may have been delayed if not impeded because the principal American players were not on the same page.[4] If the remote center model proposed in this section had been in place, those players—the national security adviser, the secretary of state, the secretary of defense, and director of the CIA would have had the opportunity for input and feedback, in real time, which could have provided for a more collaborative response to some otherwise closely monitored events. Use of a different ISP to host the virtual crisis center could provide the simplest solution.

Another aspect of virtuality involves the fact that all the tools and technologies to monitor such signals must be accessible via *virtual* means including the Internet, PDAs, wireless devices, or telephonic transfer. By analogy, once it appeared on September 11 that Washington, DC, was under attack, the president and his immediate staff were moved to a remote control center that had the technologies needed to monitor the developing situation. We suggest that similar arrangements—but in a less resource-intensive way—be developed for organizations concerned with crisis evasion. Aside from tough economic times putting a cap on new infrastructure spending, we believe that information technology resources can undergo small modifications that will have a tremendous impact in the area of crisis management.

A first step is to inventory all sources of information with which the organization should be concerned. Information signals need to be gathered from relevant sources both within and around the organization. A number of automated tools exist for this task. Such devices include scanners, automated transaction processing systems, or existing equipment that may be modified for enhancement by adjusting sensitivity variables. Existing systems are becoming increasingly sophisticated and now handle volumes of data at higher levels of detail than previously possible. Recent advances in distributed artificial intelligence have led to the proliferation of intelligent agents, which act as representations of humans in electronic environments. Such devices are common in environments such as business-to-business transaction systems, negotiation software, supply chain management systems, search engines, and web monitoring tools. Agents generate data when transacting business or on behalf of their owners, the organization, and are valuable existing sources that can be monitored.

The next step is to aggregate like-source information together (*build classes*) and establish links or relationships between like classes of sources. Those familiar with object-oriented design techniques are familiar with this approach. For example, in traditional batch processing systems of organizations, programs aggregate and process similar transactions together. At this stage it is important to ensure proper cohesiveness and coupling in systems. Each subsystem must be cohesive, that is, it must have one goal. This goal is reflected in its ability to manage the *class* of data that is involved. Links among subsystems must be coupled in a manner so as to have a smooth flow of information while preventing extensive dependence on the other subsystems. This appears to be where most signals of developing crisis get lost. While many organizations use a class of system intended for Enterprise Resource Planning (ERP), the architecture is not truly of "enterprise" but rather a hodgepodge of inherited systems, sometimes recently installed with older equipment or from other organizations they have merged with or acquired. Rather than trying to integrate these systems in an effective manner, many have tied them together loosely and without any global concept in mind. This leads to poor information movement across departments and groups in the organization. The virtual crisis center would provide a seamless map of information movements across sectors of the organization.

Signals include information and, to be useful, information must be acted upon. Failure to act on information may be related to the fact that the signal is improperly received and makes little or no sense. By example, consider what is needed to maintain a functioning photocopier. Long before the printer stops functioning, signs of its failure are present—diminishing toner strength, longer print times, poor quality, and so on. If these are monitored and acted on in a timely fashion, there will be no need to use so-called preventive mechanisms. The next step in design is to have adequate tools and technologies in place that will allow for cohesive *sensemaking*. To accomplish this, two elements must be in place.

First, a repertoire of past signals and their effects should be cataloged so that an organization can gain from cyclical information from historic feedback. Unless an organization can learn from the past, its chances for future successes in evading crisis are restricted. This requires a data warehouse that allows for interoperable and temporal databases. There is a need to be able to link to an artificial intelligence technique, for example, neural networks that will continuously learn new patterns and signal an impending crisis. Prototypes of such designs might involve the study of daily loads and traffic patterns and signal when a server is expected to fail. The second facet of sensemaking is to have adequate decision support and planning tools to establish a repertoire of "what if" scenarios. This practice facilitates the decision-making process by augmenting limitations in human processing. One of the key aspects of decision support systems is their ability to aid in problem visualization or "spatial" representation. Such approaches foster problem structuring by connecting the various components of interest, presenting the information in a meaningful manner, and calculating costs of decisions. While information systems can aid in suggesting directed information or insights and deducing patterns, they cannot generate *complete actionable* meaning. The human aspect of tacit knowledge and experience with the problem domain are employed at this stage. At a rudimentary level we can have expert systems that automate reasoning and suggest actions, but for more complex tasks human intelligence is still needed.

Second, integration of the existing information processing systems is salient. We must strive to have a seamless flow of information through the disparate and heterogeneous systems of the organization. This can be accomplished through the building of pipelines or connectors. Translators also play a critical role. Translators are programs or devices that enable us to have two disparate systems communicate. A translator either serves as the lowest common denominator in terms of a common language or can interface between schemas of two distinct languages. We are not revisiting the general discussion of data integration cost-benefits of fifteen years ago; we are calling for a judicious choice of crisis-relevant data connection between those systems not yet appropriately connected. The ability to make sense of information from different information systems will become easier in the near future with the diffusion of markup languages such as XML, which do more to describe data contained within information packets or objects.

Once integrated, the next step—the creation of the virtual center itself—involves presentation and representation of the information. This is accomplished on the Internet. The goal here is to design a Web site with all the necessary bells and whistles to make information presentable much like in the form of a car's dashboard. The use of active server pages (ASP) and other database export languages should make this relatively easy. The goal should be to make all necessary information cleanly presentable. Last, we need to ensure integrity and protection of our center. While much of the center can be made available to members of the organization, only a dedicated group of individuals should have the ability to make modifications to the core architecture. Each person in the organization should be allowed to personalize their view of the system to reflect the needs of their task, but authorization determines who will have access and at what level of security.

The requirements for establishing a remote information center in contingency planning and emergency preparedness come with some expense. But the expense is justified given our current political and economic climate. Each of the *Fortune* 200 companies (F2C) will need to have their own virtual crisis center. The sheer amount of signals generated and dissipated by these organizations coupled with their global reach and 24/7 operations demands specialized attention. It is futile to think that two F2C organizations might, in attempts to save on costs, consider sharing such a resource. If the same crisis were to hit both organizations at once, a single center would be unable to sustain the attention.

Virtual information centers will become a necessity as we face even more uncertain economic and political times. As witnessed by the tragedies of 9/11, those organizations that were not able to restore services within a couple of days after the attack never survived the disaster. The losses experienced in those few hours in terms of information and knowledge losses represented irreplaceable damage. Organizations need to be capable of reestablishing their online presence within minutes, not hours and days, after a disruption of their services. Remote crisis centers will enable them to do at least that and likely more. The clear benefit of such centers stems from an initiative that reflects preparedness and determination through actions to mitigate and possibly evade some of the consequences related to crisis.

Input Readdressed

The lifeblood of any system is its input. Organizations deal with a vast array of inputs. It is important to spend some time discussing what makes good "input." Inputs can be defined as measurements on *aspects* of objects and agents of interest. Put another way, as defined by Stevens, it is "the assignment of numbers to aspects of objects or events according to one or another rule or convention."[5] It is important to clarify an important point. Objects and agents are not measured per se; some *aspect* of them is measured. Aspects include behaviors, actions, characteristics, and the like. For example, we cannot truly measure a person, but we can measure one's motivation, stress level, an so on.

It is fair to state that our current society and way of life are predicated on having adequate measures.[6] Measures are ubiquitous: job performance, the currency we trade, cost of goods, and income, for example. It is impossible to think of life where we have inconsistent and unreliable measures. For instance, consider what would happen if two carpenters working together on furniture were to use different measures. Simple differences like the use of the metric system versus the American system could make for a painful construction experience. Similar to society, organizations need to have reliable measures in order to conduct optimal information processing, leading to better decision-making.

An adequate measure must meet several criterions. First and foremost it must adequately represent the phenomena of interest, that is, the aspect of the agent or object we are interested in. The concept of isomorphism is salient here. As pointed out by Pedhazur and Schmelkin, "measurement consists of mapping a set of objects onto a set of numbers, such that there is *isomorphism* between the objects measured and the numbers assigned to them."[7] Second measures need to be timely. Delayed or non–real-time measures in most cases are useless, for example, if one wanted the price of a stock at 9 A.M., providing the stock price at 9:15 A.M. is not appropriate. Third, measures need to be calibrated on the appropriate scale. There are four major scales—nominal, ordinal, interval, and ratio.[8] A nominal scale assigns numbers as labels for objects or agents mainly for the purposes of classification. For example, days of the week can be represented as 1, 2, 3, 4, 5, 6, and 7. "1" could represent Saturday, Sunday, or Monday; "2" would be the day that succeeds "1." It is important to note that assignment of numbers to days does not imply any kind of order; for example, day "7" is not greater or less than day "1." The ordinal scale, as the name implies, assigns numbers to objects and agents in rank order. An interval scale is an ordinal scale with the added feature of equal intervals between the ranks. The difference between a temperature reading of 45°F and 60°F is the same as the difference between 55°F and 70°F. Finally, a ratio scale is an interval scale with a true or absolute zero. Items such as income and age are measured on a ratio scale, for each of these it is not possible to have negative values. Knowledge of which type of scale a measurement is based on is critical to choosing the appropriate method of processing and interpreting it. For instance, it would be useless in most cases to compute the differences or rank order of nominally based measures. Fourth, measurements are made on indicators of the object or agent; we measure the length of the rectangle, not the rectangle. Due to the indirectness in the way measurement is conducted, it is important to have indicators that are directly affected by the agent or object or one that is highly correlated with it.[9] Otherwise, the measures we calibrate will be useless as they do not represent the phenomena of interest. For example, if one wanted to measure how intelligent a person is, using an indicator such as height or weight is a poor choice of indicator to measure.

While the above guidelines are for the most part basic, they are not *trivial*. As stated by famous physicist Lord Kelvin: "If you cannot measure it—if you cannot express it in quantitative terms—then your knowledge is of a meager and insignificant kind." In order to appropriately manage something, you need to be able to adequately measure it. Measurements are inputs, hence they are means and not the end. Measurements need to be adequately processed to lend useful information. As the old adage goes—garbage in, garbage out; it is common to find poor measurements in organizations. The hope is that through the use of sophisticated information processing techniques such as statistical analysis, somehow poor use of measures will be transformed into useful information.[10] Poor measures not only result in poor information, but also waste valuable organizational resources. The opportunity cost of resources involved in the processing of information can be quite high. Hence it is important to get our measures right in order to optimally manage information in organizations.

Processing Readdressed

Once inputs are in order, the next step involves their processing. Processing, as we have already talked about, can take multiple forms. It can be as simple as computing the average for a series of numbers, or handle more complex matters such as exploratory or data-mining activities. Moreover, it is the processing of information that leads us to actionable knowledge. While the sophistication of processing mechanisms can be varied, some universal concerns need to be attended to.

Foremost is the issue of fault tolerance. Humans are error-prone and as such, the machines we design have innate errors. While trying to avoid errors altogether may not be possible either because of technological or economic considerations, we can strive to minimize the occurrence of errors. Moreover, if errors do occur, we can devise adequate checks and balances to minimize the extent of their damage thus building a reliable system. A reliable system should behave in a predictable, consistent manner regardless of the point through which it is accessed: there should be no contradiction between the actions and state of the system at different locations, the system as a whole should do only what it was designed to do, and the system should manage or operate itself with minimal human intervention. Reliability also has the additional properties of self-management, real-time responsiveness, data recoverability, security, and the ability of a system to tolerate incorrect input.

Some basic guidelines one should adhere to while building systems to ensure reliability include the following. First, a system should be as simple as possible in order to achieve its required functions. Second, one is reminded that perfection is not necessarily reached when there is nothing to add, but nothing to take away. Third, in most systems there should be no single points of failure. Failures can come in a variety of forms, and often appear to be more creative than those anticipated by the system designer. Systems must be run through multiple rounds of testing with varying complexity of test cases to ensure that *most* faults can be detected early on; design very simple systems that have a higher chance of being correct and are easy to prove correct.

Besides reliability we must also be concerned with coupling. As stressed early on in the book, loosely coupled systems are one's best option. This will ensure that parts of the systems with errors and faults can be removed and quarantined from the rest of the system. Moreover, highly sensitive systems, such as those with classified documents, need to be secured during times of crises. Recently the Welchia virus hit the U.S. State Department's computer network.[11] Once the virus was detected, the systems housing the classified documents were able to be detached from the rest of the network. Failure to have such a feature in place can result in the whole system crashing. Many times organizations have tight coupling in place that causes cascading failures—when one part is affected, it affects another, and so on until the whole system crashes. In today's information world, the problem gets a bit more complex, as we now have interorganization systems. When two or more organizations decide to exchange information, they are now vulnerable to failures that occur in their partners' information systems, too. Some of the more sophisticated viruses can spread through to more than one network.

Additionally, one must appreciate the complexity associated with the concept of *distributed* systems. Distributed systems survive on optimal communication, but as we all know, communication is subject to noise and channel maturity. Messages between systems can be lost, corrupted, or even delivered in duplicate or out of order. Message loss is the primary communication problem with which a distributed system must cope. This is typically handled using an acknowledgement/transmission strategy. This is where a recipient acknowledges the receipt of a message prior to the sender sending the next message. By including sequence numbers in messages, damaged messages can be detected and suppressed and out-of-order messages put in order.

Fourth, the need for "currency" is important. Systems should be regarded as living organisms. As humans need to go in for regular acts of maintenance and checkups, so do systems. Most systems that fail are outdated and poorly maintained. We use the term *outdated* to reflect a system that is not keeping up with the pace of time. Recently, many computers were attacked by malicious programs, including the Blaster worm.[12] It is interesting to note that Microsoft has notified its users to update their systems via a patch available online at its Web site. Many system administrators failed in this task. This allowed for the proliferation of the worm across the Internet, which followed the schema similar to those associated with chaos theory.

Managing Users: The Need for Counterintelligence

The recent incidents including the debacles at Enron, Arthur Andersen, and the fallout in telecommunications companies require a question to be raised— could any of these have been prevented? While legislative measures have been enacted to address this concern, none may be sufficient to address the real problem. Laws are intended to outline parameters and punishments associated with crimes. Laws do not go into effect until they are exercised, which means a crime will have to be reported before action against offenders may be initiated. We are forced to face the fact that the distance between active legislation and criminal detection is vast.

Any agent (employee) who knowingly and willfully contemplates acts, conspires to act, or executes acts against the will of his/her principal (organization) is an enemy of the organization. Most organizations are owned by shareholders who appoint their board of directors to oversee the well-being of the organization. These individuals in turn are responsible for the hiring and firing of senior management personnel, such as the chief executive officer and his subordinates, the basic tenet being that these individuals will work in the best interests of their principals. But since we are again seeing separation between the entity owners, who have a pretty focused idea on what they wish to accomplish, and ultimately the employee, who may not be as attached to the company mission statement as his boss might suspect, emergent problems may occur. While most principals do act in the interest of their organization, it takes only a few managers at lower tiers to create damage.

We argue for the more prominent role of counterintelligence activities in organizations. While the field of competitive intelligence is alive and well, recently we have seen a surge of interest in the area of counterintelligence. These have taken the form of employee surveillance, background checks, security clearances, an so on. After the events of 9/11, organizations are more terrified than ever of their vulnerability to an attack. In that vein, most have beefed up their external perimeter security (for example, metal detectors, policy changes, random drug testing of screened hires), while internally not much has changed. A problem occurs when one gains a legitimate (or illegitimate) internal access to an organization's environment and then decides to do damage.

The counterintelligence unit of the firm should be likened to similar teams used in law enforcement and the military. These teams must be composed of some of the best internal minds, and they should be also external specialists. Characteristics of such individuals include their ability to be operable, flexible, adaptable, exaptable, and agile.

At the lowest level such teams must be operable. They must contribute to increasing the effectiveness and efficiencies of operations in the organization. In order to be operable, such teams must be independent of the other agents in the organization. The counterintelligence teams must be independent in function and report only to the board of directors. Having it otherwise will compromise their functionality. A committee of the board, which will also have responsibility for approving intelligence gathering and monitoring, should monitor their tasks. At the next level the team must enable an organization to be flexible and should be flexible. Flexibility is defined by range and response.[13] Range represents the alternatives of possible system changes, while response represents the reaction time needed to respond to such changes. The team efforts at this level enable an organization to perform outside its predefined bounds through modification of input consumption and output production. Flexibility calls for higher-order knowledge processing, as merely reporting on what is currently being carried out will not accomplish the goal; to carry this out one needs to go through scenario and sensitivity analysis. Adaptability is the accumulation of small changes over time in response to the changing environment.[14] Counterintelligence teams cannot be static, they need to continuously learn and adapt based on changes in the environment. Teams at this level must enable an organization to modify its structure in response to changes in the environment without drastic disruption to current form in response to changes in the marketplace. A key determinant of a team at this level is the ability to analyze and synthesize undefined signals. While adaptation is accumulation of small changes over time to improve an existing function, exaptation is accumulation of small changes that results in development of a new function. Counterintelligence teams must be able to either develop new functions or use existing functions in a nontraditional role. The first task can be achieved through identification of new opportunities for an organization to investigate, and invest into that which fosters its mission. The second task can be accomplished through utilizing knowledge generated from traditional systems in novel manners. Agility is defined as the ability to cope with unexpected changes, to survive unprecedented threats of business environment, and to take advantage of changes as opportunities.[15] A counterintelligence team at the agile level must allow for development of high quality and highly customized products and services with high information content, mobilization of core competencies, intraenterprise and interenterprise integration, localized exploitation of resources, and business scope redefinition.

A fundamental principle in management suggests that if everything were always running smoothly, there would be no need for managers. Managers are given certain authority, presumably prescribed within the value-frame of the organization, to perform actions required to keep the proverbial ship on course. While no manager can control the wind, he is expected to adjust the sails of the ship for which he is responsible. Such adjustments contribute to the organization's ability to sustain itself and keep on course; those who handle the rigging determine its ultimate success.

We suggest that organizations interested in averting crises establish independent teams designated as "untouchables" under an ad hoc intelligence gathering banner. Such teams should be comprised of internal as well as external monitoring personnel who have a proclivity for creativity, a trait that is unfortunately constrained by traditional organization schemes. The internal components must represent personnel who have a clear understanding of the organization's value system and have access to decision-makers. The external group(s) should be flexible enough to understand the organization's values yet be sufficiently detached so their input is objective. Techniques used by both groups should be established along similar lines so their language is compatible. An example of an analysis tool to aid in this effort includes semiotic models, which involve signal detection processes intended to synthesize information. All members among such cadres should be encouraged to employ programs that relate to the notions of the PCA model discussed earlier in chapter 7. Communication channels to decision-makers must be direct with the understanding that information produced by the ad hoc teams, because of its objectivity, is likely to be in conflict with other information sources. But it may be just such a conflict that produces the unexpected benefit of uncovering an unforeseen organizational vulnerability to allow the option of avoidance before a problem materializes. This is the strength of the ad hoc system focused on emergent processes.

It is quite likely that the individuals charged with forming ad hoc teams would not fit the more common description of an organizational supervisor. In the first instance this is because of the knowledge worker who is aware of the organization's faults or weaknesses, especially within a specific department. However, people in organizations soon learn that criticism of systems or certain decisions is unpopular. As a result a popular myth akin to the children's story concerning *the emperor's new clothes* is perpetuated, and this condition is unfortunate. To be effective, organizations must consciously seek criticism and be prepared to acknowledge shortcomings that need addressing. The easiest way to find the people who may offer constructive criticism is to listen! Few New York City firefighters from among the rank and file were stunned as the experts had been that the Twin Towers had been targeted for destruction. This may be because many of them live under the threat that when the reality of such catastrophe strikes, it is they, not the experts, who will be called upon to respond. Still, it is unlikely that these workers had been polled for their input prior to the disaster.

An ad hoc team represents the employment of untapped resources within the organization but does not necessarily translate into participatory management, lest that be a concern. It involves personnel in a novel, often encouraging way and serves to benefit the company and the employee who receives recognition and possible compensation for effort. This efficient use of employees to create a new knowledge base for the organization is not a new concept (Nonaka), but the ad hoc application for a specific intention is.

The counterintelligence units in organizations must monitor and protect the information assets of the organization. In doing so, they must be able to prevent unauthorized tampering with and unscrupulous application of information. Moreover, they must help alleviate concerns with misuse of information, especially with acts that involve agents within the organization. These are similar to "blue on blue" attacks in the battlefield.

"Blue on Blue" Attacks: Friendly Fire

Friendly fire, a military term, is the deployment of friendly weapons and munitions with the intent to kill the enemy or destroy his equipment and facilities resulting in unforeseen and unintentional death and injury to friendly personnel.[16] These represent blue on blue attacks in which soldiers belonging to the same side attack each other. This occurs mainly due to the poor availability of information on enemy locations and is also a function of the battlefield terrain. Battlefield terrain can impair visibility and hence increase the chance of an attack. It is interesting to note that in older wars the occurrence of fratricide was low. This was due mainly to the fact that wars were of a simpler magnitude and there were no exchanges of resources between countries. By simpler wars we mean that battlefield formations were mainly linear, hence the chance of shooting your own men was low. Moreover, there was no exchange of military arsenals between countries. Hence, if one spotted a German tank, one could be reasonably sure that Germans drove it. Today, battlefield scenarios are much more complex. Reconnaissance missions, coalition-based wars, and the like make for complex setups. Moreover, with weapons proliferation and exchanges between countries, it is no longer sufficient to just identify the type of armed vehicle, but also who is in it. It was the United States after all that provided weapons and trained bin Laden and the Taliban to fight against the Russians during the 1980s.

"Friendly fire" casualties are disturbingly common in organizations; often they are the consequence of intentional actions. Cited examples include the events leading to 9/11, but others can be found among the memos of NASA or Union Carbide. In each case the organization had information prior to disasters and elected to disregard or otherwise not to act on it. As a result, this type of friendly fire has members of the same organization attacking each other due to poor processing of information that led to crisis. Other examples involve *infighting,* a variation of "finger-pointing," as was the case involving Western intelligence sources and the claim that Iraq sought to buy weapons-grade uranium from Niger. In each case the fire is intended more to deflect attention than resolve issues related to where or how breakdowns in information flow occurred so they might be averted in the future. Such squabbling serves to weaken the intelligence sharing activities between participants, in this case, between England's MI6 and the CIA. When U.S. jets bombed Canadian soldiers on training exercises in Iraq, casualties and repercussions were placed squarely on pilot error while little public attention was focused on the conditions that allowed the incident to occur. This is tantamount to placing a simple bandage on a hemorrhaging wound; the likelihood that similar events will take place remains well within the realm of possibilities.

Organizations must clearly strive to use information wisely. In fact, information is their weapon of choice against their enemies (their competitors) and should not be a cause of infighting within the organization. Infighting can cause issues within the culture of the organization.

Organization culture, that is, how personnel interact within the context of the organization, presents the best proving ground for conditions that can prevent many of the problems associated with information problems in organizations. Culture is a learned product of group experiences that have been consistently and mutually shared.[17] Adherence to the conditions of organizational culture requires participants' total compliance and the unwavering belief among its members that the organization's way is the best way. If such conditions exist, the organization is seen as speaking with one voice; if they do not, the organization should anticipate problems. After the FBI found Robert Hanssen had been working for the Russians for over a decade, selling secrets that he personally hand-carried out of his office, they discovered someone who was living outside of their culture. Hanssen was able to provide his organization with obvious trappings associated with its culture, that is, he never complained, probably accepted assignments without complaint, dressed the part, was punctual, and had otherwise "fit" the general notion of its culture without the organization considering the possibility of a flaw.

The "flaw" had exhibited itself early in his career when Hanssen complained of the lack of recognition for his work and what he considered his contribution to the organization. He intentionally transferred his aggressions into activities that included learning and accessing digital files that involved a certain degree of computer literacy. It is likely that Hanssen was aware that other agents were either uncomfortable or reluctant to be involved with some of the bureau's computerized applications and that worked to Hanssen's advantage since he would become the "go to" guy in situations regarding computer access. Based on his frequent use of the equipment, it did not seem uncommon for him to ask for greater authority and access to more classified files. The organization encouraged but never rewarded Hanssen's apparent zeal to be of service as a "team player." And it never considered Hanssen's real motives. Although the FBI was aware that some information was likely going over to the Russians, they had erroneously attributed it to a spy ring that had been exposed earlier and never regarded the possibility that the FBI's culture had been violated.

The use of information within organizations might have prevented the embarrassment that visited the FBI as a result of the Hanssen incident. One approach would have involved a system's administrator attending to a real-time log of access by all agents to particularly sensitive documents or objects within the organization. Although the FBI computer system was not particularly sophisticated at the time Hanssen was gathering information for the Russians, the techniques for tracking file use was in place but not used. As with other information, if it is not used, it is worthless.

The idea of such oversight involves the notion of *collusion to prevent collision*. The notion of "collusion" involves agreement, involvement, and consent. If all parties who have access to information are aware that their activities are being monitored, they are less likely to take unprivileged advantage of the systems. Because such practices involve policy, the practice becomes part of the organizational culture. Involvement by the members of the organization creates conditions in which individuals are more sensitive and aware of the probability of questionable activity by users or breaches in accepted practices.

Conclusion

In this chapter we have presented illustrations from organizational models that handle information processing in distinct manners. We have seen that while the same information may be available to multiple agencies, how an agency handles the flow of information will determine whether the information is useful. Organization structures either enhance or inhibit the flow of information. This relates to how the units of the organization are coupled or related through dependencies. Interagency use of remote information centers can serve to correct deficiencies that may be present in traditional organizational designs as well as certain unanticipated dependencies because such sites are exclusively dedicated to processing information and less tied to relationships determined by organizational charts.

Other alternatives that can assist to preserve and enhance information that otherwise might be overlooked is to employ preemptive "countermeasures" intended to avert the possibilities often associated with "friendly fire." Such measures are heavily dependent on the involvement of competent personnel who serve as practitioners in their respective fields within the organization who are well acquainted with an organization's culture. Ironically, these people are often overlooked by organizations, although they represent a highly valuable asset to organizations. In the future this tendency must be addressed to correct other predictable consequences.

In concluding this text, it is our intention to address some of the future considerations affecting organizations of information. Before that, however, we will present a review of the preceding chapters as an outline, which suggests when and how an organization might tackle the task of applying the ideas presented thus far. Use of the outline will give readers a fairly good idea of where their organization stands in this new age of information dependency based on its present state of data collection and storage. New organizations should find the outline useful for establishing sound practices for the management of their information.

10

Recap and Real Time

In reviewing what has been covered, there may be a tendency for some to want to prioritize or otherwise rank topics as to which issues should be addressed first; this brings up some interesting points. While most organizations will have some of what has been discussed thus far included in their own plans, the sequential order of the chapters presented might be applied to a Gantt chart to demonstrate the order in which issues should be addressed. The time line presented is arbitrary but represents a realistic interpretation of when and how much attention should initially be given to issues related to information before permanent changes are made (Figure 10.1). The "arrows" indicate areas that require continued assessment.

Note that in the section "Organization Understanding" the topic of "entropy" is considered important enough to initiate the process of studying organizations of information. Recapping the conditions and effects of entropy, it should be remembered that once the entropic process begins, it is irreversible. For this reason it is important to review the most current and existing information and retrieve what is salvageable. By salvageable, we expect that in reviewing information status, the investigators are likely to discover some that have deteriorated from a point of initial usefulness because of the effects of entropy. Examples might include "held" information, information related to meetings that never materialized, project plans, or distribution schedules that were delayed to the point that the technology or value of the information, once considered applicable to a project, is now outdated.

The first chapter also included information that serves as the basis for grounded theory, that is, data upon which other theories may be developed. The nuances involved in *semantics* describe the ease with which information can be altered by interpretation. This error occurs because of a failure to bridge the gap between what is intended and what is interpreted. Often, this type error is the result of audience response, that is, the information

Figure 10.1 **Time Line**

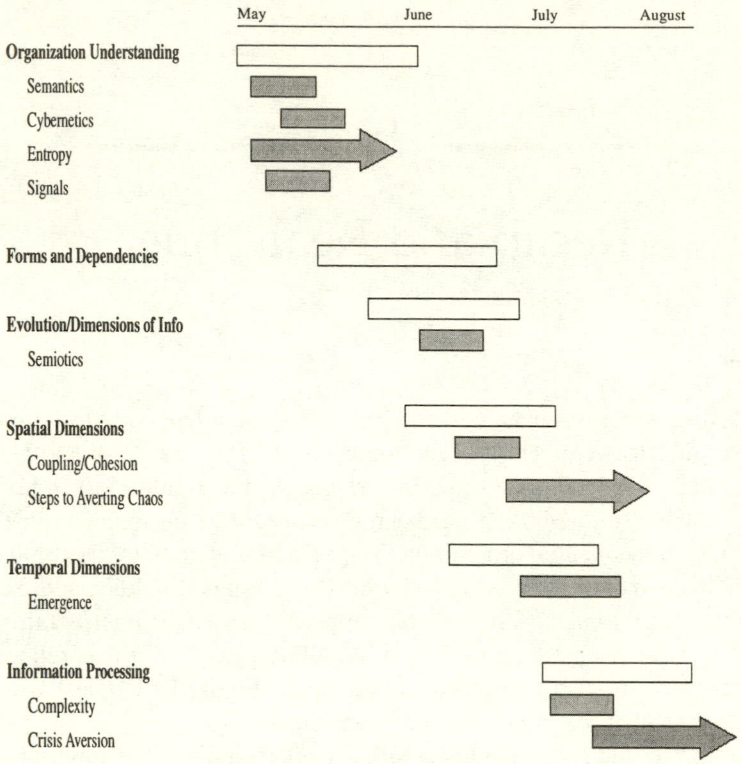

	May	June	July	August

Organization Understanding
Semantics
Cybernetics
Entropy
Signals

Forms and Dependencies

Evolution/Dimensions of Info
Semiotics

Spatial Dimensions
Coupling/Cohesion
Steps to Averting Chaos

Temporal Dimensions
Emergence

Information Processing
Complexity
Crisis Aversion

recipient *reads* something into the received message that defeats intention. This may result for a variety of reasons but is often associated with mixed agendas between those who generate information and those who receive it.

The concept of cybernetics views all entities as living things that are subject to principal laws affecting organisms. Information viewed as a living entity must be nurtured and capable of adaptation if it is to survive or evolve. Through cybernetics we see the first instance that stresses *interdependency* in the design of systems as being a vital consideration to the success and survival of information; *it is all connected.*

Both cybernetics and semantics then are connected with information and its flow because both rely on signals to convey the message. While signals are generally thought of in terms of some mechanically generated indicators, whether via smoke signals or more elaborate digital or analog telephony techniques, they are also generated through gestures, conversations, pictures, and reports. But anything along the transmission chain that is capable of distortion to a signal device also disrupts the message, regardless of the means of conveyance. By example, noise in a signal line may result in the partial transmission of a message while the body language of the listeners can indicate that they are preoccupied with other thoughts that can serve to block the intention of the message. Both examples reflect directly on the semantics and meaning of a message. Cybernetics is useful in determining whether the message has been effective despite the effects of semantics, because it weighs the interpretation and usefulness of meaning in terms of its "fit" to the task at hand. If the information fits the task at hand, that is, if it is useful, it will contribute to the adaptation process necessary to acquire knowledge. If not, the signal's message is likely to perish.

When information is successfully delivered, its concepts, related to similar messages, work to strengthen it as a candidate for knowledge within the organization, and knowledge is the basis for action. An interruption in the delivery of information serves to contribute to the defeat of any potentially useful content contained in the message because of conditions associated with entropy. Entropy represents a state of disorganization within a system, and while some purists may disagree, we maintain it also represents high degrees of uncertainty within such systems. The main effect of entropy results in a nonalterable state of conditions which, when maximized, is not reversible, that is, once something is influenced by entropy, it will never be the same. Entropy may begin slowly but once maximized, it demonstrates a plateau that represents the combining effects of existing conditions within a system and that which has been added. For information, this can indicate that data, once potentially useful, becomes engulfed by or otherwise relegated to areas other than where it was intended. At maximum entropy the information becomes ineffective to serve the conditions for which it was intended. By example, when memos to NASA that indicated the possibility of problems associated with mechanical failures during failed missions were ignored, that information was subsumed under the effects of entropy.

The chapter *Information Forms and Dependence* relates specifically to how individual organizations are arranged to handle information. Here we discuss the notions of spatial and temporal information processing to differentiate between how new and stored information is received, used, or archived into what some refer to as an "organizational memory." It is our contention that a third processing technique, evolutionary, should be employed in order to force greater attention on the relational dependence between new and stored information. Several inhibitors to information acquisition or use of information are presented in this chapter as common barriers, often unintentionally "built into" organizations because of a cultural predisposition or tendency of dependency on past practices. Old structures are the easiest targets of opportunity for information failures since they are the slowest to react and adapt to environmental changes because of an inability to recognize the difference between tacit and implicit knowledge within the organization, perception problems leading to hubris, and the lack of regard as to how information affects behavior.

To assist in overcoming some of the problems presented in the preceding chapter, chapter 4 deals with the semiotic model for information synthesis. Using a cybernetic approach, we initially compare evolution in living beings to evolution of information in order to stress the notion of adaptability for survival. In addition to many of the concepts discussed earlier in the text, this chapter demonstrates the process whereby data is synthesized to information and further qualified for the purpose of developing "actionable knowledge." Actionable knowledge involves the use of information to modify the behavior of individuals within the organization. The authors initially coined the term, but its first "public" use was during the news debriefing by the military following the capture of Saddam Hussein in describing the use of specific intelligence material to direct the mission. Chapter 4 also provides an example involving events prior to September 11 in which information gathering and sharing was far less effective, and suggests that if the steps associated with the semiotic model had been employed, those charged with national security could have been far better prepared to avert if not avoid some of the eventual consequences that may be traced to the mishandling of information.

Chapter 5 discusses the importance of how information delivery systems are arranged in order to promote both effectiveness and efficiency. The initial details in the chapter have to do with hardware, but the importance of *coupling and cohesiveness* is addressed later to emphasize how *information results* may vary depending on how information contained in any signal is conveyed. While some designs are intentionally arranged to stress one aspect (effectiveness *or* efficiency) to the detriment of the other, maximizing both presents the optimal conditions for information handling. The arrangements discussed are as applicable to organizational structures and how information traverses those structures as they are to physical stacking of devices. In concluding this chapter, the notion of chaos is addressed in terms of an unexpected condition that results because of the inattention to initial details. While the definition may be simple enough to understand the condition of chaos when it appears, it suggests that few take the time to practice the preventive techniques required to avert it. One method that may be employed toward averting conditions of chaos involves the notion of *"emergence."*

In chapter 6 the ad hoc approach, founded in emergence theory, is presented. Emergence involves an understanding of those "building blocks" that serve as the underpinning to the core functions of an organization. As with a physical building, if the foundation becomes exposed to changing conditions that are detrimental but nevertheless ignored, it is likely that problems will eventually occur. Of critical importance here is the fact that those building blocks are continually subject to change, and inattention to this fact may result in dire consequences. For example, critics of current antiterrorism plans are correct in their assessment that attention should be diverted from what terrorist groups have accomplished in the past and instead become more focused on what they are capable of now. Similarly, crisis management planners might do more by considering a variety of "what if" scenarios rather than emphasizing hypothetical conditions for recovery after expected crisis conditions occur. The success of an emergent approach to the use of information results from the *flexibility and talent* of the personnel assigned to employ ad hoc techniques in order to adapt at least some phases of organizational structure before a problem develops. This begs for the provision of "think tanks" within organizations, whose sole responsibility would involve creating theories related to conditions rather than to existing data.

If one accepts *complexity* as a condition of being dependent on the sensitivity involving activities of many agents within any system, the ideas expressed in chapters 5 and 6 become more focused; this is the intention of chapter 7. By understanding the notion of complexity, one is more prepared to take initial steps toward a program intended to avert rather than contend with crisis situations. Most research into crisis situations indicates that all were predictable in that there was adequate information available prior to the crisis which, if acted upon, could have averted subsequent conditions. Action invariably falters, however, because of a misunderstanding of the causal relations brought on by organizational dependencies and player relations that are best described in terms of complexity. Subsequent chapters described the role of game theory and how players and agents within the organization serve to enhance or inhibit information flow, and addressed optimal models of information design, including the need for learning. Now, chapter 11 looks at future concerns involving information in relation to technologies and new needs.

11

The Future of Information Processing

Predicting the future is never an easy task. Alan Kay put it succinctly: "The best way to predict the future is to invent it." In this final chapter we offer a few informed predictions on what the future of information processing might hold. We base much of our predictions on the study of the history of computing and information processing. The central discourse for much of our discussion in this book has been the idea of cybernetics. Norbert Weiner, Claude Shannon, Vannevar Bush, John von Neumann, Alan Turing, John Ash, and many others have contributed greatly to the field of cybernetics, which was developed as the science that led to the development of the current information processors. From the early days of large mainframes to the current slew of PC gadgets, the concerns for computing have been to increase performance (that is, improve the quality and speed of feedback) while making the machines more ubiquitous and pervasive (that is, reducing the size and cost) in our society. Market expectations will continue to feed this trend, focusing first on the convergence of telephony and computing. We are currently at the stage where desktops have the power once belonging to the exclusive domain of mainframes. In the future, machines will appear more like flexible sheets of lightweight portable plastic to be unrolled when required, and their power will be derived from the signals they receive. The driving force for development at this stage is entertainment, as the majority of PC users employ their machines for a variety of tasks, many of which are not directly related to "computing." But for organizations that will become more information-dependent in the future, we anticipate the immediate future in the following sections. Before we consider the future, we should first quickly review the current past.

Where We Are Today

About fifty years ago, technology reached the masses so that a radio the size of a small lunchbox could be carried and played *without wires*, thanks to transistors. At about the same time, a cathode tube powered room-size computers, and messages were sent as signals in binary code. Telephones of that time were strictly analog devices, which sent discrete signals between parties in much the same way that telephonic messages had been delivered since the turn of the century. But as technology advanced, there came the time when the term "convergence" among all of these existing appliances came into play. Convergence relates to the point where all similar technologies might be joined, where common threads tie related knowledge together. Among the electronic devices mentioned, convergence met and joined at a common spot where communication was supported by signals that carried information to individuals and organizations. And convergence indicated that faster ways to port information would have to be developed because there would be more users.

This notion proposed a method that allowed telephones and computers to communicate via devices such as modems. The next phase in communication at the point of convergence would involve signal standards for clear interpretation and transfer techniques. Bandwidth then came under consideration as more signal devices required "channeling" in the airwaves, similar to determining channel selection on a car radio. Later the size of the information content being delivered raised issues requiring stronger send-receive machinery and better delivery techniques. Today, handheld devices carry more power than the full-size computers of the early 1980s, and the best is yet to come. Yet each of the devices mentioned has but one common purpose, that is, information delivery.

Organizations are not likely to keep pace with the innovations in technology involving information delivery systems. Individuals on the other hand will make it their business to keep up with the latest changes, and some of those people will not be working for the common good. While several firms realize the competitive importance of monitoring and employing strong information technology, most do not. Our intention in presenting this book was to address the variety of issues and promote understanding with regard to information uses within organizations; essentially it is intended to assist in building bridges between what, in information, is intended and what, from information, is interpreted. The use of information, whether it is used correctly or not, *will form the organization*.

The Future

To aid in systematizing our discussion of the future, we segment it into three areas—hardware, software, and communication (or mediums). While these are three interrelated areas, treating them distinctly will help make for an easier, more digestible read. As in our discussions regarding complexity, innovation in each area will affect the other areas. Moore's Law still governs much of what takes place in the hardware development. Gordon Moore, the founder of Intel, predicted that the number of transistors on a microprocessor would double approximately every eighteen months to bring down costs associated with computing. To date this prediction has been surprisingly accurate. Hardware devices are becoming smaller, leaner, and more powerful. The PC on your desk today is cheaper in real money value than earlier models and is superior in terms of computing power. Interestingly, this came about as a case in which the tail was wagging the dog. In the early years of computing, because of restricted capacity, programmers were forced to "write lean," meaning fewer instructions so there would be memory left to execute the application. But as the public wanted more performance, more graphics, and better displays, memory types and sizes increased and software developers were encouraged to do whatever was required to produce the desired effects; the machines would catch up.

The software revolution also continues at full pace. Until quite recently you needed to be educated in the computer or information sciences to be able to program software. Today that is not really necessary. At one time a company might be required to take on a Java programmer who might command, in 1999, as much as $125 per hour to develop an application. Today a (smart) high school kid will probably do the same job during a lunch break. Software is becoming easier to write and more *open*. Extensive efforts by individuals such as Richard M. Stallman, Larry Wall, and Eric Raymond have revolutionized the concept of software from that which is produced by a few (secretively) and consumed by many to that which is openly developed by an entire community of users who share knowledge freely and improve the state-of-the-art for the betterment of the entire community.[1] The concept of *openness* is salient; software is moving out of the realm of becoming a private asset of a programmer to that which is built in a community where there is an open exchange of code, ideas, and methods. Software will also help in our ability to parse through the information. The processes of information mining and discovery will be salient as the amount of information increases at an exponential pace.

Communication mediums have also undergone radical reengineering. We have been able to increase the power of bandwidth at an astonishing pace while maintaining reliability and integrity of messages. Moreover, communication devices are able to transmit a wide range of mediums from basic data and voice to images and video; information is taking on many forms.

The future of information processing will involve a fresh perception of the role of information within organizations; information will attain the function of a commodity. Because it will assume value, it will have to be authenticated.

Recently, while attending a talk on "information integrity," one of the speakers asked the audience if anyone ever inspected the contents label on a can of Campbell's soup. His point was, what assurance does a consumer have that the can of soup one purchases has the ingredients on the label, or what guarantees are in place that assures the ingredients are in the right quantities? Now use a similar analogy when reviewing a phone or credit card bill. Most people spend time and effort inspecting the accuracy of the information presented there to ensure that it matches what is expected. We are less inclined to accept that information presented is accurate at face value. But these habits are likely to change as information certification and assurance programs are beginning to take shape; these will help make information certifiable. Moreover, there will be efforts attempted to better process varied types of human physiological and behavioral features to assist in generating authentication schemes. Information considered certifiable and valuable will not come free, even from within organizational exchanges. We expect in the near future that "information markets" will pervade most organizations. These will provide the platform for information producers to receive payment for their efforts while ensuring consumption of only truly valuable information. Just like the notion of competition in physical goods has forced producers to improve the quality of products and services offered, in turn increasing the societal (social) wealth, so too will information markets make for better information generation and dissipation in organizations.

Pervasive and Ubiquitous Computing

The idea of making information pervasive is not new and can be easily traced back to the early days of cybernetics. Wiener, who was concerned mainly with the role of feedback, was fascinated with how humans processed information and received instantaneous feedback to guide their actions; he was also intrigued with building machines that could emulate such behavior.[2] His followers Vannevar Bush, John von Neumann, and Alan Turing attacked this problem from different angles, and each attained some degree of success.[3] Early researchers in artificial intelligence, such as Marvin Minsky, also tried to develop architectures that would provide immediate feedback.[4] This led to the idea of pervasive and ubiquitous computing with the goal being to have computers nearly everywhere, intertwined and integrated with our social environments (pervasive). While in 1950s this seemed to be a dream, today it is reality. Mark Weiser in his article "The Computer for the 21st Century," stated, "The most profound technologies are those that disappear. They weave themselves into the fabric of everyday life until they are undistinguishable from them."[5] The goal of information processing in the future will include the ability to *manage the information space* (MIS*): "The manager should be able to imagine the MIS* but it should not become an illusion; the manager should be able to immerse himself or herself in the MIS* without getting lost; and the manager should be able to interact with the logical and physical organization through the MIS* without loss of control."[6]

Information will move to the foreground and technology will recede to the background. Information will direct actions, but not be so powerful so as to dictate actions. There are several objectives in pervasive and ubiquitous computing. First is to design and use *smart spaces.* Smart spaces can be physical or logical enclosures such as a boardroom or a desktop computer. The inclusion of *smartness* in such spaces enables real-time intelligent modifications to the space based on a given criterion. For example, an individual opening the door and entering the room would trigger the lights and air-conditioning being turned on, to reflect the user's preference. Some refrigerators today keep an "inventory" of the user's contents and can provide a list of consumed products before the owner goes shopping. A user's desktop could also be modified and updated to reflect given preferences. Some of these features are included in Microsoft's XP operating system. Second, developing of smart spaces enables the technology in use to become "invisible" because it moves to the background. While technology will enable better task completion, it will not interfere with the task. A third feature involves the aspect of continuous monitoring, as suggested by Suchman; a computer should continuously monitor the situation in order to proactively aid the user.[7] We also consider the aspect of seamless integration of electronic devices so as to better process information. An example of this approach is IBM's Pervasive Computing Project, which provides the following statement in their goals: *"Pervasive computing gives us tools to manage information easily. . . . We expect devices—personal digital assistants, mobile phones, office PCs, and home entertainment systems—to access that information and work together in one seamless, integrated system, Pervasive computing can help us manage information quickly, efficiently, and effortlessly."*[8]

All of these attempts are geared toward forcing information to the foreground while moving the technology to the background. Examples of this are present and surround us today. Three years ago choices in cell phones involved whether the consumer wanted digital or analog service. Today these devices are modeled after minicomputers in that they not only transmit voice, data, pictures, and video, but are capable of downloading games, e-mail, and text transmissions, and can be attached to computers for other enhanced features. A popular comic strip detective wore a mobile radio in his wristwatch during the 1950s, and by the 1960s Dick Tracy's wristwatch included a small viewing screen at a time when readers could ascribe such technology only to the imagination of a cartoonist, a classic case of life imitating art.

Central to the developments in pervasive and ubiquitous computing will be continuous striving to make feedback quicker and more robust. Feedback serves as instant gratification and complements information. Feedback no longer has to take the form of a report or large conference meeting. Today, teleconferences allow participants to see each other's reactions while speaking, allowing far better inference from feedback than a telephone call. Working models of wearable computers, pocket sensors, and real-time information synthesizers are currently available. By the end of the current year it is likely that a "collapsible" version of the personal computing device will be available to allow the user to receive e-messaging via Wi-Fi technology on a flat screen that can be "rolled up" and carried in a case the size of a fountain pen.

Biometrics

Traditional mechanisms for identity verification such as the use of personal identification numbers (PINS) or passwords are subject to easy manipulation and can be bypassed with minimal sophistication. Consider the following; most people choose passwords that are easy to remember (at least to them). Hence, they have an inclination to have a password that is either wholly or partly symbolic of some characteristic of theirs. This can be in the form of a birth date, maiden name, sibling's name, child's name, high school, or college. In the 1940s movie *It Takes a Thief*, a famous cat burglar was asked how he was so successful at stealing secrets from German embassy safes. "Not difficult," he replied. "All the combinations are Hitler's birth date." Similarly, it takes little effort to deduce one's password if details are known about the individual. Moreover, individuals have an inclination to be sloppy when it comes to password protocols. For instance, it is not uncommon to find individuals share passwords for access to information directories in organizations. Hence it is difficult to verify whether the individual who is using the password is the actual individual who was authorized. Individuals seldom change their passwords and PINS on a regular basis as this forces them to update their own memory. To add to this problem, individuals have a tendency to use the same password across multiple domains. For example, many people use the same PIN for accessing their ATM account, checking e-mails, and using a calling card.

Since passwords and PIN are the first line of defense to prevent unauthorized access to information in the organization, the current state-of-the-art can be described as weak at best. Research and development in biometrics is looking to alleviate some of these concerns.

A simple definition of *biometrics* is the use of biological (bio) signs as an indication of measurement (metrics). Today much of the work is being carried out in the use of such signs to conduct identification of a person based on their physiological and behavioral characteristics. These can take the form of handprints, voice recognition, face geometry, retinal scans, and face recognition. The oldest form of biometrics is fingerprint-matching. It is well known that every person has unique fingerprints, which can be used to deduce identity. Unlike with traditional mechanisms, the use of biometrics for identification ensures with a significant degree of confidence that the person who is gaining access to an asset or object is indeed the person who was authorized.[9] Moreover, such authentication schemes generally ensure the physical presence of the agent trying to gain access. Your retina cannot be scanned in Germany if you are in London. One benefit of such an arrangement is that there is no need to remember passwords.

Biometric-based authentication schemes will help organizations monitor which agents have access to their physical and logical environments. The Port Authority of New York has already implemented such a system, called INSPASS, at John F. Kennedy International Airport.[10] INSPASS helps in the verification of a traveler's identity electronically; a passenger must insert his/her INSPASS card at a kiosk and get their palm scanned. This verifies the passenger's identity and helps one pass through immigration in roughly fifteen seconds. As will be evident from our case on cyberterrorism in the appendix, the first line of defense to preventing unauthorized access is to monitor who enters the organization and can access its information base. Much like a nation's airports, seaports, and borders are the first line of defense against preventing unscrupulous individuals from causing damage, so are an organization's authentication schemes. Once an individual bypasses such schemes, it is difficult, though not impossible, to prevent them from causing damage. In many cases the mere penetration of a system is likely to be the most significant damage, also if nothing was hurt inside the system. Many financial firms have incurred losses due to news of credit card numbers being stolen and published in public spaces; in most cases the credit cards were never used for theft. Moreover, in the very near future, companies will have to disclose such break-ins and thefts publicly, which currently is not mandated.[11]

Information Certification and Assurance

If information is going to be truly valuable, there is a need to certify its quality and assure proper usage. Information assurance involves several dimensions. First, is to assure that the information is original and not tampered with. Originality of information is preserved mostly through the use of copyright protection mechanisms. These take two forms—legal and mechanical. As we all know, there are legal implications for plagiarizing, unauthorized duplication and distribution, and tampering with information products. For example, a video or music CD is subject to copyright laws. While laws are ostensibly effective, enforcing them is very difficult. The sheer numbers of suspected lawbreakers makes this nearly impossible. This is a classic case of supply and demand wherein there are a few products compared to many consumers. As a result, articles are illegally reproduced en masse or otherwise "bootlegged." The market becomes flooded with both legitimate and illegitimate material. Thus, rather than relying purely on legal remedies, information producers must develop other mechanisms to protect their interests. One such wave of development is in the area of digital rights management (DRM), which is concerned with maintaining rights in digital medium. DRM helps preserve the authenticity and originality of information objects through the use of passwords, permission sets, and time bombs. Unless a user has a password they will not be able to access the information. Along with a password, the user must have the necessary permission, which dictates what can be done with the documents in question. Some permissions allow only reading the document on the screen, some allow reading and copying, others may not allow printing, and so on. These permissions are set by the creator of the document based on their needs of information preservation. Virtual "time bombs" are becoming common today. These are mechanisms that delete or wipe out an information object after a specific period of time. Recently, movie producers have come up with DVDs that will self-destruct in forty-eight hours.[12] This is a means of ensuring the DVD is viewed only for the length of time to which the purchaser is entitled.

As information protection mechanisms get more sophisticated, so do mechanisms that can break them. Recently there has been an onslaught of lawsuits brought against individuals who share copyrighted songs.[13] What is interesting here is that many of the perpetrators are being caught because they trade or exchange music on known public platforms on the Internet. While legal sanctions may be brought against such platforms, for example, Napster, they are less effective against individuals who practice private one-on-one sharing or exchanges among their peers. Devices to duplicate informational product are abundant. Today there are devices that can make near-perfect copies of complete DVDs in less than twenty minutes.[14] Proponents for the device state that it can be used to make legitimate backup copies of one's data, while the music and motion picture lobbyists argue that it makes illegal duplication easier.

Information assurance schemes will also be used to alleviate some of the current concerns with unsolicited electronic messages, most commonly known as spam. We have all fallen victims to receiving unnecessary and sometime just plain rude messages in our inboxes. Besides being a nuisance, such messages waste the resources of the receiver. They take up disk space and time in terms of processing of the message. In the case of MasterCard, of the company's eight hundred thousand incoming messages for the month of July 2003, 50 percent were tagged as spam.[15] As much as a third of most organizations' e-mail resources are spent on dealing with spam. Assurance and smart schemes are being developed to help filter information and provide assurance of its quality. These use a combination of artificial intelligence schemes to detect the probability of a message being spam. Moreover, over time the tool builds a blacklist of spam senders and quarantines any future messages. One reason why the fight against spam has intensified over the past year has been the surge in the number of computer viruses. Most of these are proliferated via e-mails. Viruses, like their biological counterparts, attach themselves to legitimate programs in the victim's computer. The virus acts as a miniprogram and, once opened, may give instructions to delete all word processing programs or databases. More complicated and more destructive programs may be delivered via "worms" which, as the name implies, have the ability to bore through files in search of root directories, which affects not only programs but can corrupt an operating system or the computer itself. Consumers today, demanding faster access to information, are using a technology intended to take advantage of greater bandwidth, most commonly through digital subscriber lines (DSL). A major concern with DSL involves the fact that the consumer's line is "open" all the time, which leaves their location address exposed. With dial-up service a user is exposed to nefarious attacks only during the time they are "online." DSL users may ask for dynamic addresses from their subscribers so the code that identifies them is "scrambled," that is, constantly changed so it would be more difficult to expose them. Users are reminded to use current versions of antivirus software, especially the type that allows for "updates" of virus definitions. They should also be aware that there is a difference between an antivirus program that states it is capable of detecting 100 percent and isolating any virus program, and those that say they can defeat 100 percent of the viruses they detect; if a virus cannot be detected, it cannot be defeated.

A major aspect of *information assurance* involves information standardization and tagging. Information on objects and agents is too often referred to in multiple ways and means; hence any effort to process it collaboratively becomes cumbersome. Efforts are under way by many industries to tag information systematically and standardize information labels. Consider that

UCCnet, a division of the Uniform Code Council, is working on systematizing and standardizing product names and descriptions that are currently inaccurate and inconsistent, resulting in cost overruns and poor collaboration in supply chains.[16] The biggest hurdle in the success of such information tags and standardization is the cleaning up of legacy systems. For many companies it takes years and millions of dollars in revenues to clean up their existing databases before they can be standardized. Moreover, since we live in a global world, the global community from raw materials producers to final retailers must accept standards; only then will the true effort of data synchronization be realized.

Information Mining

Today we are able to access richer quality in data. Data is available at a much more micro level, so there is more of it, and equipment affords this access at a rather frequent pace. Shopping marts and grocery stores do not need to guess customer-buying behaviors; from those who are online, they have it. The use of discount and preferred cards entitles us to some discounts, but it gives the stores something much more valuable—our data. This data can be used for product targeting, advertising, planning shop layouts, and more. If used efficiently and effectively, such information will allow a store to alert us to products of our liking, target discounts, offer sensible product bundles, and create other promotions. As we advance through the information age, the granularity at which information will be available will only get finer. We can also expect the mediums of information collection to get richer from static data to images, then voice and video. The frequency at which information will be gathered from objects and agents will also accelerate. An organization must hence *mine* such information for value. It is impossible to physically inspect each piece of information due to the large volume; attempting such a task is futile and would lead to information overload. Instead, researchers use intelligent *assistants* or miners that will sift through these large collections and highlight valuable patterns or intricacies, which can then be inspected. The gamut of tools and technologies that enable such automated discovery of patterns, trends, and associations from collections of data are called data mining tools. We, however, posit that the changing nature of *data* being collected will reflect a move toward *information* mining rather than just pure data mining. Temporal, archived information will be mined for the innovative trends and patterns that contributed to the organization's core successes. Spatial information will be mined for discovery of real-time associations between the archived information and the changing environment. When Coke decided to change its basic formula, it was responding to interpretive marketing information that was *spatial* without much regard to what had been its greatest strength as represented in its archived, *temporal* history; the results were disastrous. The use of *evolutionary* information processes, for example, the semiotic model, provides for the reduction in time normally associated with filtering new information to determine if it belongs in the organizational memory.

Information mining should not be regarded as an item of luxury for organizations. Many types of organizations are required by the government to conduct such exercises. With the signing of the Patriot Act, banks and financial institutions are being required to conduct extensive analysis of their databases to lend information of suspicious activity. Mining of their databases and across databases of their counterparts in the industry will reveal suspicious patterns of financial behavior such as money laundering, funding terrorists, and the like.[17] Information mining in most cases today is passive. Once the transactions are executed and processed, analysis is conducted as a postmortem to deduce if a suspicious transaction has occurred. By then the agent perpetrating the transaction may be long gone. Research and prototypes are under way in what we call real-time information mining. These are going to pick up steam as the next crucial enablers to information processing. The use of artificial intelligence mechanisms is critical to their effectiveness.[18] Real-time information mining will call for monitoring of environments, dealing with changing information, and making decisions based on past information all simultaneously. Some of these systems are already in place to deal with enterprise network security management. By detecting patterns in intrusion detection and scanning large amounts of data, the systems will become smart enough to recognize a potential break-in before it occurs. When these systems first go live, there will a lot of false positives. Over time the system will learn how to minimize such errors. Once again the notion of feedback is critical. Through repeated cycles of negative feedback and positive reinforcement, systems will become smarter and more effective, eventually attempting to reach near-zero false positives.

Information mining and processing will also become more automated through the use of *assistants*. These assistants known today as intelligent agents will become commonplace in organizations. As defined by Hayes-Roth, "Intelligent agents continuously perform three functions: perception of dynamic conditions in the environment, action to affect conditions in the environment, and reasoning to interpret perceptions, solve problems, draw inferences, and determine actions."[19] This involves the notion of agency; we have agents in practically every aspect of commerce today. An agent is someone who acts on our behalf to attain a predefined goal.[20] Financial brokers trade securities on our behalf; lawyers represent their clients; so on and so forth. Use of agents saves people time and money as they perform specialized tasks on behalf of the contracting party. In the realm of information science, agents are specific applications with predefined goals, which can run autonomously. Like their human counterparts, they perform specific functions. A prime example of intelligent agents is in search engines on various Internet Web sites. These agents help in retrieval of documents based on user-defined criteria. Intelligent agents and assistants are common today in most software. Consider the Microsoft Office Suite, the sometimes annoying yet helpful *office assistant* helps answer queries through the use of natural languages. Most Internet shopping sites have product comparison agents that help us compare products on different attributes such as price, reputation, and quality. FinCEN is an agency of the U.S. Treasury Department that overlooks policies and implementations and detects money laundering in an effort to support federal, state, local, and international law authorities. All cash transactions involving dollar amounts above ten thousand dollars need to be reported and analyzed. This amounts to approximately 10 million transactions a year, which cannot be manually monitored. The FinCEN Artificial Intelligence System (FAIS) uses a multiagent cooperative system to weed through this large data space and search for fraud and abnormalities through the use of neural network and other pattern-matching techniques.[21] Once patterns are established, organizations can isolate relevant information, which it may isolate and analyze. Future businesses, proficient at data mining, may parse specific information profiles into large data sections for resale to smaller companies interested in specific information. The smaller companies would employ techniques used in data mining but would actually, because they are looking at specific information, be involved in the exploration of "data marts."

Information Markets

If information is truly valuable to an organization, its value should be measurable.[22] This idea was asserted by E.L. Thorndike (1914), "If a thing exists, it exists in some amount; and if it exists in some amount, it can be measured," and Lord Kelvin, "If you haven't measured it you don't know what you are talking about." Information is being priced and valued today, though not as pervasively as one would want it to be. Taking an economic approach to the management of information has several intriguing benefits. First, it provides a means to value such assets in the organization. Second, it acts as an incentive mechanism for the generation of robust and ideal information while curtailing the issues of generating myth-information and information hoarding.

Consider the following cases. Fujitsu, the Japanese firm, developed a knowledge-market-based system in 1993.[23] This electronic market (housed on their intranet) allows its system engineers to buy and sell knowledge. When a system engineer (information provider) contributes knowledge to the system, they set its price. Information consumers can then search for specific information and view its associated price. If one decides to purchase the information nugget, a fee is charged to their department. The information package will then be made accessible electronically. This system is constantly monitored and updated. Over time, information objects that do not get traded are archived or disposed off. In this manner, the most valuable items stay in the market while less than ideal ones will eventually leave. This mechanism serves as an ideal platform to reward employees for the insights they provide. Infosys has implemented an internal knowledge market called K-Shop. Employees can submit research papers, project experiences, and other types of knowledge goods through a Web site. When a document is submitted to the K-Shop, experts review the document, and if found suitable publish it. The reviewer and author are compensated via knowledge currency units (KCU). Each reader of the document must pay a certain number of KCUs for utilization of the document. KCUs can be redeemed for cash and other gifts. These KCUs thus help in serving as an incentive and also rating the quality of knowledge provided.

Mathematical and simulation proofs of the intricacies of the knowledge and information markets have shown the validity of pricing mechanisms to address several issues. Due to the pricing scheme, every agent of the organization is motivated to produce and sell only knowledge that is felt will give the maximum return or profit. Hence, if we have two agents who have knowledge on a particular object, assuming quality being equal, the one who can produce it cheaper and faster will enjoy a greater benefit over the other. This is due to the fact that this agent can set a lower price and still retain a profit. Similarly, given the same situation and holding the price constant, the agent who can deliver a better-quality object will enter the market by contributing the object. The other agent will not do so, as he stands no chance of making any profit. In this manner the issues of myth-information get curtailed, as only superior information enters the market; myth-information and distorted information, even if they enter, will eventually not exist in the market. It has also been shown that a market mechanism forces people to keep their knowledge current. This is akin to a technology market with its influx of new products and services; a producer has two options, increase the quality and currency of the product, or lower its price. Moreover, unless the original producer of the information object has a competitive edge, that is, can update the good at a lower price than another agent in the market, the producer will lower the original goods price. Hence, this forces members of the organization to not only generate good information once, but also keep up their generation advantages. Many of these markets operate on the premise that, in order to purchase someone else's knowledge, you must also produce and contribute to the market. Hence it is in the best interest of every organizational member to contribute to the market, while accounting for the above-mentioned considerations, in order to garner revenue, which can be used for the purchase of others' knowledge.

While information markets have the potential to help an organization, they can also hurt if used in a naive or unscrupulous manner. Gatekeepers, for example, middle managers, could intentionally restrict the flow of information or access to knowledge. This can be accomplished by hoarding information or by placing exorbitantly high prices on knowledge. This can result in the organization being held "hostage" by the gatekeepers. Moreover, while mathematical proofs assume that employees behave rationally, in real life, as the Enron case has demonstrated, there are exceptions. While the proofs recognize an ideal state, several classic crisis studies demonstrate that when human nature comes into play, ideal, even rational, states can quickly deteriorate. To prevent similar types of events in the future, organizations must have far better methods with which to address information, especially that which signals impending crisis.

While information markets are starting to surface, several questions still need to be answered before they will become prominent. The first is, how should information be advertised? Unlike traditional physical goods, information goods cannot be given away as trials or in parts. If information is given out, why should someone pay for it? Research is being executed in the development of appropriate information advertising strategies. One idea that has been fairly popular has been extracted from academia. Instead of sharing the complete information object, generate "metainformation" on the object. This is akin to the abstract or executive summary found in most papers. Metainformation is information about information. On reviewing the metainformation and other available data, such as the number of times it was accessed, purchased, and ratings of consumers, one will be in a position to make a decision regarding the information object. Second is the question of black markets in organizations. Black markets are also called underground or illegal markets and pose several problems to their legitimate counterparts. Knowledge is costly to produce but cheap to reproduce, that is, it has high fixed costs but low marginal costs.[24] Hence, it is with ease that knowledge can be duplicated and replicated. Take for instance a text document; using a few clicks of the mouse, one is able to create a duplicate version of it. Moreover, with a few more clicks, one can e-mail it to a peer. Information markets in organizations will fail if people choose to spread knowledge outside of it, that is, in black markets. For example, if an agent purchases a certain knowledge object from the market and then shares it with his team members via private e-mail or by printing out copies of it, his team members have no incentive to participate in the market and actually reward the knowledge provider. In rare cases we can also see a reverse black market. This is where a knowledge provider sells knowledge outside the market for a higher price. This happens in cases where employees fear making their knowledge available to all agents in a competitive pricing setting and choose to share it with a few. Organizations must strive to curtail such actions as, in the long run, they will be detrimental to the market. Of the many strategies available to curtail the development of black markets, we find the following to be the most successful. First, there must be some kind of an organizationwide declaration or law condoning private one-to-one exchange of knowledge objects when access to the free market is available. This is similar to the notion of copyright laws. Some exceptions will exist, as in examples of "knowledge" held by executives on strategic aspects of the organization should not be made privy to all members and will call for private exchanges. Second, recent advances made in digital rights management technology are proving to be a viable solution to the problem. Knowledge objects can be password-protected, available on read-only basis, and their printing could be disabled, for example. The last issue is reminiscent of the chicken-and-the-egg debate. An information market will not survive without critical mass, and people will not join the market unless information is present. Hence, attracting and jump-starting the market always presents challenges. The use of early incentives and top management endorsement has been shown to aid in this challenge.

Open Source Software

The open-source movement began in 1984, when Richard Stallman developed an alternative to the popular UNIX operating system. Stallman made the software freely available to anyone to use and change and distribute, subject with one condition—any changes made to the code must be shared openly with anyone seeking access to the code. In 1991, Linus Torvalds, a Finnish college student, added a kernel to Stallman's code along with a few other accessories, leading to the development of Linux. The idea behind open source is fairly neat. Software code is made open so that programmers can read, redistribute, and change it to meet task requirements and also help the software to evolve. This kind of coding is in sharp contrast to the traditional model of programming, where each piece of code was a private asset of the programmer. As such, sharing of code was absent or poorly done, as the many holes and bugs in software were the result of poor linking of disparate code modules. The open source initiative aims to change this, making code as transparent as possible. Though still in its budding stage, it is receiving a warm reception from the programming community. The promise of open-source is the move away from expensive proprietary software toward commodity- and component-based development.[25] An organization is no longer restricted to purchase a complete suite from one vendor; instead, components can be purchased and integrated with ease. Moreover, since the code will be open, in-house developers can view it and decide if they have the capability to modify the code themselves. If they lack capability, they can solicit advice from newsgroups and other user communities or pay for it. The open-source movement is going to be interesting. Many questions remain unresolved yet, such as the ownership of code, piracy issues, risk issues, and acceptance of the new paradigm.

Managing the Future

In this chapter we have given some attention to current developments in the field of science that have bearings on information processing in organizations. Our discussion is not intended to be exhaustive; rather it is in many ways restrictive. It is important that managers keep abreast of other developments in the field to maintain the semblance of a competitive edge. Failure to experiment with new technology or the tendency to hold dear to the present can and probably will be costly. It is important to appreciate and support creativity and experimentation and to understand that failure involves the first steps toward success. This is where many managers and scholars often miss the point. Unless one experiments with new ideas and solutions, innovation will not occur. Holding on to old ideas without updating them to meet realities of the current environment is a sure way to lose competitive position both in industry and academia. Academicians should not ignore industry in a reciprocal fashion. Too often academics are too busy looking for the next *great theory* without regard to the changing *reality* in the practitioner's world. This results in "espoused theories," which could work in an ideal world but are impractical without insufficient attention given to "theories in use." Practitioners should also appreciate academic theory; academicians know how to rigorously test an idea, and an academic may be a good source for unbiased, perhaps naive, insights on problems and issues that exist in organizations. Kurt Lewin said," There is nothing as practical as good theory."

By the very nature our field, change is certain. Current technology will get obsolete and new developments will take their place. Appreciating change and jumping on every bandwagon are two different things. The field of information systems and management has been subject to new buzzwords—

e-commerce, business process reengineering, knowledge management, and the like. Dunnette, in a classic article in *American Psychologist,* described some of the fashions academicians go through. New buzzwords and fashions in the literature are common. Academicians for the most part can be split into two groups. The first group is *fashion-conscious*, constantly trying to mimic the newest trends in language and practice. This practice generally has a short shelf life, as new trends are common. The second group practices consistency as a religion and simply resists change. The optimal position would be *fashion-neutral.*

Certainly, by the time this book is released, business jargon will have adopted another dozen or so new buzzwords; the information mechanics used in this book should assist in deciding whether such use of language has meaning or value.

Epilogue

Throughout this work our attention has been focused on a variety of notions involving information sciences and their impact on the development of organizations. While the concept is not new and is certainly evolving, it has been our intent to pull a number of the unifying themes together and demonstrate how they relate to the phenomena encompassing organizations of information. To accomplish this we view organizations in terms of systems, as both involve some interaction by design intended to produce specific results, goals, or purposes. How organizations and systems function is dependent on information that yields unique input intended to modify behavior of the elements involved in the structure, and such modification has an influential effect on all elements composing the structure. For managers this idea is particularly salient in reference to decision-making because of organizational interdependencies. Theorists recognize that the consequences of decisions involve certain aspects, including the ability to "self-regulate" system activities (cybernetics), the interdependencies and resultant actions within organizations (complexity), bottom-up rather than exclusive top-down changes to hierarchy (emergence), the likelihood of unforeseen consequences because of inattention to initial conditions (chaos), and the conditions of rules and players in the organization (game theory); everything is situational and everything hinges on information.

It is important to remember—and easy to forget—that system approaches involve both social and managerial considerations.[1] Both students of research and educators should be aware that this notion focuses attention on the fact that social psychology, philosophy, and behaviorism contribute to and influence information flow and effects on organizations. And though information sciences have used extensive quantitative analysis in an effort to seek order among the complex variables associated with information and organizations, the human factor drives the mechanism. As such, uncertainty will always play a part. We have discussed how Claude Shannon creatively applied the notion of uncertainty to information systems through the second law of thermodynamics, that is, entropy. It is the uncertainty of information and the attendant consequence and impact on organizations that serves as the basis of this book.

While we have presented several examples of crisis related to the information theories presented in this book (many more could be applied), none has had the obvious impact as those leading to the events of September 11. Three years later, despite the government's published intention to combine twenty-three agencies under one umbrella for the explicit purpose of gathering and sharing information on concerns of national security to benefit all levels of government, little if anything has been accomplished. This may be tied to any number of reasons or rationales, but the principal reasons are lack of understanding of what constitutes the system that would be required and, just as important, an obvious lack of creativity. For example, analyst Bruce Berkowitz suggested that the government's currently drafted policies regarding issues of cybersecurity "bore an uncanny resemblance to the draft plan unveiled three years earlier."[2] This poses a frightening specter of things to come if the conditions leading to September 11 represent our nation's best new defense in the use of information that may be attached to future threats.

A little over one hundred years ago, Charles H. Duell, commissioner of the U.S. Patents Office, proclaimed, "Everything that can be invented has been invented." Those who currently subscribe to the notion that information, while important, has no real effect on organizations are subscribing to a similar, deterministic, and doomed philosophy. It is not without irony that one of the greatest challenges for those involved in information technologies requires them to communicate the ideas of theorists and concepts referenced in this work to those who have the authority to make decisions. If this feat is not accomplished, it is unlikely that quotes coming from any U.S. authority in as little as fifty years will have any significance.

Gödel's Incompleteness Theorem maintains that all logical systems of any complexity are, by definition, incomplete; each of them contains, at any given time, more true statements than can possibly be proved according to its own defining set of rules. Similarly, while we have provided the basis for the development of rules associated with information that will help organizations understand the increasing dependence on information and actions, investigation of this process must continue.

Information, and specifically information leading to actionable knowledge, makes the organization, and the organization can be constructed from information. We have drawn extensively from existing literatures such as semiotics, communication theory, information theory, chaos, information systems, economics, and even history to drive home our arguments. Additionally, we have revisited the notions of emergence, complexity, and chaos theory, critical topics too often passed over as too abstract to be practical, yet they are essential if organizations are to understand their real relation to information as each that impacts information and the ability for the organization to effectively adapt within its environment.

As with most resources, our text is replete with related references, many of which should be explored by those interested in any of the topics we have discussed. We have provided a working model that any group can apply to information synthesis in their organization. The semiotic model has been presented in publications related to information technologies to describe lost opportunities, which if attended to during critical events may have averted organizational disasters.[3] Failure to attend to organizational inhibitors that defeat information restrict the system's ability to react, or adapt, to changing environmental conditions. Such conditions can lead the organization to entropy, a state of disorder that, when maximized, cannot be recovered to any semblance approximating the original state or conditions. Such was the case during the information gathering processes prior to September 11, and it is likely that similar conditions exist today in organizations involved with power consumption, transportation, economics, public safety, intelligence gathering, and manufacturing. While technology provides a number of answers as to the "how" we can best access information, the question as to "what" constitutes good and valuable information must continue to be addressed. We believe this text provides a primer for this task.

Douglas Engelbart, in *Augmenting the Human Intellect,* stated that each of us, given our fields of specialization, can contribute collectively to problem-solving, as everything is interrelated. Improvements in one area can trigger cascading improvements in other areas.[4] We hope this text has lit the fire for such synthesis and symbiosis.

Appendix A

Cyberterrorism and Medical Errors

A major tenet of our discussion involves semiotics. We have outlined the evolutionary model of knowledge generation and application in preceding chapters. Here, we portray how the model can be applied to the study of two classes of problems—cyberterrorism and medical errors. Our goal is to show the veracity of the model in the study of problems from varied disciplines.

Cyberterrorism

During the past two years there has been a lot of attention given to terrorism.[1] As a direct result of the events of September 11, 2001, much of the attention has been directed toward countermeasures intended to protect airports, physical plants, or multinational concerns, though little attention has been given to the concept of *cyberterrorism*. A critical reason that concerns for *cyber*terrorism are regarded as a bastard stepchild to physical terror attacks may be associated with the pejorative context in which the word *"cyber"* has come to be misused. Mention "cybersomething" and that "something" is immediately cast into the realm of a *"virtual,"* nonreal world comprised and cloaked amid electronic signals, digital representations, and binary symbols. A popular antonym for cyber is "actual." The question becomes, can something be *represented as cyber* while at the same time be *regarded as actual?* The answer is as close as your word processor. The words typed on your page are the digital representations of something that may be printed; the virtual is transformed to actual by the execution of a keystroke. Soft copy becomes hard copy based on the intention of the user. The cyber aspect we will address involves elements of *control* vis-à-vis our semiotic framework, a control model that does not seek to describe conventional control procedures. The purpose of this approach is to prescribe a model in order to understand the nature of cyberterrorism and the associated effects of cyberattacks.

Merriam-Webster's Dictionary defines terrorism as "the systematic use of terror especially as a means of coercion" and terror as "a state of intense fear [when] violence is committed by groups in order to intimidate a population or government into granting their demands." The United Nations defines terrorism in terms of transnational implications and classifies it among crimes "most worrisome to the public." We propose the following working definition for cyberterrorism: "A purposeful act, personally or politically motivated, that is intended to disrupt or destroy the stability of organizational or national interests through the use of electronic devices that are directed at information systems, computer programs, or other electronic means of communications, transfer, and storage."[2]

Concerns over cyberterrorism should not be regarded as mere paranoia, and a short historic review of network evolution helps ground these concerns in terms of governing dynamics. In 1972 when Rob Metcalf attempted to demonstrate the power of his "Ethernet" project to visiting AT&T executives, his system crashed, much to the delight of the guests who represented Ma Bell. Based on their observations, these executives felt that their jobs were secure and reported that packet switching would never affect their business.[3] The next year Cerf and Kahn developed a "protocol" which, if employed through a common "gateway" to other computers, allowed for wide-range digital communications between different systems. By 1983 this Transfer Code Protocol/Internet Protocol (TCP/IP) had become the standard application for network traffic. Within ten years the World Wide Web had been established, and browsers to link various sites had been developed for ease in navigation. Now, thirty years from inception, the Internet stands about where telephonic advances stood circa 1900. In 1972 the military and certain universities communicated between twenty-five sites. Today that number is approaching 100 million. As use of networks becomes more ubiquitous, so does the opportunity for illegal or terror-related activities become more attractive. In 1972 security concerns involved precautions against the guessing of passwords. Today the possibility of distributed attacks by terrorists could literally bring down the Internet. Transnational groups, often considered unsophisticated, view the Internet as a tool of convenience to add to their arsenal for terror. It was not until 1999, for example, that Saudi Arabia first opened its country to Internet access. Almost immediately the U.S. intelligence community detected communications related to terrorist activities, including plans for terror attacks on U.S. soil.[4]

Types of Cyberterrorism

While it may not be possible to agree on a precise definition of what constitutes cyberterrorism, many scholars have looked at ways to categorize types of cyberattacks. For instance, the Center for the Study of Terrorism and Irregular Warfare, housed at the Naval Postgraduate School, issued a report, "*Cyberterror: Prospects and Implications*," in which three levels of cyberterror acts were described.[5] First is *simple-unstructured*, representing the more rudimentary kinds of attacks against individual systems using easily accessible tools. In 1999 it was reported that twelve of the thirty terrorist groups deemed foreign terrorist organizations (FTO) by the United States Department of State had their own Web sites.[6] Deployment of worms or viruses would fall under this category. Second is *advance-structured*, which represent more sophisticated attacks against multiple systems. In order to effect such attacks, the hacker must modify existing hacking tools or create variants. A third type involves *complex-coordinated* attacks that are capable of causing mass disruptions to multiple targets either concurrently or sequentially. These require superior target analysis, command and control, and intelligence. Examples of this type of assault includes *swarming*, an interesting approach where the dispersed nodes of a network of small (and perhaps some large) forces converge on a target from multiple directions. The overall aim is the sustainable pulsing of force or fire. Once in motion, swarm networks must be able to coalesce rapidly and stealthily on a target, then dissever and redisperse, immediately ready to recombine for new attacks.[7] Members of the research institute at the Naval Postgraduate School estimated that it would take a group two to four years to develop capabilities to undertake an advanced-structured attack and six to ten years to execute a complex-coordinated attack.

We view cyberterrorism under two lights: as either *conventional* or *unique* attacks. We can consider conventional attacks as overt attacks and unique attacks are covert. Conventional attacks involve disruption to information infrastructures through use of viruses, worms, "Easter eggs," time bombs, or distributed denial of service (DDOS) attacks against servers. Yahoo, eBAy, and Amazon.com have all suffered from DDOS attacks that have periodically shut them down. Some conventional attacks *appear* covert but are not. Easter eggs require the user to find the embedded code and issue specific instructions to open and activate them. Time bombs are exactly what they sound like; they are "fused" to detonate at a specific time because of some intervention. One example is when an employee slips in a program with instructions to delete company files if his Social Security number is not present in the payroll database. The day this guy gets fired, things start going wrong.

Other extremes involve mirroring of actual and testing applications, which causes utter confusion among end users. The recent and recurring ILOVEYOU, Melissa, and Na CIH viruses, which attacked tens of millions of users and involved billions of dollars in damage, were little more than a costly nuisance. [8] In 1997 the U.S. Department of Defense, in conjunction with the National Security Agency (NSA), conducted "Eligible Receiver," a surprise operation to examine vulnerabilities in critical infrastructures. They found that the power grid and emergency 911 systems had weaknesses that were subject to exploitation using *publicly available tools.*[9]

Unique attacks are a variant of cyberterrorism in which the use of legitimate electronic outlets to facilitate communication among terrorist groups is conducted. For example, the passing of innocent messages on discussion groups found on the Internet can be used as a mode of communication between terrorist operatives. This may be accomplished using techniques such as steganography, which hides one piece of information inside another. For example, a compressed image (JPG format) file allows a lot of room for embedding other data. In the proper hands, the image is ignored and literally dissolved to reveal the hidden message.

There is a saying that "a conservative is a liberal that was mugged the day before." Perhaps definitions regarding cyberterrorism work the same way. Cyberthreats or actions against banks or brokerage houses in which the institution's system is taken "hostage" for ransom is a crime involving terrorism, although the offenders may not be directly from a recognized terrorist group. In 1997 a group calling itself the Chaos Computer Club managed to corrupt an integral part of a popular accounting program that allowed them to steal funds from users of the program.[10] This feat damaged personal accounts while doing harm to the program vendor's reputation, as both found themselves vulnerably exposed to a type of terrorism, although the perpetrators were not on anyone's "terrorist list." Similar cyberattacks, typically performed for personal reasons, could be defined as e-crimes. Recently, the *New York Times*[11] suggested that such crimes are likely to target not only cash from bank accounts but increasingly more the pilfering of valuable information like "business development strategies, new product specifications or contract bidding plans." Statistics mentioned in the article suggest that by January 2003 the number of such attacks may exceed twenty thousand per month. The average losses in a survey of cyberattacks conducted by the FBI and the Computer Security Institute were a staggering $2 million. However, losses were even bigger per occurrence for those respondents who lost proprietary company information (average $6.5 million) or financial fraud (average $4.6 million). Over 70 percent of these incidents were perpetrated by insiders, presumably because they have the knowledge necessary to penetrate the systems. And the situation is likely to get worse before it gets better, particularly in the United States, which already leads in e-crime statistics because of sheer volume of population and access to computers as compared to other countries. We consider e-crimes as a subset of all cyberterrorist activities. One could conduct e-crimes at the local level, which we define as the lower levels of the semiotic model. However, as the natures of these crimes emerge through the semiotic discourse, they will lend themselves to be classified as acts of terrorism. Hence the emergence of e-crimes from a local to the global level is of interest. As will be explained, prevention and controls are easier to deploy at the lower levels than at the higher semiotic levels. We now apply the model presented in chapter 4 to studying cyberattacks.

A Semiotic Discourse to Cyberterrorism

Cyberterrorism at the morphological level is restricted to singular acts on objects executed by individual agents. Typical concerns at this level involve the activities of crackers, or hackingagents, who conduct malicious acts to attain self-fulfilling goals. For instance, a cracker might bring down a Web site through detonation of denial of service attacks intended to prevent access to the site. Some ignore the threat of crackers in discussions about cyberterrorism, but we argue that studying the behavior of crackers is relevant. Crackers have the ability to cause harm to organizations through their acts; analyzing their patterns of operations can provide insights into the weaknesses of systems and infrastructure. It is interesting that once caught, crackers are often asked to provide companies with information intended to better protect systems from assault.

Objects of concern at the morphological layer include Web sites, listservs, and portals maintained by terrorist cells and factions. Web sites such as www.alneda.com have been suspected of carrying messages from bin Laden and Mullah Omar.[12] These sites have also been regarded as likely suspect mediums that transfer low-level operational information among its disparate cells.[13] Items posted on such Web sites can serve two purposes. First, such items assist to further the cause of terrorist groups and cells through wide-scale, easily produced propaganda. Second, they act to serve as communication forums between distributed terrorist cells. This can occur through the use of coded messages or text with hidden meanings. Some terrorist and guerrilla groups have even begun to use U.S. government property for propaganda against American interests. For instance, the Revolutionary Armed Forces of Colombia (FARC)[14] had their Web site hosted at the State University of New York at Binghamton; similarly the Tupac Amaru Web site [15] has been operating at the University of California at San Diego.[16] Both groups are on the U.S. State Department's list of international terrorist groups. Today we are also seeing the deployment of "intelligent agents" on the Internet.[17] An intelligent agent is software that assists users and acts on their behalf. A terrorist can deploy an intelligent agent to carry out malicious acts in cyberspace without human intervention. Most of the e-crimes as defined earlier would fall under this categorization. A well-known case of computer crime involved two accountants from Cisco Systems, who used the company's computer system to issue themselves nearly $8 million in company stock. [18]

In the context of cyberterrorism at the empirical level, we are concerned with finding groupings among similar perpetrators and origins of attacks. Groupings of like agents based on characteristics gauged at the morphological level will help us in the identification of "groups" or "cells." Moreover, the grouping of like objects, for example, domain name servers (DNSs) or Internet protocols (IPs) from which signals are emitted at similar time frames or regularities, will help us monitor and predict outcomes. If we were to consider a denial of service attack, we would find most could be traced back to a well-defined cluster of IPs from which the attack originated. Fortunately, e-crimes are not yet known to have happened at any higher level than morphological. Presumably the coordination effort that it may take would outstrip the capabilities of the traditional profile of the e-crime perpetrator. However, cyberterrorism could also include an organized set of attacks with financial purposes to fund subsequent terrorist efforts, very much like how the Irish Republican Army (IRA) attacked physical banks in Northern Ireland. Therefore, the considerations put forward in the next few sections should also be heeded by organizations concerned about being targeted.

At the syntactical level, detecting patterns and relationships will help us predict cyberterrorist activities. For example, assume the following attack scenario: [19] a number of computerized bombs are placed across a city, each of which transmits unique numeric patterns to peer bombs. If one bomb stops transmitting, all bombs detonate simultaneously. This attack involves syntactical cyberterrorism. The interdependency associated with the information infrastructure, which is in place today, makes the execution of syntactical cyberattacks attractive. Taking one hub down can cause a cascading effect to other nodes on the network. A key determinant to success in this type of attack is how well relationships are defined across heterogeneous agents and objects. Consider the Army Knowledge Online portal (AKO).[20] The framework for the portal is an open standards-based system, making it easier for army maintenance engineers to develop and revise software on the platform. AKO provides a single entry point into a growing knowledge management system that enables greater sharing among army communities. It enables enhanced communication between army personnel and their civilian friends.[21]

For security purposes, the army relies on its own telecommunications systems rather than the local systems in host nations like Germany, Italy, and the United Kingdom AKO is meant to be a very usable and nonhostile environment for army personnel to work in. To break in the AKO, one would need syntactical knowledge. One would need to know more than just the local telecommunications infrastructure, but also how is it related to the U.S. Army's telecommunications hosting system.

Most of the cyberterrorism literature in our opinion is focused on the semantic level. Attacks at this level are concerned with the destruction of national information infrastructures and causing large-scale disruptions. The environment for such attacks is not restricted to particular organizations or entities, but is more national or international in scope. To execute these attacks, the offender must have prerequisite skills, including those needed at the previous levels, as well as some sense of systemic knowledge. The systemic knowledge should be regarded as "insider knowledge," including how to exploit weaknesses in a system to cause havoc in the system under attack in order to produce a cascading effect throughout the network.

At the final level, pragmatics, the cumulative information gained through use of the model provides the basis for action by decision-makers. This stage synthesizes everything learned through successive layers in the chain and requires a response. Responses may be to act directly and/or dissipate information gained from any of the layers. It is likely advantageous to "recycle" the information gleaned and start the semiotic process a second time in order to filter information further. A second run is more sensitive to timing and redundancy, that is, information that is picked up the second time is likely more valuable because it validates earlier information, while at the same time some things picked up the first time may have to be discarded as not useful so they do not clutter this second run with noise. Assume for example, that a power grid fails on the West Coast and the model is being employed to determine if the failure is related to a possible terrorist attack. By the second cycle, if a similar incident happens anywhere else in the country, while rational suspicion might suggest something is going on, much of the refinement work addressing who is likely suspect will have been accomplished during the first cycle.

Management of Cyberterrorism

The practice of cyberterrorism, not surprisingly, has its roots in game theory. Game theory implies conflict, which in some ways mirrors everyday life. Game theory studies conflict between thoughtful and potentially deceitful opponents. And for a situation to constitute a game setting, there must be the potential for a winner and a loser. A potential threat may materialize because of something as mundane as faulty system design, natural conditions brought on by a power outage, or some deliberately heinous plot on the part of a saboteur or terrorist. The opportunity for winning often favors the most prepared, regardless of which side the player represents.

Experts in game theory insist on specific terms to represent the events of such conflicts between players. These terms consist of the game, the rules, and the moves.[22] For our purposes, the system environment in its totality determines the game, which in practice should conform to a specific set of doctrines governing convention within the system. If the system environment were baseball, three strikes and you are out; if football, four downs to make a first down; if it were a nuclear reactor, control critical mass conditions; each represents a part of the essential doctrines defining the game. In the cyberworld, specific paths (channels and addresses) establish early strategy and determine access to the playing field.[23] The distinction between the term "cyberterrorism" and terrorist *use* of cyberspace [24] is critical here as it determines what constitutes the game. This missed distinction lies in the fact that the *use* need not be widespread; rather it must be, and is, focused. Much of the discussion on cyberterrorism has been restricted to efforts intended to comprehend the effect of large-scale attacks on the national information infrastructures such as the Department of Energy and defense systems (at the semantic level). This approach is myopic and confounds more fundamental threats to security that should be addressed. It also affords the opportunity for the perpetuation of the problems associated with Stoll's cuckoo's egg metaphor.[25] Stoll reminds us that the cuckoo relies on the ignorance of its species to perpetuate its survival when it deposits eggs in the nests of other birds that raise the interloping hatchlings as their own.

The game in the abstract should not be confused with the rules. Rules are provided to address how the game should be played. Rules are determined in an exact sense and apply to both sides. If you play the game you are not fined or ejected, but you might be if you break the rules. There may be times when the player may opt to violate a rule intentionally. If a particular game imposes time limitations and a player intentionally violates a rule to either suspend or accelerate a temporal advantage, that player does so for a tactical advantage. A cyberattack might be deliberately designed for discovery with the intention of launching a second attack during a time while resources are committed to investigating the first assault. In other scenarios, game rules are intentionally violated because of the player's misunderstanding of the game.

Within game theory the most compelling aspect related to our discussions are the moves, which in turn, determine *die spiel,* the play within the game. In chess, for example, there are three generally accepted phases of play:

beginning, middle, and end. This illustration is provided because it gives a good sense as to how moves and play are related. On the other hand, chess may not be the best example of a game because of certain mathematical algorithms associated with the available alternatives. But the phases of play should demonstrate how a situation becomes more complex as the game evolves. Each player's strategy is restricted at the beginning, but their initial play is for position and the control of the board's center. By midgame their strategies have been exposed and the subsequent moves are intended to establish strength, generally determined by the placement and number of remaining pieces. But even this may not be enough if, during the end game, their moves reflect weakness in their play. The game is always decided in the end *spiel*. Assuming the nation's resources had been more clearly focused on consequences associated with cyberterrorism, there is a great likelihood that the al-Qaeda plans for the World Trade Center might have been exposed by midsummer 2001.[27] In a briefing given in late September 2001, FBI assistant director Ronald Dick, head of the United States National Infrastructure Protection Center (NIPC), told reporters that the hijackers had used the Net, and "used it well."[27] Thus a critical part of playing the cyberterrorism game is perception of the reality associated with the threat and bringing appropriate resources to bear.

It is not enough for today's managers to presume that since a plan is available, the associated strategy as a whole will yield the desired results without careful regard to the parts making up the whole plan. Such posturing serves as an inhibitor to the organization. Organizational or system complexity may create unexpected interactions of failure (that) are sufficient to bring whole systems down.[28] While the rules of the game provide provisions to prevent this from happening, the individual actions of a player may at times make it inevitable. Moreover, the notion of sequential games merits attention—who will act first? Unless managers of organizations act first preemptively by putting up controls and checks to deter the acts of cybercrimes and terrorism, the perpetrator has the upper hand and will conduct a first strike. The loss of conducting a first strike in terms of effort is much lower than the potential catastrophe.

In addition to the schism mentioned during the introduction of our discussion of cyberterrorism, a larger problem related to the concepts of cyberterrorism has to do with perception. Because large corporations and governments place such little value on creativity, they are, as entities, not very creative and therefore generally lack the ability for anything more than linear approaches in their thinking to problem-solving.[29] Consider the budgets used to combat cyberthreats. It is not too far of a stretch to look at how organizations spend their money in order to determine where their priorities rest. For example, Washington's cyberczar Richard Clarke has noted that companies generally spend more money for coffee than for countermeasures related to cybersecurity.[30] Similar apathy at the federal level has prompted a request for a nearly two-thirds increase in funding for matters related to digital security post-9/11, which is tantamount to closing the barn doors after the cows have all gone. Following the attack that brought down two of the world's largest buildings on America's eastern seaboard, the government responded by providing the nation with an unintelligible color-coded alert system in an effort to provide the perception that something was being done to prevent similar events. Of course, the alert system represents little more than a reaction, and a weak one at that, and if it had been in place on September 10 it could not have prevented what transpired the following day. But the attention given the impact of the events of September 11 will garner far greater press than the events that preceded the attack because of our nation's neurosis. To obviate the conditions that allowed the assault on our nation to occur in the first place, Washington will fuel this condition using buzzwords included in prophecies that promise a "digital Waterloo," an "electronic Pearl Harbor," or "an electronic Chernobyl" in an effort to maintain or increase the public's anxiety.[31] If these pundits of protection were more focused on the uses and defenses involving the tools of cyberwarfare, they might be less worried about the pork they can pack into weak legislation and more concerned with the activities among the powerful Sunni minority, the Wahhabi and Akhanan Muslaheen (the Islamic Brotherhood) who may have produced software packages for some of the United States' security services.

The attention on terrorism, virtual and real, raises new issues of grave concern among the security-minded guardians in our nation and businesses. Any methods in the approach to seek solutions to either of these concerns should not be regarded as distinctively different since both represent the potential for crisis. A new paradigm of crisis indicates that the focus is now directed more on early detection and prevention than on the recuperation associated with the probabilities and consequences of threats.[32] The new questions involve, "What can be done to prevent . . ." rather than, "How could we have prevented . . ." and accountability becomes increasingly important. Efforts to separate cybercrime from cyberterrorism should be eliminated since such notions merely represent a semantic distinction with no concluding difference; both involve the intent to destroy. Although the threat of cyberterrorism *occurs in the symbolic world* of binary digits, semiotics is used to make sense of signs, their meanings and associations, and their evolution, and can be an effective tool in detecting and defeating cyberthreats. Some assert that the cyberthreat of terrorism is merely that, and without a substantive example that the threat provides actual damage or death through its use, it should not at this time be allowed to drain scarce resources that perhaps have better use elsewhere. We end with the following recent news item: In early December 2002, U.S. Customs raided the offices of the Ptech Corporation, a Boston-based company that handled sensitive military and national security information, including software development for products used by FBI counterterrorism units.[33] ABC's *Nightline* reported that Yassin al-Qadi, a Saudi millionaire with possible ties to bin Laden, underwrites that company.[34] In the wrong hands, this type of cyberinformation *can result* in consequences as deadly as those caused by any car bomb or nuclear bomb.

Medical Errors

Medical errors[35] emerge when there is lack of efficient and effective processing of information. Medical errors and mistakes are the most commonly reported negative press for the health care industry. The National Academy of Science's Institute of Medicine estimates that 44,000 to 98,000 people die from medical errors each year.[36] This is greater than the number of people who die annually in automobile accidents. The National Institutes of Medicine estimated that of the 770,000 adverse-drug-related events each year, about 28 percent to 95 percent are classified as preventable errors. Some attribute as many as 100,000 deaths per year to such errors.[39]

The lack of efficient and effective processing of information can be traced to either fallacies in humans or machines. Recently a blood-typing error at Duke University resulted in a seventeen-year-old being given the wrong lungs and heart.[38] The hospital authorities confirmed that the doctor did not check the patient's blood type prior to conducting the surgery, which caused her body to reject the new organs and resulted in irreversible brain damage. In another case a woman went through a double mastectomy only to realize that she did not have cancer in the first place.[39] Health care enterprises are the most knowledge-intensive organizations.[40] The keys for survival in these organizations are the effective and efficient generation and dissipation of data, information, and knowledge. Even though this realization is pervasive and ubiquitous among the academic and practitioner community, little if any effort has been undertaken to systematically study the occurrence of medical errors. We apply the semiotic model to understand the nature and variety of medical errors and their causes.

Semiotic Discourse to Medical Errors

In health care enterprises, objects of interest at the morphological layer include drugs, equipment, machinery, and computer systems. Each of these systems emits information in a basic sense or is used upon the emission of information from other devices. Agents are the medical professionals and staff members of the hospital. Here we are concerned with each item in an isolated fashion. Errors at this junction have to do with the misuse of individual medical items. Put another way, medical errors here have to do with utilizing the wrong information emitted by a single agent or object. A good example here will be the case of Jessica Santillan, who was given the wrong lungs and heart due to negligence by a doctor in checking the blood type. [41] This was a clear case in which the doctor failed to appropriately calibrate the sources of information he needed to be aware of prior to conducting a medical process. He missed a valuable source of information, "blood type," that resulted in a patient's death. This individual data item was the cause of the medical error. Another example of a medical error at this stage occurred when a pub was faxed sensitive medical information from Portsmouth NHS Trust.[42] The fax contained sensitive financial, medical history, and drug-related information on patients. The error occurred due to the fact that the pub shared the same fax number as a social security office, but with a different area code. This occurred despite the fact that the area code was clearly printed on all literature. Here the error was caused due a single information nugget, "an area code of a fax number." In summary, at the morphological stage, errors can be traced to a single medical device or piece of information that was poorly administered.

In health care enterprises, we are also concerned with the grouping of like objects and agents—*empirics*. We have classes of physicians, surgeons, nurses, pharmacists, and so on that represent the grouping of agents based on their tasks and expertise. We can also have groupings of similar objects such as a class for syringes, blood dispensers, drugs, and the like. One can also dig a level deeper and have subclasses, such as the various types of physicians— family health, internal medicine, gynecologist, for example. An error at this level occurs when empirical calculations go wrong. Empirical calculations are widely conducted in the medical field. Some examples include calculations to determine dosages of drugs, the number of days a patient needs to be attended to, and similar information. A good example of an error at this level is the case of Gloria Renteria, who was admitted to a hospital for back pain. She was discharged and asked to take 2.5-milligram tablets of Glyburide to control her blood sugar level.[43] The pharmacy, however, gave her 5-milligram tablets of the drug, thus making an empirical error in calculation. Twenty days later she was admitted back into the hospital and died due to a case of hypoglycemic encephalopathy, which is most commonly attributed to Glyburide overdose. Another error in this class occurred when an infant received ten times the normal dosage required to stimulate his breathing at

Stevens Hospital.[44] According to doctors, "It was not written down wrong; it was not administered wrong . . . the only possible [explanation] was in the dilution." Once again there was an error in calculating the appropriate strength of the drug—an empirical error. In the above cases errors were made in conjunction with the administering or handling of information related to groups of objects. In the first case, the wrong strength of tablets was administered, while in the second example the wrong strength of dosage. In summary, at the empirical level wrong calculations are made on similar objects, which result in errors. These calculations are most commonly represented as strengths or number of units of a drug that gets administered.

In health care enterprises, we can see syntactical behavior when cross-functional staff members interact on an engagement or operation. For example, it is routine for an operation room to have a nurse, an anesthesiologist, a surgeon, and other specialists as needed. The syntactical level is concerned with errors that might occur when these multiple classes of individuals come together. Syntactical connections do not have to be synchronous, that is, all agents or objects interacting simultaneously, as in the operation room. An example of an asynchronous connection can be seen where a physician sends a prescription to a pharmacist to be filled. Of interest here is the interaction of two different classes of agents also if it is not synchronous. Errors at this level emerge from the syntactical mishandling of information. This can be in the form of information distortion as it moves among multiple classes of workers who may be coming at the piece of information with different contexts. As an example of an error at this level, consider the following. A man was wrongly issued medication for breast cancer even though his doctor prescribed him medication for palsy.[45] The patient deduced the error when the pharmacist asked him to refrigerate the medication; his past medication for palsy never needed refrigeration. The cause of this error was attributed to the fact that the physician's handwriting was illegible. Another example would be the case of Linda McDougal, who went through a double mastectomy even though she did not have cancer.[46] Three separate individuals from the hospital had mixed up the names on the slides with pathology sheets, resulting in wrong connections being made. The pathologist picked up the wrong paperwork with the slides and failed to check for syntactical integrity between the names on the identification papers and those on the slides. Hence a well patient was subjected to cancer treatment while an ill patient was told to go home as she was doing well. These examples show the errors that can occur when information passed between agents of different classes in the hospital is not verified or is destroyed due to the communication channel. In summary, at the syntactical level, errors occur when two or more classes of agents and objects interact on poorly administered and managed information. Most of the time such errors occur due to information transfer and inconsistencies among the various classes of objects and agents found in hospitals.

At the semantic level we are concerned with errors that occur at the facility or practice level. At this level the context of interest is the "organization" in question. This could be either an entire medical facility or a section of it (practice). Organizational practices such as poor training of personnel, lack of adequate staff on hand, and the like are of interest here. These practices make up the semantic context in which agents and objects conduct actions. The errors that occur due to the organizational practices and procedures in place are defined as semantic errors. Consider the following incident that occurred at Queen's Medical Centre in Nottingham.[47] Two drugs were given to an untrained doctor who thought that they were both supposed to be injected in the spine. The wrong administration of the drugs led to damage to the patient's nervous system. This case illustrates the situation, where the semantic meaning of correct actions (the administration of two drugs) is wrong in the context of the system. The drugs were not supposed to be introduced in the spine. One cause for the error was the fact that organizational procedures in place at the hospital allowed an untrained doctor to administer drugs without supervision—a semantic error. Another example of a semantic error resulting from poor training and incorrect assignment of personnel is the following—Clare Lewis, an eleven-year-old girl died after a pituitary tumor operation. The nurse wrongly diagnosed Clare's pain and suffering after the operation. She thought Clare was having intracranial pressure and hence deferred immediate action. Clare stopped breathing and was intubated and died shortly thereafter.[48] No doctor was consulted in the postoperation diagnosis by the nurse. Hence the error that occurred is semantic, as it was a function of poor organizational practices in place.

In the context of health care enterprises, medical errors at the pragmatic level can be considered akin to gross negligence or intended malpractices. This is where a medical professional(s) knowingly and willfully apply their pragmatic knowledge to deceive and/or cause harm to patients. There is no excuse for errors at this level as these cannot be considered as errors in the purest sense. Instead, these are willful acts that are aimed to apply information for the benefit of unscrupulous tasks. At the pragmatic level we are concerned with situations where the knowledge of medicine or information related to medical agents or objects is knowingly altered for unscrupulous purposes. Consider the following case—the Green Cross Company in Osaka, Japan, sold untreated products (actually infected with HIV) despite being aware of the risks that they posed. Corporate executives influenced ministry inspectors to play down the risks of untreated blood products. About 1,800 hemophilic people received the infected products, resulting in 500 deaths and the remaining being HIV-infected. The executives were jailed and asked to provide compensation.[49] The executives here knew pragmatically the dangers of untreated blood. Yet they decided not to abide by the pragmatics of the medical profession and hide such information. Moreover, they used the information to influence external parties (ministry inspectors), that is, members outside their defined environment (the Green Cross Company) to also manipulate the information. This resulted in a large number of deaths and numerous people being infected. Another type of error that occurs at this level includes misrepresentation of medical expertise in courts of law. Dr. Alan Williams, a forensic pathologist, was found tampering with evidence by not disclosing microbiology tests.[50] This act led to errors in legal judgments in several cases.

Management of Medical Errors

The concept of emergence is salient in this framework. In most cases the magnitude of errors emerges from bottom layers to the top layers. For instance, empirically calculated errors occur on the objects or agents identified at the morphological layer. Similarly, syntactic and semantic errors are generated on empirical sets of objects or agents. Pragmatic level errors (or acts of negligence) have their grounding in the behavior of objects and agents at the lower levels. Hence, managers must focus their attention on error containment at the lowest levels; these, if not controlled, will balloon into complex problems. The old adage "a stitch in time saves nine" holds true here. If we were to organize our information generating and dissipating objects and agents strategically and optimally at the morphological layer, many of the errors could be prevented. If not prevented, they can be at least be detected before grave harm is caused. It is hence not surprising that much of the current state of the art of medical information systems seeks to help organizations manage information with a morphological focus. The future of wireless applications in hospitals is deemed to aid in remote patient monitoring and the promotion of real-time data entry and control.

Management must also begin to streamline information controls at the morphological layer. The use of bar code technology is now pervasive in health care organizations. This, coupled with mechanisms such as color-coding of files and redundancy checks on information before administration of treatment, should reduce the likelihood of medical errors at the empirical and syntactical layers. The notion of redundancy is critical here. Unless we have redundant checks and controls in place, errors are bound to occur. Redundancy in control ensures that multiple screening occurs, which lowers the likelihood that errors will occur. Hence, we recommend that management move away from cost-cutting measures, as making the health care organization leaner will sacrifice redundancy, making errors more likely to occur. Moreover, practices such as handwriting of prescriptions and movement of paper-based records should be terminated. These practices cause much of the syntactically flavored errors. With the new Health Insurance Portability and Accountability Act (HIPAA) rules and regulations, much of the controls should begin to take shape, which will hopefully reduce errors. Ensuring effective and efficient syntactical and empirical processing of information will also have us better prepared for acts of terrorism. For instance, if a hospital in downtown Chicago receives a patient who has been exposed to anthrax, this data can be made accessible to neighboring operations in order to check the spread of disease. Data mining tools have a huge potential to aid us in these activities. Errors at the pragmatic level cannot be truly called "errors" or "mistakes." These are willful acts and need to be dealt with as such. Hence, managerial intervention, while suitable, cannot deter a person from committing such acts. These acts must be stopped by proper education and societal controls.

The above two cases illustrate the use of the semiotic model to study information processing in two different settings. It is our hope that these illustrations move you to begin thinking of other problems where the model lends application. More important, we hope these cases have provided you a means to improve on the model and develop new frameworks. While we have not elaborated on the spatial and temporal dimensions in the case studies, these can very easily be incorporated and synthesized with the semiotic dimension.

Appendix B

Bibliography and Suggested Readings

The articles and books listed below have been useful resources for us in our quest to understand information processing in organizations. We share them to provide you with references for further reading; many of these complement the works found in the notes for each chapter. Moreover, all of the works below have pointers to more resources for suggested readings.

Abernathy W.J. and K. Clark. "Innovation: Mapping the Winds of Creative Destruction." *Research Policy*, 14, 1985: 3–22.

——, and J.M. Utterback. "Patterns of Industrial Innovation." *Technology Review*, 80, 1978: 40–47.

Ackoff R. "Management Misinformation Systems." *Management Science*, 11(4), 1967: 147–56.

Aguilar F. *Scanning the Business Environment.* New York: Macmillan, 1967.

Ajzen I. "The Theory of Planned Behavior." *Organizational Behavior and Human Decision Processes*, 50, 1991: 179–211.

Argyris C. *Knowledge for Action: A Guide to Overcoming Barriers to Organization Change.* San Francisco: Jossey-Bass, 1993.

Arrow K. *The Limits of Organization.* New York: Norton, 1974.

Barney J.B. "Firm Resources and Sustained Competitive Advantage." *Journal of Management*, 17, 1991: 99–120.

Bertalanffy L. "General System Theory." *General Systems: Yearbook of the Society for the Advancement of General Systems Theory*, ed. L. Bertalanffy and A. Rapoport. Ann Arbor, MI: Society for General Systems Research, 1956: 1–10.

Boisot M. *Knowledge Assets: Securing Competitive Advantage in the Information Economy.* Oxford: Oxford University Press, 1998.

Bruns W.J. and F.W. McFarlan. "Information Technology Puts Power in Control Systems." *Harvard Business Review*, vol. 65, 5, 1987: 89–94.

Campbell J. *Grammatical Man.* New York: Simon & Schuster, 1982.

Chandler A. *The Visible Hand: The Managerial Revolution in American Business.* Cambridge, MA: Harvard University Press, 1977.

Churchman C.W. *The Design of Inquiring Systems.* New York: Basic Books, 1971.

Ciborra C. *Teams, Markets, and Systems: Business, Innovation, and Information Technology.* Cambridge: Cambridge University Press, 1993.

Cohen M.D. "Individual Learning and Organizational Routine: Emerging Connections." *Organization Science*, 2, 1991: 135–39.

Cohen W. and D. Levinthal. "Absorptive Capacity: A New Perspective on Learning and Innovation." *Administrative Science Quarterly*, 35, 1990: 128–52.

Crosby P.B. *Quality Is Free.* New York: McGraw-Hill, 1979.

Cyert R.M. and J.G. March. *A Behavioral Theory of the Firm.* Englewood Cliffs, NJ: Prentice-Hall, 1963.

Daft R.L. and G.P. Huber. "The Information Environments of Organizations." *Handbook of Organizational Communication*, ed. F.M. Jablin, L.L. Putman, K.H. Roberts, and L.W. Porter. Newberry Park, CA: Sage, 1987: 130–64.

———, and A.Y. Lewin. "Where Are the Theories for the New Organizational Forms: An Editorial Essay" *Organization Science*, 4(4), 1993: R1–R6.

———, and K.E. Weick. "Toward a Model of Organizations as Interpretation Systems." *Academy of Management Review*, 9(2), 1984: 284–95.

Davenport T.H. *Process Innovation: Re-engineering Work Through Information Technology.* Boston: Harvard Business School Press, 1993.

———, and J.C. Beck. *The Attention Economy: Understanding the New Currency of Business.* Boston: Harvard Business School Press, 2002.

De Geus A. *The Living Company.* Boston: Harvard Business School Press, 1997.

Deming W.E. *Out of Crisis.* Cambridge, MA: MIT Center for Advanced Engineering, 1982.

Denrell J. and J.G. March. "Adaptation as Information Restriction: The Hot Stove Effect." *Organization Science*, 12(5), 2001: 523–38.

Drucker P.F. *The Post-Capitalist Society.* Oxford, UK: Butterworth-Heinemann, 1993.

Eisenhardt K.M. "Agency Theory: An Assessment and Review." *Academy of Management Review*, 14(1), 1989: 57–74.

———. "Building Theories from Case Study Research." *Academy of Management Review*, 14(4), 1989: 532–50.

———, and J.A. Martin. "Dynamic Capabilities: What Are They?" *Strategic Management Journal*, 21, 2000: 1105–21.

Feldman M. and J. March. "Information in Organizations as Signal and Symbol." *Administrative Science Quarterly*, 26, 1981: 171–86.

Festinger L. *A Theory of Cognitive Dissonance.* Palo Alto, CA: Stanford University Press, 1957.

Galbraith J.R. *Designing Complex Organizations.* Reading, MA: Addison-Wesley, 1973.

———, and E.E. Lawler, III. *Organizing for the Future: The New Logic for Managing Complex Organizations.* San Francisco: Jossey-Bass, 1993.

Ghoshal S. and E. Westney. "Organizing Competitor Analysis Systems." *Strategic Management Journal*, 12(1), 1991: 17–31.

Gould S.J. and E.V. Vrba. "Exaptation—A Missing Term in the Science of Form." *Paleobiology*, 8(1), 1982: 4–15.

Granovetter M. "The Strength of Weak Ties." *American Journal of Sociology*, 78, 1973: 1360–80.

Hamel G. and C.K. Prahalad. *Competing for the Future.* Boston: Harvard Business School Press, 1994.

Holland J.H. *Adaptation in Natural and Artificial Systems.* Ann Arbor: University of Michigan Press, 1975.

———. *Emergence: From Chaos to Order.* Oxford, UK: Oxford University Press, 1998.

Huber G. "Organizations' Information Systems: Determinants of Their Performance and Behavior." *Management Science,* 28(2), 1982: 138–55.

———. "A Theory of the Effects of Advanced Information Technologies on Organizational Design, Intelligence, and Decision Making." *Academy of Management Review,* 15(1), 1990: 47–71.

———. "Organizational Learning: The Contributing Processes and the Literatures." *Organization Science,* 2(1), 1991: 88–115.

———. "Organizational Learning: A Guide for Executives in Technology-Critical Organizations." *International Journal of Technology Management,* 11(7), 1996: 821–32.

———, and W.H. Glick. *Organizational Change and Redesign: Ideas and Insights for Improving Performance.* New York: Oxford University Press, 1993.

Kauffman, S.A. *The Origins of Order: Self-Organization and Selection in Evolution.* New York: Oxford University Press, 1993.

———. *At Home in the Universe: The Search for Laws of Self-Organization and Complexity.* New York: Oxford University Press, 1995.

Kogut B. and U. Zander. "Knowledge of the Firm, Combinative Capabilities, and the Replication of Technology." *Organization Science,* 3(3), 1992: 383–97.

Lave J. *Cognition in Practice: Mind, Mathematics, and Culture.* Cambridge, UK: Cambridge University Press, 1988.

Lawrence P.R. and W. Lorsch. *Organization and Environment: Managing Differentiation and Integration.* Homewood, IL: Irwin, 1967.

Levinthal D.A. and J.G. March. "A Model of Adaptive Organizational Search." *Journal of Economic Behavior and Organization,* 2, 1981: 307–33.

———. "The Myopia of Learning." *Strategic Management Journal,* 14, 1993: 95–112.

Levitt B. and J.G. March. "Organizational Learning." *Annual Review of Sociology,* 14, 1988: 319–40.

Lewin A.Y. "Application of Complexity Theory to Organization Science." *Organization Science,* 10(3), 1999: 215.

Lewis D. and A. Weigert. "Trust as a Social Reality." *Social Forces,* 63(4), 1985: 967–85.

Machlup F. "Theories of the Firm: Marginalist, Behavioral, Managerial." *American Economic Review,* 57, 1967: 201–20.

Mackay D. *Information, Mechanism, and Meaning.* Cambridge, MA: MIT Press, 1969.

Mandler G. *Mind and Emotion.* New York: Wiley, 1975.

Mansfield E. *Industrial Research and Technical Innovation.* New York: Norton, 1968.

March J.G. and R.M. Cyert. *A Behavioral Theory of the Firm.* Prentice-Hall, 1963.

———, and Z. Shpira. "Managerial Perspectives on Risk and Risk Taking." *Management Science,* 33(11), 1987: 1404–18.

———, and H.A. Simon. *Organizations.* Oxford, UK: Basil Blackwell, 1958.

———, and R.I. Sutton. "Organizational Performance as a Dependent Variable." *Organization Science,* 8(6), 1997: 698–706.

Miles R.R. and C.C. Snow. *Organizational Strategy: Structure and Process.* New York: McGraw-Hill, 1978.

Minsky M. *The Society of Mind.* New York: Simon & Schuster, 1985.

Mintzberg H., D. Raisinghani, and A. Theoret. "The Structure of Unstructured Decision Processes." *Administrative Science Quarterly*, 21(2), 1976: 246–75.

Mitroff I.I. "On Management Myth-Information Systems." *Management Science*, 21(4), 1974: 371–82.

―――. "Management Myth Information Systems Revisited: A Strategic Approach to Asking Nasty Questions about System Design." *The Human Side of Enterprise*, ed. N. Bjorn-Anderson. Amsterdam: North-Holland, 1980.

―――, and M.C. Alpaslan. "Preparing for Evil." *Harvard Business Review*, March–April 2003: 109–16.

―――, and T. Pauchant. *Transforming the Crisis-Prone Organization*. San Francisco: Jossey-Bass, 1992.

Nadler D., M. Gerstein and R. Shaw. *Organizational Architecture: Designs for Changing Organizations*. San Francisco: Jossey-Bass, 1992.

Nelson R. and R. Winter. *An Evolutionary Theory of Economic Change*. Cambridge, MA: Belknap, 1982.

Nonaka I. "The Knowledge-Creating Company." *Harvard Business Review*, 69(6), 1991: 96–104.

―――. "A Dynamic Theory of Organizational Knowledge Creation." *Organization Science*, 5(1), 1994: 14–37.

―――. "Creating Organizational Order: Self-Renewal in Japanese Firms." *California Management Review*, 30(3), 1998: 57–73.

―――, and N. Konno. "The Concept of 'Ba': Building a Foundation for Knowledge Creation." *California Management Review*, 40(3), 1998: 40–54.

―――, and H. Takeuchi. *The Knowledge-Creating Company: How Japanese Companies Create the Dynamics of Innovation*. New York: Oxford University Press, 1995.

O'Reilly C. "Individuals and Information Overload in Organizations: Is More Necessarily Better?" *Academy of Management Journal*, 23(4), 1980: 684–96.

Orr J. "Talking about Machines: An Ethnography of a Modern Job." Cornell University, Ph.D. Thesis, 1990.

Penrose E.T. *The Theory of the Growth of the Firm*. New York: Wiley, 1959.

Perrow C. *Organizational Analysis: A Sociological View*. London: Tavistock, 1970.

―――. *Complex Organizations: A Critical Essay*. New York: Random House, 1986.

Polanyi M. *Personal Knowledge*. Chicago: University of Chicago Press, 1958.

Popper K.R. *The Logic of Scientific Discovery*. London: Hutchinson, 1959.

Pounds W. "The Process of Problem Finding." *Sloan Management Review*, 1(2), 1969: 1–19.

Schumpeter J.A. *The Theory of Economic Development*. Cambridge, MA: Harvard University Press, 1934.

―――. *Capitalism, Socialism, and Democracy*. Cambridge, MA: Harvard University Press, 1942.

Scott Morton M.S. *The Corporation of the 1990s*. New York: Oxford University Press, 1990.

Senge P.M. *The Fifth Discipline: The Art and Practice of The Learning Organization*. New York: Doubleday, 1990.

―――. "Learning to Alter Mental Models." *Executive Excellence*, 11(3), 1994: 16–17.

―――, and J.D. Sterman. "Systems Thinking and Organizational Learning: Acting Locally and Thinking Globally in the Organization of the Future." *European Journal of Operating Research* 59(1), 1992: 137–50.

Shannon C. and W. Weaver. *The Mathematical Theory of Communications*. Urbana: University of Illinois Press, 1947.

Shrivastava P. "A Typology of Organizational Learning Organizations." *Journal of Management Studies*, 20(1), 1983: 7–28.

Simon H.A. *The Sciences of the Artificial*. Cambridge, MA: MIT Press, 1997.

———. "Bounded Rationality and Organizational Learning." *Organization Science*, 2(1), 1991; 125–34.

Stamper R. *Information*. London: Batsford, 1973.

———. "Semantics." *Critical Issues in Information Systems Research*, ed. R.J. Borland and R.A. Hirscheim. New York: Wiley, 1987.

Starbuck W. "Learning by Knowledge-Intensive Firms." *Journal of Management Studies*, 29, 1992: 713–40.

Szulanski G. "Exploring Internal Stickiness: Impediments to the Transfer of Best Practice with the Firm." *Strategic Management Journal*, 17, 1996: 27–43.

Teece D.J. "Research Directions for Knowledge Management." *California Management Review*, 40(3), 1998: 289–92.

———, G. Pisano and A. Shuen. "Dynamic Capabilities and Strategic Management." *Strategic Management Journal*, 18(7), 1997: 509–33.

Thietart R.A. and B. Forgues. "Chaos Theory and Organization." *Organization Science*, 6(1), 1995: 19–31.

Thompson J.D. *Organizations in Action*. New York: McGraw-Hill, 1967.

Tushman M.L. and C. O'Reilly. "Ambidextrous Organizations: Managing Evolutionary and Revolutionary Change." *California Management Review*, 38, 1996: 8–30.

———, and P. Anderson, "Technological Discontinuities and Organizational Environments." *Administrative Science Quarterly*, 31, 1986: 439–65

Von Hippel, E. *The Source of Innovation*. Oxford: Oxford University Press, 1988.

———. "Sticky Information and the Locus of Problem-Solving: Implications for Innovation." *Management Science*, 40(4), 1994: 429–39.

Von Krogh G., K. Ichijo, and I. Nonaka. *Enabling Knowledge Creation: How to Unlock the Mystery of Tacit Knowledge and Release the Power of Innovation*. New York: Oxford University Press, 2000.

———, and J. Roos, eds. *Managing Knowledge: Perspectives on Cooperation and Competition*. London: Sage, 1996.

———, J. Roos, and K. Slocum. "An Essay on Corporate Epistemology." *Strategic Management Journal*, 15, 1994: 53–71.

Walsh J.P. and G.R. Ungson. "Organizational Memory." *Academy of Management Review*, 16(1), 1991: 57–91.

Walsham G. *Interpreting Information Systems in Organizations*. Chichester: Wiley & Sons, 1993.

Weick K.E. ed. *Cognitive Processes in Organizations*. Greenwich, CT: JAI Press, 1979.

———. "The Nontraditional Quality of Organizational Learning." *Organization Science*, 2(1), 1991: 116–24.

———. "The Role of Renewal in Organizational Learning." *International Journal of Technology Management*, 11, 1996: 738–46.

———, and M.G. Bougon. "Organizations and Cognitive Maps: Charting Ways To Success and Failure." *The Thinking Organization*, ed. H. Sims, Jr., and D. Gioia. San Francisco: Jossey-Bass, 1986.

————, and K.H. Roberts. "Collective Mind in Organizations: Heedful Interrelating on Flight Decks." *Administrative Science Quarterly*, 38(3), 1993: 357–81.

Wiener N. *Human Use of Human Beings.* Boston: Avon Books, 1954.

Weiser M. "The Computer for the 21st Century." *Scientific American*, 265(3), 1991: 94–104.

Wenger E. *Communities of Practice: Learning, Meaning, and Identity.* Cambridge: Cambridge University Press, 1998.

Williamson O.E. *Markets and Hierarchies.* New York: Free Press, 1975.

————. "Transaction-Cost Economics: The Governance of Contractual Relations." *Journal of Law and Economics*, 22, 1979: 233–61.

————. "The Economics of Organization: The Transaction Cost Approach." *American Journal of Sociology*, 87, 1981: 548–77.

Yates J. and W.J. Orlikowski. "Genres of Organizational Communication: A Structurational Approach to Studying Communication and Media." *Academy of Management Review*, 17(2), 1992: 299–326.

Zuboff S. *In the Age of the Smart Machine: The Future of Work and Power.* New York: Basic Books, 1988.

Notes

Notes to Preface

1. C.E. Shannon, "A Mathematical Theory of Communication," *Bell Systems Technical Journal*, 50, 1948: 279–423 and 623–56.

2. See K.C. Desouza and T. Hensgen, "On 'Information' in Organizations: An Emergent Information Theory and Semiotic Framework," *Emergence: A Journal of Complexity Issues in Organizations and Management*, 4(3), 2002: 95–114. See also K.C. Desouza and T. Hensgen, "Semiotics of 9/11," *IT Professional*, 5(2), 2003: 61–64.

Notes to Chapter 1

1. See K.C. Desouza and T. Hensgen, "On 'Information' in Organizations: An Emergent Information Theory and Semiotic Framework," *Emergence: A Journal of Complexity Issues in Organizations and Management*, 4(3), 2002: 95–114. See also K.C. Desouza and T. Hensgen, "Semiotics of 9/11," *IT Professional*, 5(2), 2003: 61–64.

2. See J. Newman, "Some Observations on the Semantics of Information," *Information Systems Frontiers*, 3(2), 2001: 155–67.

3. L. Wittgenstein, *Philosophical Investigations* (New York: Macmillan, 1953).

4. G. Hardin, "The Tragedy of the Commons," *Science*, 162, 1968: 1243–48.

5. See R.L. Ackoff, "Management Misinformation Systems," *Management Science*, 14(4), 1967: 147–56; A. Ramaprasad and A. Rai, "Envisioning Management of Information," *Omega: The International Journal of Management Science*, 24(2), 1996: 179–93; Desouza and Hensgen, "Semiotics of 9/11"; A. Ramaprasad and P.J. Ambrose, "The Semiotics of Knowledge Management," in *Proceedings of the Workshop on Information Technology Systems*, Charlotte, NC, December, ACM Press, 1999; A. Ramaprasad, K.C. Desouza, and K-T. Mak, "MIS*: Management of Information Space," in *Proceedings of the First Pre-ICIS Human Computer Interaction Workshop*, Barcelona, Spain, 2002.

6. See N. Wiener, *Cybernetics, or Control and Communication in the Animal and the Machine* (Cambridge, MA: MIT Press, 1948); L. von Bertalanffy, *General System Theory: Foundations, Development, Applications* (New York: Braziller, 1975); R.W. Ashby, *An Introduction to Cybernetics* (London: Chapman & Hall, 1956).

Notes to Chapter 2

1. P. Drucker, *The Age of Discontinuity* (New York: Harper & Row, 1968).
2. R.S. Rosenbloom and E. Pruyne, "Polaroid Corp.: Digital Imaging Technology in 1997," *Harvard Business School Case*, 9–798–013, 1997.
3. J.A. Baker, *Future Edge* (New York: William Morrow, 1992), pp. 16–17.
4. V. Bertalanffy, *General Systems Theory* (New York: George Braziller, 1968).
5. E.T. Hall, *The Silent Language* (New York: Anchor Books, 1990), p. 108.
6. Ibid.
7. This example originally appeared in K.C. Desouza, and T. Hensgen, "Every Citizen a Missile: The Need for an Emergent Systems Approach for Law Enforcement," *Government Information Quarterly*, 20(3), 2003: 259–80.
8. N. Wiener, *The Human Use of Human Beings* (New York: Avon Books, 1954), p. 106.
9. Ibid., p. 106.
10. Dr. W. Ross Ashby, a contributing founder of cybernetics and systems theory, developed several insights during the 1950s related to current work in complexity and adaptive systems. His most-known work is *An Introduction to Cybernetics* (London: Chapman & Hall, 1956).
11. See I.I. Mitroff and T. Pauchant, *Transforming the Crisis Prone Organization* (San Francisco: Jossey-Bass, 1992). See also I.I. Mitroff, "Cutting through the Confusion," *Sloan Management Review*, 29(2), 1988: 15–20.
12. See J. Campbell, *Grammatical Man* (New York: Simon and Schuster, 1982).
13. B. Engelbert, *Ludwig Boltzmann: Man, Physicist, Philosopher* (Woodbridge, CT: Ox Bow Press, 1983).
14. Campbell, *Grammatical Man*, p. 25.
15. C.E. Shannon and W. Weaver, *The Mathematical Theory of Communication* (Urbana-Champaign: University of Illinois Press, 1963).
16. Desouza and Hensgen, "On 'Information' in Organizations."
17. Wiener, *Human Use of Human Beings*, p. 31.
18. Shannon and Weaver, *Mathematical Theory of Communication*.
19. M.S. Feldman and J.G. March, "Information in Organizations as Signal and Symbols," *Administrative Science Quarterly*, 26, 1981: 171–86.
20. See Campbell, *Grammatical Man*; and Wiener, *Human Use of Human Beings*.
21. Some of the classic papers on information and the organization are F. Aguilar, *Scanning the Business Environment* (New York: Macmillan, 1967); R. Cyert and J. March, *A Behavioral Theory of the Firm* (Englewood Cliffs, NJ: Prentice Hall, 1963); R. Daft and K. Weick, "Toward a Model of Organizations as Interpretation Systems," *Academy of Management Review*, 9(2), 1984: 284–95; G.P. Huber, "Organizational Learning: The Contributing Processes and the Literatures," *Organization Science*, 2(1), 1991: 88–109; K. Weick, *The Social Psychology of Organizing*, 2d ed. (New York: Random House, 1979); Feldman and March, "Information in Organizations as Signal and Symbols."
22. M. Polanyi, *The Tacit Dimension* (New York: Doubleday, 1967).
23. R. Nelson and S. Winter, *An Evolutionary Theory of Economic Change* (Cambridge: Harvard University Press, 1982).
24. Polanyi, *Tacit Dimension*. I. Nonaka, "The Knowledge-Creating Company," *Harvard Business Review* (November–December 1991): 96–104. See also Nonaka, I.,

"A Dynamic Theory of Organizational Knowledge Creation," *Organization Science*, 5(1), 1994: 14–37, and I. Nonaka and H. Takeuchi, *The Knowledge-Creating Company* (New York: Oxford University Press, 1995).

25. See R.L. Ackoff, *Redesigning the Future* (New York: John Wiley & Sons, 1974), p. 8.

26. See B.B. Mandelbrot, *Les Objets Fractals: Forme, Hasard et Dimension* (Paris: Flammarion, 1975).

Notes to Chapter 3

1. K. van Lehn, *Architectures of Intelligence* (New Jersey: Lawrence Erlbaum Associates, 1991).

2. J.S. Brown and P. Duguid, *The Social Life of Information* (Boston: Harvard Business School Press, 2000), p. 200.

3. See Celgene Corporation's Web site: www.celgene.com/thalomid/

4. See K.C. Desouza and T. Hensgen, "On 'Information' in Organizations: An Emergent Information Theory and Semiotic Framework," *Emergence: A Journal of Complexity Issues in Organizations and Management*, 4(3), 2002: 95–114. See also K.C. Desouza and T. Hensgen, "Semiotics of 9/11," *IT Professional*, 5(2), 2003: 61–64.

5. H.A. Simon, *The Sciences of the Artificial* (Cambridge, MA: MIT Press, 1994), pp. 86–89.

6. C. Argyris and D. Schon, *Theory in Practice: Increasing Professional Effectiveness* (San Francisco: Jossey-Bass, 1974).

7. I. Nonaka and T. Nishiguchi, eds., *Knowledge Emergence* (New York: Oxford University Press, 2001), p. 33.

8. See D. Vaughan, *The Challenger Launch Decision: Risky Technology, Culture, and Deviance at NASA* (Chicago: University of Chicago Press, 1996). See also I.I. Mitroff and G. Anagnos, *Managing Crises before They Happen: What Every Executive Needs to Know About Crisis Management* (New York: Amacom, 2001), and W.H. Starbuck and F.J. Milliken, "Challenger: Fine-Tuning the Odds until Something Breaks," *Journal of Management Studies*, 25, 1988: 319–40.

9. See CNN News, "Texaco Investigator: Tape Analysis Shows No Racial Slur" (November 11, 1996); available at www.cnn.com/US/9611/11/texaco/index.html. See also CNN News, "Texaco Boycott to Go Forward, Despite Lawsuit Settlement" (November 16, 1996); available at www.cnn.com/US/9611/16/texaco/. See K. Eichenwald, "Blowing the Whistle, and Now Facing the Music," *New York Times*, March 16, 1997.

10. J.G. Saxe, *The Blind Men and the Elephant: John Godfrey Saxe's Version of the Famous Indian Legend*, pictures by Paul Galdone (New York: Whittlesey House, 1963).

11. L. Festinger, *A Theory of Cognitive Dissonance* (Stanford, CA: Stanford University Press, 1957).

12. Brown and Duguid, *Social Life of Information*, pp. 119–20.

13. B. Jowett, trans., *The Great Books*, vol. 7, *The Dialogues of Plato* (Chicago: University of Chicago Press), pp. 388–401.

14. See www.computer.org/history/development/1952.htm

15. R. Weston, "UNIVAC: The Paul Revere of the Computer Revolution," available at ei.cs.vt.edu/~history/UNIVAC.Weston.html

Notes to Chapter 4

1. See *Webster's Dictionary.*

2. C. Darwin, *On the Origin of Species by Means of Natural Selection, or The Preservation of Favored Races in the Struggle of Life* (London: J. Murray, 1885).

3. T.R. Malthus, *An Essay on the Principle of Population, or, A View of Its Past and Present Effects on Human Happiness: With an Inquiry into Our Prospects Respecting the Future Removal on Mitigation of the Evils which It Occasions* (Washington, DC: Roger Chew Weightman, 1809).

4. E.C. Moore, *Charles S. Peirce: The Essential Writings* (New York: Harper & Row, 1972), p. 165.

5. B. Krause, *The Basis of Human Evolution* (New York: Harper & Row, 1964), pp. 67–68.

6. Ibid., p. 67.

7. M. Polanyi, *Personal Knowledge* (Chicago: University of Chicago Press, 1958); M. Polanyi, *The Tacit Dimension* (New York: Anchor Day Books, 1966).

8. J.S. Brown and P. Duguid, *The Social Life of Information* (Boston: Harvard Business School Press, 2000), p. 134.

9. See K.C. Desouza, "Barriers to Effective Knowledge Management: Why the Technology Imperative Seldom Works," *Business Horizons*, 46(1), 2003: 25–29, and K.C. Desouza, "Strategic Contribution of Game Rooms to Knowledge Management: Some Preliminary Insights," *Information & Management*, 41(1), 2003: 63–74. See also K.C. Desouza, "Barriers to Effective Use of Knowledge Management Systems in Software Engineering," *Communications of the ACM*, 46(1), 2003: 99–101, and K.C. Desouza, "Facilitating Tacit Knowledge Exchange," *Communications of the ACM*, 46(6), 2003: 85–88.

10. C.S. Peirce, *Peirce on Signs* (Chapel Hill: University of North Carolina Press, 1991).

11. See www.bu.edu/wep/Papers/Cogn/CognSkag.htm

12. See A. Greimas, *Structural Semantics* (Lincoln: University of Nebraska Press, 1983), and A. Greimas, *On Meaning: Selected Writings in Semiotic Theory*, P.J. Perron and F.H. Collins, trans. (London: Frances Pinter, 1987).

13. U. Eco, *A Theory of Semiotics* (Bloomington: Indiana University Press/London: Macmillan, 1976).

14. See W.E. Odom, *Fixing Intelligence: For a More Secure America* (New Haven, CT: Yale University Press, 2003) and A.M. Dershowitz, *Why Terrorism Works: Understanding the Threat, Responding to the Change* (New Haven: Yale University Press, 2002).

15. P.B. Anderson, *A Theory of Computer Semiotics: Semiotic Approaches to Construction and Assessment of Computer Systems* (Cambridge, UK: Cambridge University Press, 1997); R.J. Clarke, K. Liu, and P.B. Anderson, eds., *Information, Organization, and Technology: Studies in Organizational Semiotics* (Boston: Kluwer Academic Publishers, 2001); K. Liu, *Semiotics in Information Systems Engineering* (Cambridge, UK: Cambridge University Press, 2000); P. Watzlawick, J.H. Beavin, and D.D. Jackson, *Pragmatics of Human Communication: A Study of Interactional Patterns, Pathologies, and Paradoxes* (New York: Norton, 1967).

16. See A. Ramaprasad and P.J. Ambrose, "The Semiotics of Knowledge Management," in *Ninth Workshop on Information Technology and Systems* (Charlotte, NC: 1999).

17. S. Kiesler and L. Sproull, "Group Decision Making and Communication Tech-

nology," *Organizational Behavior and Human Decision Processes*, 52, 1992: 96–123; Desouza, "Strategic Contribution of Game Rooms to Knowledge Management," Desouza, "Facilitating Tacit Knowledge Exchange."

18. K.C. Desouza, "Dissipation of Intelligence," *Competitive Intelligence Magazine*, 6(5), 2003: 65–67.

19. W. Hoge, "Blair Aide Says Presentation of Iraqi Arms Dossier Was Mishandled," *New York Times*, June 6, 2003.

20. J. Steinberg, "*Times* Reporter Steps Down Amid Criticism," *New York Times*, May 29, 2003, and Anonymous, "Witness and Documents Unveil Deceptions in a Reporter's Work., *New York Times*, May 11, 2003.

21. P. Wait and W.P. Dizard, III, "HSD Official Obtained Ph.D. from Diploma Mill," May 30, 2003; available at www.washingtontechnology.com/news/1_1/daily_news/20849–1.html

22. K.C. Desouza, "Intelligent Agents for Competitive Intelligence: Survey of Applications," *Competitive Intelligence Review*, 12(4), 2001: 57–63, and G.M. Marakas, *Decision Support Systems in the 21st Century* (Englewood Cliffs, NJ: Prentice-Hall, 1998).

23. See K.C. Desouza and T. Hensgen, "On 'Information' in Organizations: An Emergent Information Theory and Semiotic Framework," *Emergence: A Journal of Complexity Issues in Organizations and Management*, 4(3), 2002: 95–114. See also K.C. Desouza and T. Hensgen, "Semiotics of 9/11," *IT Professional*, 5(2), 2003: 61–64.

24. Odom, *Fixing Intelligence*.

25. Ibid.

26. C. Hartshorne, P. Weiss, and A.W. Burks, eds. *Collective Writings*, vol. 8, (Cambridge, MA: Harvard University Press, 1958).

27. See F. de Saussure, *Course in General Linguistics*, W. Baskin, trans., (London: Fontana/Collins, [1916] 1974); F. de Saussure, *Course in General Linguistics*, R. Harris, trans., (London: Duckworth, [1916] 1983).

28. S.K. Langer, *Philosophy in a New Key: A Study in the Symbolism of Reason, Rite and Art* (New York: Mentor, 1951), p. 61.

29. I.A. Richards, *The Philosophy of Rhetoric* (London: Oxford University Press, 1932).

30. C. Lévi-Strauss, *Structural Anthropology*, C. Jacobson and G.S. Brooke, trans. (Harmondsworth: Penguin, 1972), p. 91.

31. See I. Nonaka, "The Knowledge Creating Company," *Harvard Business Review* (November–December 1991): 96–104; I. Nonaka, "A Dynamic Theory of Organizational Knowledge Creation," *Organization Science*, 5(1), 1994: 14–37; I. Nonaka and H. Takeuchi, *The Knowledge-Creating Company* (New York: Oxford University Press, 1995); I. Nonaka and N. Konno, "The Concept of 'Ba': Building a Foundation for Knowledge Creation," *California Management Review*, 40(3), 1998: 40–54; Polanyi, *Personal Knowledge*; Polanyi, *The Tacit Dimension*.

32. See J. Sturrock, ed., *Structuralism and Since: From Lévi-Strauss to Derrida* (Oxford: Oxford University Press, 1979); J. Sturrock, Structuralism (London: Paladin, 1986); C.K. Oggen and I.A. Richards, *The Meaning of Meaning* (London: Routledge & Kegan Paul, 1923).

33. I. Nonaka and H. Takeuchi, *The Knowledge-Creating Company*.

34. H.A. Simon, *The Sciences of the Artificial* (Cambridge, MA: MIT Press, 1997).

35. See F. de Saussure, *Course in General Linguistics*, [1916] 1974, p. 112; also de Saussure, *Course in General Linguistics*, [1916] 1983, p. 113.

36. B.S. Bloom, D.R. Drathwohl, and B.B. Masia, *Taxonomy of Educational Objectives: The Classification of Goals* (New York: David McKay Company, 1956).

37. This case study originally appeared in Desouza and Hensgen, "On 'Information' in Organizations: An Emergent Information Theory and Semiotic Framework," and in their "Semiotics of 9/11."

38. C. Dickey and A. Nagorski. "Who's the Mastermind," *Newsweek Web Exclusive,* 2001; available at www.msnbc.com/news/627496.asp

39. Ibid.

40. K. Anderson, "US Intelligence Efforts Fractured," BBC News, May 18, 2002; available at news.bbc.co.uk/1/hi/world/americas/1994710.stm

41. T. Clancy, *Debt of Honor* (New York: Simon & Schuster, 1982).

42. B. Hodge and G.R. Kress, *Social Semiotics* (Ithaca, NY: Cornell University Press, 1988).

43. D. Dörner, *The Logic of Failure* (Cambridge, MA: Perseus Press, 1996).

Notes to Chapter 5

1. B. Kogut and U. Zander, "What Firms Do? Coordination, Identify, Learning," *Organization Science*, 17(5), 1996: 502–18.

2. E. Wenger, *Communities of Practice* (Cambridge: Cambridge University Press, 1998).

3. See A. Ramaprasad and A. Rai, "Envisioning Management of Information," *Omega*, 24(2), 1996: 179–93, and K.C. Desouza and T. Hensgen, "On 'Information' in Organizations: An Emergent Information Theory and Semiotic Framework," *Emergence: A Journal of Complexity Issues in Organizations and Management*, 4(3), 2002: 95–114. See also A. Ramaprasad, K.C. Desouza, and K-T. Mak, "MIS*: Management of Information Space." In First Pre-ICIS HCI/MIS Workshop, Barcelona, Spain, 2002, and K.C. Desouza and T. Hensgen, "Semiotics of 9/11," *IT Professional*, 5(2), 2003: 61–64.

4. See S.P. Borgatti and R. Cross, "A Relational View of Information Seeking and Learning in Social Networks," *Management Science*, 49(4), 2003: 432–45; R. Cross and L. Prusak, "The People Who Make Organizations Go—or Stop," *Harvard Business Review*, 80(6), 2002: 104–12; R. Cross, N. Nohria, and N. Parker, "Six Myths about Networks—and How to Overcome Them," *Sloan Management Review*, spring, 2002: 67–75; R. Cross, A. Parker, L. Prusak, and S.P. Borgatti, "Knowing What We Know: Supporting Knowledge Creation and Sharing in Social Networks," *Organizational Dynamics*, 30(2), 2001: 100–20; M.S. Granovetter, "Economic Action and Social Structure: The Problem of Embeddedness," *American Journal of Sociology*, 91(3), 1985: 481–510; A. Kleiner, "Karen Stephenson's Quantum Theory of Trust, *Strategy+Business*, 29, 2003: 2–14; D. Krackhardt and J.R. Hanson, "Informal Networks: The Company behind the Chart," *Harvard Business Review*, 71, 1993: 104–11.

5. T.H. Davenport and K.C. Desouza, "Re-Using Intellectual Assets," *Research Note*, Institute for Strategic Change, Accenture, 2003; K.C. Desouza, J.J. Raider, and T.H. Davenport, "Intellectual Asset Re-Use in Software Development," *Research Note*, Institute for Strategic Change, Accenture, 2003; R.J. Thomas, K.C. Desouza, and J.J. Raider, "A Life-Cycle Perspective on Intellectual Assets," *Research Note*, Institute for Strategic Change, Accenture, 2003; J.J. Raider, R.J. Thomas, and K.C. Desouza, "Intellectual Asset Reuse: A Comparison of Two Units in a Consulting Firm," *Research Note*, Institute for Strategic Change, Accenture, 2003; T.H. Davenport, R.J.

Thomas, and K.C. Desouza, "Reusing Intellectual Assets," *Industrial Management*, 45(3), 2003: 12–17.

6. C. Stoll, *Cuckoo's Egg* (New York: Pocket Books, 1989).

7. R. Lewin, *Complexity: Life on the Edge of Chaos* (Chicago: University of Chicago Press, 1999) pp. 63–64.

8. M. Page-Jones, *The Practical Guide to Structured System Design* (Englewood Cliffs, NJ: Yourdon Press, 1980 [1988]).

9. Ibid.

10. Ibid., and J.A. Hoffer, J.F. George, and J.S. Valacich, *Modern Systems Analysis and Design* (New York: Addison-Wesley, 1999).

11. This illustration originally appeared in K.C. Desouza and T. Hensgen, "Every Citizen a Missile: The Need for an Emergent Systems Approach for Law Enforcement," *Government Information Quarterly*, 20(3), 2003: 259–80. Two common approaches to regression are general and hierarchical. In general regression, each variable explains its portion of the variance of the phenomena, and any common variance explained by more than one variable is given to the R square. In hierarchical regression, the order of entry is important. The first variable explains its portion of variance and is given credit for any common variance it shares with other variables. Then the second variable enters the model and explains its share along with anything it has in common with the variables yet to enter. As a result, the last variable gets credit for very little, even though it may explain an important section of the variance.

12. Page-Jones, *The Practical Guide to Structured System Design*.

13. E. Lorenz, *The Essence of Chaos* (Seattle: University of Washington Press, 1996); J. Gleick, *Chaos: Making a New Science* (New York: Viking Penguin, 1988).

14. H.L. Lee, V. Padmanabhan, and S. Whang, "The Bullwhip Effect in Supply Chains," *Sloan Management Review*, 33, 1992: 93–102; H.L. Lee, V. Padmanabhan, and S. Whang, "Information Distortion in a Supply Chain: The Bullwhip Effect," *Management Science*, 43(4), 1997: 546–58.

15. J. Gollub and T. Solomon, "Chaos Theory," in *Academic American Encyclopedia*, vol. 4, ed., K.A. Ranson (Danbury, CT: Grolier, 1996), pp. 282–83.

16. See K.C. Desouza and A. Ramaprasad, "Toward a Knowledge Management Maturity Model," *Working Paper*, Department of Information & Decision Sciences, University of Illinois at Chicago, 2003.

Notes to Chapter 6

1. L.R. Pondy and I.I. Mitroff, "Beyond Open Systems Models for Organizations," in *Research in Organizational Behavior*, ed. B.M. Staw (Greenwich, CT: JAI Press, 1979), pp. 3–39.

2. K.E. Boulding, "General Systems Theory: The Skeleton of Science," *Management Science*, 12, 1956: 197–207.

3. R.L. Daft and K.E. Weick, "Towards a Model of Organizations as Interpretation Systems," *Academy of Management Review*, 9(2), 1984: 284–95.

4. B. Hedberg, "How Organizations Learn and Unlearn," in *Handbook of Organizational Design*, ed. P. Nystrom and W. Starbuck (New York: Oxford University Press, 1981), pp. 1–27; Daft and Weick, "Towards a Model of Organizations as Interpretation Systems."

5. B.G. Glaser and A.L. Strauss, *The Discovery of Grounded Theory: Strategies for Qualitative Research* (New York: Aldine de Gruyter, 1967).

6. B. Hedberg, P.C. Nystrom, and W.H. Starbuck, "Camping on Seesaws: Prescriptions for a Self-Designing Organization," *Administrative Science Quarterly*, 21(1), 1967: 41–65.

7. A.M. Pettigrew, "The Character and Significance of Strategy Process Research," *Strategic Management Journal*, 13 (winter special issue), 1992: 5–16; A.M. Pettigrew, "Studying Strategic Choice and Strategic Change. A Comment on Mintzberg and Waters: 'Does Decision Get in the Way?' " *Organization Studies*, 11(1), 1990: 6–11.

8. E.S. Vrba and S.J. Gould, "The Hierarchical Expansion of Sorting and Selection," *Paleobiology*, 12(2), 1986: 217–28.

9. S.J. Gould and E.S. Vrba, "Exaptation: A Missing Term in the Science of Form," *Paleobiology*, 8(1), 1982: 4–15.

10. S.J. Gould, "Exaptation: A Crucial Tool for Evolutionary Psychology," *Journal of Social Issues*, 47, 1991: 43–65.

11. S.N. Salthe, *Development & Evolution: Complexity and Change in Biology* (Cambridge, MA: MIT Press, 1994).

12. M. Waldrop, *Complexity: The Emerging Science at the Edge of Order and Chaos* (New York: Simon & Schuster, 1992), p. 218.

13. S. Kovoor-Misra and N. Maria, "Timing Is Everything: The Optimal Time to Learn from Crises," *Review of Business*, 21(3), 2000: 31–36.

14. C. Perrow, *Normal Accidents* (Princeton, NJ: Princeton University Press, 1999), p. 265.

15. P. Pawlowsky, "The Treatment of Organizational Learning in Management Science," in *Handbook of Organizational Learning and Knowledge*, ed. M. Dierkes, A.B. Antal, J. Child, and I. Nonaka (Oxford, UK: Oxford University Press, 2001), p. 6.

16. W.J. Orlikowski and J. Yates, "It's About Time: Temporal Structuring in Organizations," *Organization Science*, 13(6), 2002: 684–700.

17. C. Perrow, *Normal Accidents*, p. 141.

18. J.P. Kotter, "Leading Change: Why Transformation Efforts Fail," *Harvard Business Review*, 73(2), 1995: 59–67; J.D. Duck, "Managing Change: The Art of Balancing," *Harvard Business Review*, (May–June 1996): 81–90; J.P. Kotter, "Managing Change: The Power of Leadership," Balanced Scorecard Report (January 15, 2002); J.P. Kotter, *Leading Change* (Boston: Harvard Business School Publishing, 1996).

19. M. Waldrop, *Complexity*, p. 146.

20. L. Festinger, *A Theory of Cognitive Dissonance* (Palo Alto, CA: Stanford University Press, 1957).

21. M. Waldrop, *Complexity*, pp. 241–42.

22. Ibid., p. 279.

23. C. Perrow, *Normal Accidents*, p. 270.

24. M. Polanyi, *Personal Knowledge* (Chicago: University of Chicago Press, 1958); M. Polanyi, *The Tacit Dimension* (New York: Anchor Day Books, 1966); I. Nonaka, "The Knowledge-Creating Company," *Harvard Business Review* (November–December 1991): 96–104; I. Nonaka, "A Dynamic Theory of Organizational Knowledge Creation," *Organization Science*, 5(1), 1994: 14–37; I. Nonaka and H. Takeuchi, *The Knowledge-Creating Company* (New York: Oxford University Press, 1995); I. Nonaka and N. Konno, "The Concept of 'Ba': Building a Foundation for Knowledge Creation," *California Management Review*, 40(3), 1998: 40–54.

25. I. Nonaka and T. Nishiguchi, *Knowledge Emergence* (Oxford, UK: Oxford University Press, 2001), p. 124.

26. W. Cohen and D. Levinthal, "Absorptive Capacity: A New Perspective on Learning and Innovation," *Administrative Science Quarterly*, 35, 1990: 128–52.

27. D.S. Fox, "The Inner Servant," *Discovery Magazine*, 23(2), February 2002.

28. R. Dawkins, *The Extended Phenotype: The Long Reach of the Gene* (Oxford, UK: Oxford University Press, 1982).

29. Ibid.

30. A. Lynch, "Units, Events, and Dynamics in Memetic Evolution," *Journal of Memetics—Evolutionary Models of Information Transmission*, 2, 1998. Available at jom-emit.cfpm.org/1998/v012/lynch_a.html

31. A. Hitler, *Mein Kampf* (Boston: Houghton Mifflin, 1943), p. 635.

32. Ibid.

33. Glaser and Strauss, *Discovery of Grounded Theory.*

34. D.H. Kim, "The Link between Individual and Organizational Learning," *Sloan Management Review*, 35(1), 1993: 37–50.

Notes to Chapter 7

1. M. Waldrop, *Complexity: The Emerging Science at the Edge of Order and Chaos* (New York: Simon & Schuster, 1992), p. 11.

2. Ibid.

3. T. Hensgen, K.C. Desouza, and G.D. Kraft, "Games, Signals, and Processing in the Context of Crisis Management," *Journal of Crisis and Contingencies Management*, 11(2), 2003: 67–77.

4. I. Mitroff, "Crisis Management: Cutting through the Confusion," *Sloan Management Review*, 29(2), 1988: 15–20.

5. E. Lorenz, *The Essence of Chaos* (Seattle: University of Washington Press, 1996), p. 167.

6. F.W. Nietzsche, *Beyond Good and Evil* (Buffalo, NY: Prometheus Books, 1989).

7. C. Langton, *Artificial Life* (Reading, MA: Addison-Wesley, 1989).

8. Ibid.

9. Ibid.

10. Ibid.

11. S.N. Salthe, *Evolving Hierarchical Systems* (New York: Columbia University Press, 1985); J.H. Holland, *Emergence: From Chaos to Order* (Oxford, UK: Oxford University Press, 1998).

12. H.A. Simon, *Reasons in Human Affairs* (Stanford, CA: Stanford University Press, 1983).

13. S.N. Salthe, *Evolving Hierarchical Systems*, p. 84.

14. J.H. Holland, *Emergence: From Chaos to Order.*

15. R. Dawkins, *The Selfish Gene* (Oxford, UK: Oxford University Press, 1990).

16. C. Perrow, "Organizing to Reduce the Vulnerabilities of Complexity," *Journal of Contingencies and Crisis Management*, 7(9), 1999: 150–55.

17. Associated Press, "Experts Warned of Weak Power Grid" (August 15, 2003). Available at www.wired.com/wireless/story/0,2278,60057–00.html

18. P. Lagadec, *Preventing Chaos in a Crisis: Strategies for Prevention, Control, and Damage Limitation* (Cambridge, MA: McGraw-Hill, 1993).

19. I. Mitroff, T. Pauchant, and P. Shrivastava, "The Structure of Man Made Organizational Crisis," *Technological Forecasting and Social Change*, 33(3), 1988: 83–107; P. Lagadec, *States of Emergency: Technological Failures and Social Destabili-*

zation (London, UK: Butterworth-Heinemann, 1990); K.H. Roberts, "Some Characteristics of High Reliability Organizations," *Organization Science*, 1, 1990: 160–77; K.E. Weick, "Enacted Sensemaking in Crisis Situations," *Journal of Management Studies*, 24(4), 1988: 305–17; K.E. Weick, "The Collapse of Sensemaking in Organizations: The Mann Gulch Disaster," *Administrative Science Quarterly*, 38(4), 1993: 628–52.

20. T.C. Pauchant and R. Douville, "Recent Research in Crisis Management: A Study of 24 Authors' Publications from 1986 to 1991," *Industrial and Environmental Crisis Quarterly*, 7(1), 1993: 43–66.

21. P. Shrivastava, I. Mitroff, D. Miller, and M. Miglani, "Understanding Industrial Crises," *Journal of Management Studies*, 25(2), 1988: 283–303.

22. C.M. Pearson and J.A. Clair, "Reframing Crisis Management," *Academy of Management Review*, 23, 1998: 59–76.

23. C. Roux-Dufort and E. Metias, "Building Core Competencies in Crisis Management through Organizational Learning," *Technological Forecasting and Social Change*, 52, 1999: 113–27.

24. Pearson and Clair, "Reframing Crisis Management," p. 60.

25. M.W. Browne, "Rescuers Create a MASH Unit for Hundreds of Stricken Animals," *New York Times*, April 4, 1989; K.E. Goodpaster and A.K. Delehunt, "Exxon Corp.: Trouble at Valdez," Harvard Business School Case, 9–390–024, 1989.

26. D. Döerner, *The Logic of Failure: Strategic Thinking in Complex Situations* (Reading, MA: Perseus Books, 1989).

27. S. Fink, *Crisis Management: Planning for the Inevitable* (New York: American Management Association, 1986).

28. J. Preble, "Integrating the Crisis Management Perspective into the Strategic Management Process," *Journal of Management Studies*, 34(5), 1997: 769–91.

29. Mitroff, "The Structure of Man Made Organizational Crisis."

30. R. Clausius, *Mechanical Theory of Heat*, 1st part (Paris: Lacroix, 1868); R. Clausius, *Memories on the Application of the Mechanical Theory of Heat to the Electric Phenomena*, 2d part (Paris: Lacroix, 1869).

31. I. Wilson, "Realizing the Power of Strategic Vision," *Long Range Planning*, 25(5), 1992: 18–28.

32. Pearson and Clair, "Reframing Crisis Management."

33. S. Kovoor-Misra, "A Multidimensional Approach to Crisis Preparation for Technical Organizations: Some Critical Factors," *Technological Forecasting and Social Change*, 48, 1995: 143–60.

34. Mitroff, "The Structure of Man Made Organizational Crisis."

35. Ibid.

36. C. Perrow, *Normal Accidents: Living with High-Risk Technologies* (New York: Basic Books, 1984).

37. C.F. Camerer and H. Kunreuther, "Decision Processes for Low Probability Events: Policy Implications," *Journal of Policy Analysis and Management*, 8(4), 1989: 565–92; S. Belardo and J.R. Harrald, "A Framework for the Application of Group Decision Support Systems to the Problem of Planning for Catastrophic Events," *IEEE Transactions on Engineering Management*, 38(4), 1992: 400–11; S. Belardo and H.L. Pazer, "Scope/Complexity: A Framework for the Classification and Analysis of Information-Decision Systems," *Journal of Management Information Systems*, 2(2), 1985: 55–72.

38. Weick, "Enacted Sensemaking in Crisis Situations."

39. Fink, *Crisis Management: Planning for the Inevitable.*

40. C. Perrow, *Normal Accidents*, p. 78.

41. K.H. Roberts, "Some Characteristics of High Reliability Organizations," *Organization Science*, 1, 1990: 160–77.

42. P. Shrivastava, *Bhopal: Anatomy of a Crisis* (Cambridge, MA: Ballinger, 1987).

43. B.M. Staw, L.E. Sandilands, and J.E. Dutton, "Threat-Rigidity Effects in Organizational Behavior: A Multilevel Analysis," *Administrative Science Quarterly*, 26, 1981: 501–24.

44. Shrivastava, *Bhopal: Anatomy of a Crisis.*

45. Weick, "Enacted Sensemaking in Crisis Situations."

46. Ibid., p. 54.

47. E.N. Lorenz, *The Essence of Chaos* (Seattle: University of Washington Press, 2001), p. 45.

48. I. Prigogine, *The End of Certainty* (New York: Free Press, 1997), p. 71.

Notes to Chapter 8

1. See Y. Awazu, K.C. Desouza, and J.R. Evaristo, "Stopping Runaway Information Technology Projects," *Business Horizons*, 47(1), 2004: 73–80. Most of the quotations and data have come from this paper, conducted under this research project.

2. J. Brockner, "The Escalation of Commitment to a Failing Course of Action: Toward Theoretical Progress," *Academy of Management Review*, 17(1), 1992: 39–61.

3. F. Aguilar, *Scanning the Business Environment* (New York: Macmillan, 1967), p. 18.

4. L. Fahey and W. King, "Environmental Scanning for Corporate Planning," *Business Horizons*, 20(4), 1997: 61–71.

5. H.A. Simon, *The Sciences of the Artificial* (Cambridge, MA: MIT Press, 1997).

6. T.H. Davenport and J.C. Beck, *The Attention Economy* (Boston: Harvard Business School Press, 2001).

7. Simon, *Sciences of the Artificial.*

8. J.S. Hammond, R.L. Keeney, and H. Raiffa, "The Hidden Traps of Decision Making," *Harvard Business Review*, September–October, 1998: 47–58.

9. M.J. Prietula and H.A. Simon, "The Experts in Your Midst," *Harvard Business Review*, January–Feburary, 1989: 120–24.

10. CNN News, "Diplomat: U.S. Knew Uranium Report Was False," July 7, 2003. Available at www.cnn.com/2003/ALLPOLITICS/07/06/sprj.irq.uranium/index.html Also CNN News, "Ex-Envoy: Uranium Claim Unfounded," July 8, 2003. Available at www.cnn.com/2003/US/07/07/cnna.wilson/index.html

11. See G. Hamel and C.K. Prahalad, *Competing for the Future* (Boston: Harvard Business School Press, 1994); C.K. Prahalad and G. Hamel, "The Core Competency of the Company," *Harvard Business Review*, 68(3), 1990: 79–91. See also G. Hamel, *Leading the Revolution* (Boston: Harvard Business School Press, 2000).

12. L. Festinger, *A Theory of Cognitive Dissonance* (Palo Alto, CA: Stanford University Press, 1957).

13. C. Perrow, *Organizational Analysis: A Sociological View* (London: Tavistock, 1970), and C. Perrow, *Complex Organizations: A Critical Essay* (New York: Random House, 1986).

14. H. Montgomery, "Decision Roles and the Search for Dominance Structure: To-

wards a Process Model of Decision-Making," in *Analyzing and Aiding Decision Processes*, ed. P. Humphreys, O. Svenson, and A. Vari (Amsterdam: North-Holland, 1983).

15. See G. Whyte, "Escalating Commitment to a Course of Action: A Reinterpretation," *Academy of Management Review*, 11(2), 1986: 311–21; G. Whyte, "Decision Fiascoes: Why They Occur and How to Prevent Them," *Academy of Management Executive*, 5(3), 1991: 23–31; D. Kahneman and A. Tversky, "The Psychology of Preferences," *Scientific American*, 246(1), 1982: 160–73; D. Kahneman and A. Tversky, "Prospect Theory: An Analysis of Decisions Under Risk," *Econometrica*, 47(2), 1979: 263–91; J. Brockner, "The Escalation of Commitment to a Failing Course of Action: Toward Theoretical Progress," *Academy of Management Review*, 17(1), 1992: 39–61; and H. Garland, "Throwing Money After Bad: The Effect of Sunk Costs on the Decision to Escalate Commitment to an Ongoing Project," *Journal of Applied Psychology*, 75(6), 1990: 728–31.

16. W.P. Strobel and J.S. Landa, "CIA: Assessment of Syria's WMD Exaggerated," *Miami Herald*, July 15, 2003. Available at www.miami.com/mld/miamiherald/6310763.htm

17. P. Dickson, *The Official Rules* (New York: Delacorte Press, 1978), p. 149.

18. H.J. Smith, M. Keil, and G. Depledge, "Keeping Mum as the Project Goes Under: Toward an Explanatory Model," *Journal of Management Information Systems*, 18(2), 2001: 189–227.

19. M. Olson, *The Logic of Collective Action: Public Goods and the Theory of Groups* (Boston: Harvard Business School Publishing, 1971).

20. See K.M. Eisenhardt, "Agency Theory: An Assessment and Review," *Academy of Management Review*, 14(1), 1989: 57–74, and P.D. Harrison and A. Harrell, "Impact of 'Adverse Selection' on Manager's Project Evaluation Decisions," *Academy of Management Journal*, 36(3): 635–43.

21. K.C. Desouza, T. Hensgen, and Y. Awazu, "Lost in the Big Picture" *Across the Board*, 41 (1), 2004: 9–10.

22. E. Mach, *Realization and Mistake* (Leipzig: Ambrosius Barth, 1905).

23. J. Reason, *Human Error* (Cambridge: Cambridge University Press, 1990).

24. Ibid.

25. G. Mandler, *Mind and Emotion* (New York: Wiley, 1975).

26. D. Woods, "Visual Momentum: A Concept to Improve the Cognitive Coupling of Person and Computer," *International Journal of Man-Machine Studies*, 21(3), 1984: 229–44.

27. I. Janis, *Victims of Groupthink* (Boston: Houghton Mifflin, 1972), p. 11.

28. J. Sully, *The Human Mind: A Test-Book of Psychology* (New York: D. Appleton, 1982).

29. Reason, *Human Error*.

30. Aguilar, *Scanning the Business Environment*, and M. Feldman and J. March, "Information in Organizations as Signal and Symbol," *Administrative Science Quarterly*, 26, 1981: 171–86.

31. K.C. Desouza, "Intelligent Agents for Competitive Intelligence: Survey of Applications," *Competitive Intelligence Review*, 12(4), 2001: 57–63.

Notes to Chapter 9

1. G.A. Miller, E. Galanter, and K.H. Pribram, *Plans and Structure of Behavior* (New York: Holt, Rinehart & Winston, 1960).

2. See www.thewbalchannel.com/print/2051921/detail.html?use=print

3. M. O'Malley, "Seven Steps to Measure Homeland Security," *New Dem Daily*, September 10, 2002.

4. CNN.com, "Report: White House Sakes Up Iraq, Afghanistan Oversight," October 7, 2003.

5. S.S. Stevens, "Measurement, Statistics, and the Schemapiric View," *Science*, 161, 1968: 849–56, 850.

6. See P.H. DuBois, *A History of Psychological Testing* (Boston: Allyn & Bacon, 1970); H. Wainer, *The First Four Millennia of Mental Testing: From Ancient China To the Computer Age* (Princeton, NJ: Educational Testing Service); N. Campbell, *What Is Science?* (New York: Dover, 1952).

7. E.J. Pedhazur and L.P. Schmelkin, *Measurement, Design, and Analysis: An Integrated Approach*, 3d ed. (New York: Holt, Rinehart, & Winston, 1991), p. 17.

8. S.S. Stevens, "Mathematics, Measurement, and Psychophysics," in *Handbook of Experimental Psychology*, ed. S.S. Stevens (New York: Wiley, 1951).

9. Pedhazur and Schmelkin, *Measurement, Design, and Analysis*.

10. Ibid.

11. Associated Press, "State Department Computers Hit by Virus," *New York Times*, September 23, 2003.

12. K. Semple, "Computer 'Worm' Widely Attacks Windows Versions," *New York Times*, August 13, 2003; B. Krebs and J. Krim, "Internet Worm Targets Windows," *Washington Post*, August 13, 2003.

13. M. Barad and S.Y. Nof, "CIM Flexibility Measures: A Review and a Framework for Analysis and Applicability Assessment," *International Journal of Computer Integrated Manufacturing*, 10(1–4), 1997: 296–308; N.D.C. Slack, "Focus on Flexibility," in R. Wild, ed., *International Handbook of Production and Operations Management*, (London: Cassell, 1989), pp. 50–73.

14. Slack, "Focus on Flexibility."

15. H. Sharifi and Z. Zhang, "A Methodology for Achieving Agility in Manufacturing Organizations," *International Journal of Production Economics*, 62, 1999: 7–22.

16. C.L. Pritzker and B.J. Cline, "A Mounted Cooperative Target Identification System for Marine Corps [electronic version]," *Marine Corps Gazette*, 87(1), 2003: 50–52.

17. E.H. Schein, *Organizational Culture and Leadership* (San Francisco: Jossey-Bass, 1985), p. 7.

Notes to Chapter 11

1. See E.S. Raymond, "The Cathedral and the Bazaar," *First Monday*, 1998. Available at www.firstmonday.dk/issues/issue3_3/raymond/; von E. Hippel and G. von Krogh, "Open Source Software and the 'Private-Collective' Innovation Model: Issues for Organization Science," *Organization Science*, 14(2): 209–23; von E. Hippel, "Innovation by User Communities: Learning from Open-Source Software," *Sloan Management Review*, 42(4), 2001: 82–86.

2. N. Wiener, *The Human Use of Human Beings* (New York: Anchor Books, 1950); N. Wiener, *I Am a Mathematician* (Cambridge, MA: MIT Press, 1956).

3. V. Bush, "As We May Think," *Atlantic Monthly*, July 1945; A. Turing, "Computing Machinery and Intelligence," *Mind*, 59(236), October 1950; J. von Neumann, *The Computer and the Brain* (New Haven, CT: Yale University Press, 1958); V. Bush, "Memex Revisited," in *Science Is Not Enough* (New York: William Morrow, 1967).

4. M. Minsky, *Society of Mind* (New York: Simon & Schuster, 1985).

5. M. Weiser, "The Computer for the 21st Century," *Scientific American*, September 1991.

6. A. Ramaprasad, K.C. Desouza, and K-T. Mak, "MIS*: Management of Information Space," in *Proceedings of the First Pre-ICIS Human Computer Interaction Workshop*, Barcelona, Spain, 2002.

7. L. Suchman, *Plans and Situated Actions* (New York: Cambridge University Press, 1987).

8. See IBM Pervasive Computing Web site www-3.ibm.com/pvc/pervasive.shml

9. We do not claim to say that biometrics authentication schemes cannot be bypassed. However, these are much more difficult to conduct and are not domains for kids' play. Traditional passwords can be broken by individuals possessing basic skills taught at the high school level.

10. See www.panynj.gov/aviation/jfkinspassframe.htm

11. "Bill Would Require Companies to Notify Customers When Accounts Are Hacked" Ted Bridis, The Associated Press, June 27, 2003.

12. Anonymous, "Self-destruct Files to Secure DVDs, CDs," CNN News, June 17, 2003.

13. A. Harmon, "The Price of Music: The Overview; 261 Lawsuits Filed on Music Sharing," *New York Times*, September 9, 2003.

14. George V. Hulme, "Copyright Battle Goes To Court," *InformationWeek*, May 15, 2003. Available at www.informationweek.com/story/showArticle.jhtml? articleID=10000045

15. T. Kontzer, "Outsmarting Spam," *InformationWeek*, September 1, 2003, 18–20.

16. M. Hayes, "In Sync," *InformationWeek*, June 16, 2003, 30–34.

17. E.C. Cuneo, "Beyond Compliance," *InformationWeek*, February 24, 2003. Available at www.informationweek.com/shared/printableArticle.jhtml? articleID= 8700528

18. K.C. Desouza, *Managing Knowledge with Artificial Intelligence* (Westport, CT: Quorum Books, 2002).

19. B. Hayes-Roth, "An Architecture for Adaptive Intelligent Systems," *Artificial Intelligence: Special Issue on Agents and Interactivity*, 72, 1995: 1–2.

20. K.C. Desouza, "Intelligent Agents for Competitive Intelligence: Survey of Applications," *Competitive Intelligence Review*, 12(4), 2001: 57–63.

21. H.G. Goldberg and T.E. Senator, "The FinCEN AI System: Finding Financial Crimes in a Large Database of Cash Transactions," in *Agent Technology: Foundations, Applications, and Market*, ed. N.R. Jennings and M.J. Wooldridge (Berlin: Springer, 1998).

22. Parts of this section have appeared in K.C. Desouza and Y. Awazu, "Constructing Internal Knowledge Markets: Considerations from Mini-Cases," *International Journal of Information Management*, 23(4), 2003: 345–53; K.C. Desouza and Y. Awazu, "'Need to Know'—Organizational Knowledge and Management Perspective," *Information Systems Knowledge Management*, 4(1), 2004: 1–14; K.C. Desouza, S. Yamakawa, and Y. Awazu, "Pricing Organizational Knowledge: An Imperative," *Ivey Business Journal*, 67(7), September–October, 2003: 1–5; K.C. Desouza, Y. Awazu, and S. Yamakawa, "Facilitating Knowledge Management through Market Mechanism," *Working Paper*, 2003. For mathematical treatments on the topic of information markets, see Desouza, Awazu, and Yamakawa (2003); it contains formulations and mathematical proofs for some of our assertions.

23. K.C. Desouza and Y. Awazu, "Redesigning Human Resources Management Systems," *HR Magazine*, 2003.

24. C. Shapiro and H.L. Varian, *Information Rules* (Boston: Harvard Business School Press, 1999).

25. C. Koch, "Your Open Source Plan," *CIO Magazine*, March 15, 2003. Available at www.cio.com/archive/031503/opensource.html

Notes to Epilogue

1. J.M. Shafritz and S.J. Ott. *Classics of Organizational Theory*, 3d ed. (Belmont, CA: Wadsworth Publishing, 1992), p. 265.

2. B. Berkowitz, *The New Face of War* (New York: Free Press, 2003), p. 176

3. K.C. Desouza and T. Hensgen, "Semiotics of 9/11," *IT Professional*, 5(2), 2003: 61–64

4. D. Engelbart, "Augmenting the Human Intellect: A Conceptual Framework," AFOSR-3223 under contract AF 49 (638)-1024, SRI Project 3578 for Air Force Office of Scientific Research (Menlo Park, CA: Stanford Research Institute, 1962).

Notes to Appendix A

1. These originally appeared in K.C. Desouza and T. Hensgen, "A Semiotic Emergent Framework to Address the Reality of Cyber Terrorism," *Technology Forecasting and Social Change*, 70(4), 2003: 385–96; T. Hensgen, K.C. Desouza, J.R. Evaristo, and G.D. Kraft, "Playing the 'Cyber Terrorism Game' Towards a Semiotic Definition," *Human Systems Management*, 22(2), 2003: 51–61.

2. Desouza and Hensgen, "A Semiotic Emergent Framework to Address the Reality of Cyber Terrorism," p. 386.

3. Ironically, this is the same position Western Electric, the telegraph company, took when it passed on Edison's telephone design because they viewed it at the time as impractical.

4. K.C. Desouza and T. Hensgen, "On 'Information' in Organizations: An Emergent Information Theory and Semiotic Framework," *Emergence: A Journal of Complexity Issues in Organizations and Management*, 4(3), 2002: 95–114.

5. B. Nelson, *Cyberterror: Prospects and Implications* (U163.C982, 1999) (Monterey, CA: Center for the Study of Terrorism and Irregular Warfare, 1999).

6. T. McGirk, "Wired for Warfare," *Time*, October 11, 1999.

7. D. Arquilla, D. Ronfeldt, and M. Zanini, "Networks, Netwar and Information-age Terrorism," in *Countering the New Terrorism*, ed. I.O. Lesser, B. Hoffman, J. Arquilla, D.F. Ronfeldt, M. Zanini, and B.M. Jenkins (Santa Monica, CA: Rand, 1999).

8. R.J. Clarke, K. Liu, P.B. Andersen, and R.K. Stamper, eds., *Information, Organization, and Technology: Studies in Organizational Semiotics* (Boston: Kluwer Academic Publishers, 2001).

9. Ibid.

10. S. Kettmann, "Chaos Hackers Seek Order," *Wired News*, December 29, 1999. Available at www.wired.com/news/culture/0,1284,33312,00,html

11. B. Tedeschi, "Crime Is Soaring in Cyberspace," *New York Times*, January 27, 2003.

12. A. Iqbal, "Site Claims Bin Laden's Message," *United Press International*, February 2, 2002.

13. P. Eng, "Feds Search Boston-area Computer Firm Suspected Links to Al Qaeda," ABC News, December 6, 2002. Available at more.abcnews.go.com/sections/gma/dailynews/terror_raid021206.html

14. This site was removed from university servers and is now hosted at members.tripod.com/~farc

15. See burn.ucsd.edu/~ats/mrta.htm

16. R. Collier, "Terrorist Get Web Sites Courtesy of U.S. Universities," *San Francisco Chronicle*, May 9, 1997.

17. K.C. Desouza, "Intelligent Agents for Competitive Intelligence: Survey of Applications," *Competitive Intelligence Review*, 12(4), 2001: 57–63, and K.C. Desouza, *Managing Knowledge with Artificial Intelligence* (Westport, CT: Quorum Books, 2002).

18. Tedeschi, "Crime Is Soaring in Cyberspace."

19. B.C. Collin, "The Future of Cyberterrorism: Where the Physical and Virtual Worlds Converge," 11th Annual International Symposium on Criminal Justice Issues, 2002. Available at afgen.com/terrorism1.html

20. J. Lyons, *Semantics*, vol. 1 (Cambridge: Cambridge University Press, 1977).

21. K. Liu, *Semiotics in Information Systems Engineering* (Cambridge: Cambridge University Press, 2000).

22. J. von Neumann and O. Morgenstern, *Theory of Games and Economic Behavior* (Princeton, NJ: Princeton University Press, 1972).

23. T. Hensgen, K.C. Desouza, and G.D. Kraft, "Games, Signals, and Processing in the Context of Crisis Management," *Journal of Crisis and Contingencies Management*, 11(2), 2003: 67–77.

24. M. Conway, "Reality Bytes: Cyberterrorism and Terrorist 'Use' of the Internet," *First Monday*, 7(11), November 2002. Available at firstmonday.org/issues/issue7_11/conway/index.html

25. C. Stoll, *The Cuckoo's Egg* (New York: Doubleday, 1989).

26. Desouza and Hensgen, "On 'Information' in Organizations: An Emergent Information Theory and Semiotic Framework."

27. R.L. Dick, "Information Technology—Essential Yet Vulnerable: How Prepared Are We for Attacks?" Testimony before the Subcommittee on Government Efficiency, *Financial Management and Intergovernmental Relations* (September 26, 2001). Available at reform.house.gov/gefmir/hearings/2001hearings/0926_computer_security/0926_dick.htm

28. C. Perrow, *Normal Accidents: Living with High-Risk Technologies* (New York: Basic Books, 1984), and C. Perrow, "Organizing to Reduce the Risk of Vulnerabilities of Complexity," *Journal of Contingency and Crisis Management*, 7(3), 1999: 150–55.

29. Hensgen, Desouza, and Kraft, "Games, Signals, and Processing in the Context of Crisis Management."

30. J. Wynne, "White House Advisor Richard Clarke Briefs Senate Panel on Cybersecurity," February 14, 2002, available at usinfo.state.gov/topical/global/ecom/02021401.htm

31. Ibid.

32. Hensgen, Desouza, and Kraft, "Games, Signals, and Processing in the Context of Crisis Management."

33. Anonymous, "Feds Search Boston-Area Computer Firm Suspected of Links to Al Qaeda," ABC News, December 6, 2002. Available at more.abcnews.go.com/sections/gma/dailynews/terror_raid021206.html

34. B. Ross, "CIA Circulates List of Saudis Accused of Funneling Money to Bin

Laden," ABC News, November 25, 2002. Available at more.abcnews.go.com/sections/wnt/dailynews/ross_saudi021125.html

35. K.C. Desouza, Y. Awazu, D. Thomas, and D. Zhang, "Information Integrity in Healthcare Enterprises: Strategies for Mitigation of Medical Errors," *International Journal of Healthcare Technology and Management*, 6 (2), 2004: 175–89; Y. Zhang, D. Thomas, Y. Awazu, and K.C. Desouza, "Human-Machine Strategies for Decision Support," in Proceedings of the Americas Conference on Information Systems, Tampa, Florida, August 4–5, 2003.

36. M.K. McGee, "Mission: Critical," *InformationWeek*, May 19, 2003.

37. S. Gupta, "When MDs Mess Up," *Time*, March 10, 2003, 66–70.

38. Ibid.

39. Anonymous, "Mastectomy Mistake Patient: 'I Was in Shock,' CNN News, January 20, 2003, available at www.cnn.com/2003/HEALTH/01/20/cnna.-mastectomy.mistake/index.html

40. Desouza and Hensgen, "On 'Information' in Organizations: An Emergent Information Theory and Semiotic Framework."

41. Anonymous, "Services Set for Teen in Transplant Mix-Up," CNN News, February 25, 2003, available at www.cnn.com/2003/HEALTH/02/25/transplant.error/index.html; See also Gupta, "When MDs Mess Up."

42. Anonymous, "Private Medical Records Faxed To Pub," BBC News, April 12, 2001, available at news.bbc.co.uk/1/hi/health/1274552.stm

43. J. McBride, "Man Files Suit, Blames Death on Medical Error," *Amarillo Global News*, April 30, 2003.

44. S. Salyer, "Jury Awards $456,600 in Malpractice." HeraldNet.com, April 22, 2003.

45. R. Allen, "Drug Mix-Up Leads N.B. Couple to File Official Complaint," www.canadaeast.com, April 26, 2003.

46. Anonymous, "Mastectomy Mistake Patient: 'I Was in Shock.'"

47. Allen, "Drug Mix-Up Leads N.B. Couple to File Official Complaint."

48. K. Kilpatrick, "Apology Marks New Ear in Response to Medical Error, Hospital Says," *Canadian Medical Association Journal*, 168(6): 757.

49. J. Lamar, "Drug Company Bosses Jailed for Selling HIV Infected Products," *British Medical Journal*, 320: 601.

50. C. Dyer, "Pathologist at Heart of Case Faces GMC Investigation," *The Guardian*, January 30, 2003.

Index

About the Authors

Kevin Desouza has served as a consultant to numerous corporations in the areas of knowledge management, competitive intelligence, and strategic management of information. He has authored *Managing Knowledge with Artificial Intelligence* (2002), and over sixty referred articles published in management and research journals. He serves on the editorial boards on premier journals and is an associate editor of the *Journal of Information Science and Technology*. His research interests include knowledge management, national security, and military intelligence. He is currently completing his doctoral work at the University of Illinois at Chicago. When he is not working on research, he enjoys playing rugby and football, traveling, and sampling exquisite wines.

Tobin Hensgen is the principal administrator for Paradigm, Inc. (NFP) and a doctoral candidate at Loyola University of Chicago. He received his bachelor's degree from the University of Pittsburgh and an MBA from the Stuart Graduate School of Business, and Masters of Public Administration from the Armour Graduate School, Illinois Institute of Technology. He has been an invited lecturer on several topics ranging from telecommunications and security to crisis planning and has had articles published in outlets such as *Emergence: A Journal of Complexity Issues in Organizations and Management, Across the Board, Human Systems Management, Journal of Crisis and Contingency Management, IT Professional, Government Information Quarterly,* and *Technology Forecasting and Social Change*, many of which have been referred by other authors. His research interests include semiotics and entropic aspects of information, automated processes, knowledge management, national security, crisis management, and military intelligence.